All Men and Both Sexes

All Men and Both Sexes

Gender, Politics, and the False Universal in England, 1640–1832

HILDA L. SMITH

The Pennsylvania State University Press
University Park, Pennsylvania

Library of Congress Cataloging-in-Publication Data

Smith, Hilda L., 1941–
All men and both sexes : gender, politics, and the false universal in England, 1640–1832 /
Hilda L. Smith
p.   cm.
Includes bibliographical references and index.
ISBN 0-271-02181-0 (cloth : alk. paper)
ISBN 0-271-02182-9 (pbk. : alk. paper)
1. Sex role—England—History. 2. Sexism in language—England—History. I. Title

HQ1075.5.G7 S58 2002
305.3'0942—dc21

2001055952

This work is dedicated to
Charlote Carmichael Stopes and Ruth Kelso,
two scholarly pioneers

✤ *Contents* ✤

This study began two decades ago in preparation for a paper I offered at the Berkshire Conference on Women's History in 1981, entitled "Masculinity as a Political Concept in English Thought." In that paper I raised questions about the meaning of masculinity. As used by historians, masculinity has been associated with anthropologically-based concepts of aggression, territoriality, and sexual initiative. Instead, I contended that men's standing in the past and in the present has been determined more by status than by attributes, and that such status developed from the simple fact that they were male, not that they had particular "masculine" characteristics. Not all men were always included in that status, but their omission was tied most closely to their inability to pursue independent actions, and the reasons behind that inability were tied above all to class and nationality. Over the last two decades, valuable work has been done on the degree to which sexual orientation has also defined large numbers of men outside the category of the independent male representing both himself and his nation, and such work modifies the assertions I made in 1981. But it does not undercut the paper's basic contention, that the simple fact of being male has been the single most important criterion for a man's political and social standing.

In addition, as I read a large range of seventeenth-century works for my annotated bibliography, *Women and the Literature of the Seventeenth-Century: An Annotated Bibliography Based on Wing's Short Title Catalogue*, co-compiled with Susan Cardinale, I became aware of the rigid divisions of early modern people according to three mutually exclusive categories: age, condition, and sex. Only men were placed within the first two categories, while the last was reserved for women. This meant that male occupational status was continually employed in contrast to "women and girls" so that women's sexual identity was treated as comparable to men's work identity. In addition, terminology indicating age was limited to nouns associated with males, or gender-neutral terms such as "child" were used interchangeably with gender-specific ones such as "boy."

These two insights led me to develop the concept of the false universal, and the arguments associated with it; namely, that we best understand men and women's unequal power relationships and relegation to different roles and geographical settings (normally identified as public and private) by pursuing the strong association with, and relationships between broad terms such as "human," "people," and "human nature," with the more restricted terms "man" or "men," and the related disassociation with terms such as "women," "woman," and "female." This led me to explore the ways in which so-called universal language or goals were more apt to exclude women than more limited, directed language. Such usage has received little attention because of its ubiquitous nature and the lack of significance given to phrases such as "the brotherhood of man" or the "brotherhood of nations" as terms that did not directly or indirectly exclude women. It is only when one reviews language, descriptors, and analyses of terms standing for the species and compares them with terms and descriptions representing the male sex, and then contrasts these with comparable discussions of women by the same author, or in similar works, that their falsely universal nature becomes clear.

Over the years, I expanded my analysis of these mutually exclusive categories, and the myriad ways in which man became conflated with human. Most useful have been those texts that advised young men and women for adulthood. Also helpful have been those portions of writings that introduce definitions to be applied later. It is necessary to link these broad and abstract terms and definitions to the more specific and limited examples that follow. Here one grasps most clearly just who an author means when he/she employs supposedly inclusive terms such as people, person, human, human nature, and humanity. It is here that the false universal emerges most clearly.

My search for such materials has led me to a range of early modern works, as well as manuscripts, covering a number of topics and differing social circumstances. I have read advice literature to sons and daughters, educational programs and reform, discussions of training for apprentices, detailed listings of apprentices and those gaining the freedom through guild membership, arguments of political rights for increasing numbers of men, satirical and popular accounts of men and women's place within the public sphere, and the distinct routes outlined for men and women to obtain adult status (if such term could be used for women's journey). And here is the rub: must one change the definition of terms such as "adult" (which has been linked not simply to amassing a certain numbers of years but to economic and political independence and mature judgment) when applying them to women, who were seen as following a very different path to economic and political dependence and subordination within a family unit. To consider such a quandary one must first confront it by counterposing different portions of a single work, and similar works directed to each sex, to test the degree to which they were comparable or fundamentally incompatible.

In pursuing these efforts I have used materials at the British Library Rare Books and Manuscripts divisions, Bodleian Library's (Oxford University) books and manuscripts, rare works at the Houghton Library (Harvard University), the Folger Shakespeare Library, the Huntington Library, the Beinecke Library (Yale University), books and manuscripts at the Guildhall Library, and works at Dr. Williams' Library and the Friends' Library, London. I have received support for research trips from the Charles Phelps Taft Memorial Fund and the University Research Council at the University of Cincinnati, a Mayers Fellowship from the Huntington Library, and a Travel to Collections grant from the National Endowment for the Humanities. I have consulted with a number of individuals concerning this project, including Charles Gray, Barbara Todd, Berenice Carroll, Lois Schwoerer, Merry Wiesner, Melinda Zook, Judith Zinsser, Mihoko Suzuki, Frank Palmeri, Susan Wiseman, Ann Thompson, Christine Anderson, Willard Sunderland, and Maura O'Connor. I much appreciate their advice and corrections. As with others, any errors remain mine.

I wish to thank the staff of Pennsylvania State University Press, especially Peter Potter, for bringing this publication to fruition, and to the outside readers, who offered valuable substantive and stylistic suggestions.

I would like to acknowledge the excellent work done by Pat Rimmer in the index.

I would also like to thank my grown sons and grandson for bringing joy and different responsibilities to my life over these last few years.

Introduction

The Concept of the False Universal

Definitional Concerns

A study of the emergence of individualism and liberalism in seventeenth-century England requires a better understanding of the gender in addition to the class and ideological components of the period. While analyses of individualism have stressed its central importance to values embedded in the modern state, few studies have focused on the falsely universal language used by those presenting its principles during the 1600s. Such language has hidden the omission of those (especially women) not fitting the definitional parameters of this individual. Historians have concentrated too easily on abstract and supposedly inclusive terminology and given too little attention to the contextual and exemplary base upon which such terminology is grounded. In suggesting the concept of a "false universal" as crucial to understanding the operation of gender in seventeenth-century social and political institutions and beyond, I propose a method of organizing realities and ideas that have previously been viewed as unconnected.

Much of the theory and research in gender studies, whether focusing on the past or present, has offered documentation and explanations for the exclusion of women from certain social and political roles. As a corollary, scholars have offered evidence and explanations for women's relegation to a different set of discrete roles. As an alternative, such scholarship has focused on the masculine qualities of political writings that traditionally have been deemed universal (or gender neutral) and have centered on particular feminine qualities associated with both inherent sexual differences and the nature of a separate sphere for women. In contrast, this study will illuminate the nature of women's exclusion, and what remains following such exclusion, through an exploration of how falsely universal (or supposedly inclusive) terminology has been at the heart of values underlying current sex roles.[1] I will argue that this false universal has been more effective, and thus more harmful, in establishing constraints on women's place in society than the values that overtly exclude them.

Feminist scholars have discussed the sexist nature of language from the earliest development of women's studies.[2] They focus especially on terms such as the generic "man" and note that such terms obscure the fact that "man" as an individual male and "man" as human are used interchangeably in ways that have denied women a place in history or anthropological studies, or social science models. One prevalent solution to this dilemma has been to avoid such terms, and to use "person," "women and men," "humans," or "humanity" when referring to inclusive terms that hide women's existence. The concept of the false universal, as I employ it here, differs from this common usage in two ways: first, it involves more than a question of language and embodies

---

1. It is difficult to pinpoint any one work, or even set of works, in identifying feminist scholarship on the nature of citizenship generally and the gender implications of liberal thought or the evolution of individualism. Works that have had considerable influence include Carole Pateman, *The Sexual Contract* (Stanford: Stanford University Press, 1988), and Judith Butler and Joan W. Scott, *Feminists Theorize the Political* (New York: Routledge, 1992). From the perspective of feminist political thought, see Wendy Brown, *Manhood and Politics: A Feminist Reading in Political Theory* (Totowa, N.J.: Rowman and Little-field, 1988), and Christine Di Stefano, *Configurations of Masculinity: A Feminist Perspective on Modern Political Theory* (Ithaca: Cornell University Press, 1991). Primary themes of these works include the gendered nature of citizenship, a public/private split which has denied women a place in the state, special qualities that women's different life patterns and values could contribute to politics, and the harmful impact of women's exclusion on political, diplomatic and military policies.

2. Such discussion is to be found generally among works on the nature of feminist scholarship. For an early and influential attempt to grapple with the negative impact of men's control of naming, see Mary Daly, *Beyond God the Father: Toward a Philosophy of Women's Liberation* (Boston: Beacon Press, [1973]), and for women's studies collections that treat the issue, see Jo Freeman, *Women: A Feminist Perspective*, 4th ed. (Mountain View, Calif.: Mayfield Pub. Co., 1989), and Virginia Sapiro, *Women in American Society: An Introduction to Women's Studies*, 2nd ed. (Mountain View, Calif.: Mayfield Pub. Co., 1990).

a broader social phenomenon of not seeing or perceiving women in certain contexts, and that women are not conceived as having inherent qualities or relevant experiences for the categories from which they are omitted. Feminists have also urged an end to sexist language to overcome such invisibility by not allowing "man" to stand for "human" or "he" or "him" to stand for "she", "her," or "they." Yet that solution may perpetuate or even exacerbate the problem. If one simply uses "he and she" but discusses a reality that either ignores women or is based on a male model of experience, then one gives an even stronger impression that women are included when they are not. For example, editors at university and trade presses encourage authors to use gender-neutral language but have less influence over the content of works and whether the range of human experience is included. Thus, the language may be gender neutral but hide the reality that the text itself is far from being so. This is why, in this book, I use a masculine noun or pronoun when I believe that the author only meant a man, or male experience, in a particular text. The concept of the false universal, therefore, emerges from both the categories that early modern authors used to obscure their omission of women and the experiences and perceptions they linked to men alone that underlay those categories.

While examples of the false universal abound, it emerged for me most significantly in two separate instances: one a literary, the other a visual example. In reviewing *Athenian Mercury,* a popular periodical of the 1690s that was reprinted in compilations in the early eighteenth century, I was struck by its use of the phrase "all men and both sexes." Partially to gain a profit, the editors openly sought women for their subscribers and correspondents. The phrase "all men and both sexes" emerged from this goal and the editors' attempts to reach not simply men of all classes but women as well. As I reviewed this language, and similar examples, I was struck by the manner in which early modern authors divided human beings into three mutually exclusive categories: age, condition, and sex. Membership in one did not include membership in another, and the qualities of one did not affect the qualities of the others. Thus, I noted that the term "all," as in "all men" consistently meant all conditions or classes of men and referred to social rank and economic status, not to designations of either age or sex. When authors wanted to be inclusive in terms of class, they used the term "all," but the term did not include women or boys; they belonged to separate divisions. (Girls were determined by sex and not age and fell under categories tied to gender definitions rather than those linked to age.) This led the editors of *Athenian Mercury,* when arguing that they were more inclusive than the Royal Society in their efforts to bring knowledge to a broader audience, to stipulate that they meant for this knowledge to reach not merely "all men," but "both sexes" as well.[3]

The second example appears in the visual imagery of a stained-glass illustration of the *Seven Ages of Man* in the Main Reading Room of the Folger Shakespeare Library in Washington, D.C. While I had been generally familiar with the language spoken by Jacques in the second act of Shakespeare's comedy *As You Like It*, viewing this illustration of the stages of aging led me to understand how broad-based the false universal was. A female figure appears only once, as a mother holding an infant, illustrating life's first stage. While one might accept that women were legitimately omitted (although I would not) from discussions of citizenship, the state, or the public realm, surely no one would assume that they were not a part of the aging process. But here, and in many works discussing personal development, education, and the nature of childhood and adulthood, it became clear that women were indeed as missing from false universals that readers or viewers assumed included them—such as child, youth, adult, old age—as they were from political false universals. In reviewing works that discussed the qualities associated with human beings moving through various stages of life, I realized that those stages were open only to males. Any demarcations in a woman's life span were tied to sexual changes and social relationships and were indicated, in the early modern period, by the broad categories used in legal and literary works, namely "maid, wife and widow."

Shakespeare, in introducing the discussion of the seven ages, illustrates an unacknowledged shift from considerations of both sexes to the false universal of the male sex standing for all. In the following passage portraying human existence as drama, he begins by including both men and women and then, without explanation, jumps to a single man embodying the stages of life.

---

3. The *Mercury*, organized and published by the Athenian Society, was founded by John Dunton and had John Norris (the Platonist) among its editors. The *Athenian Mercury* went through a range of printings and name changes from volume 1, which appeared as the *Athenian Gazette* in 1691. *The Athenian News; or, Dunton's Oracle* was joined in 1710 by *The ... Athenian Mercury Resolving the Most Nice and Curious Questions propos'd by the Ingenious of either Sex* (London: Printed by T. Darrock and sold by J. Morphew at most Booksellers Shops in Town and Country, 1710). The editors of the Athenian Society were quite purposeful about their usage in the following comments about Bacon, Descartes, and the Royal Society: "Tis true it was great to cast off Authoritys, and to have recourse alone to Reason and Experiment, the only sure Foundation of all Learning. But tho the Treasure of Knowledge increas'd so vastly, yet the Possessors of this Treasure did not grow much more numerous than of old"; from *A Supplement to the Athenian Oracle, Being a Collection of the Remaining Questions and Answers in the Old "Athenian Mercuries ..." To which is prefix'd the "History of the Athenian Society,"* (London: Printed for Andrew Bell, 1710), 8–9.

Fig. 1 "The Seven Ages of Man," stained-glass window in the Main Reading Room of the Folger Shakespeare Library, Washington, D.C.

> All the world's a stage,
> And all the men and women, merely players;
> They have their exits and their entrances,
> And one man in his time plays many parts
> His acts being seven ages.

This shift acknowledges women's place in the drama of life while utilizing the medieval trope of its ages as pertaining only to men.

The mutually exclusive categories of age, condition, and sex that appeared regularly in early modern English works do not mean that in reality women were not a part of either the aging process or lacked rank or class standing. But it does mean that they were not simply omitted or overlooked, but definitionally were excluded from the qualities attached to those categories. They did not possess the characteristics of childhood because they were denied the ability to advance to independent adulthood. As individuals who lacked economic independence, they did not occupy positions that defined status as separate from women's sexual functions or their connections to individual men and to family. While women might have done what they were definitionally excluded from doing, discussions of these supposedly human categories were based only on male models.

This study looks beyond a continuum of political writings ranging from classic political theory to popular tracts that speculate on the relationship of the individual citizen to the state—and to those about him—to falsely universal constructions concerning human nature broadly. This false universal will be introduced through three sets of writings significant to the development of seventeenth-century society, and to republican, liberal, and individualist values. The first is the massive political literature of the mid-seventeenth century. The second consists of educational treatises and discussions of aging that place a male maturation process at the heart of adulthood and public responsibility. The third involves works that describe the nature of independence—economic, familial, political—and the necessity of independence to function as a person capable of judgment or public action. The concept of the false universal reveals similarities among this set of assumptions and realities, which offer a gendered understanding of the modern individual. Although these three sets of works are distinct, each revolves around the process of becoming, and the actions attached to, an adult man. The false universal reveals how those realities, rather than secondary characteristics associated with "masculinity," were at the heart of the values attached to the modern individual.

Fig. 2 Catalogue cover from special exhibit at the Musée national des arts et tradition populaires, Paris, 1995. As in the Folger stained-glass window, male figures represent the stages of human aging. In this instance, however, a woman is inserted not only in the earliest stage as a mother holding the infant male but in the stage that illustrates the lover. While sexual identity does not change, the alteration in dress is clear from Renaissance aristocracy to bourgeois respectability.

Although the evolution of this individual was gradual (with early elements existing within Christianity and the Greek polis), for the modern period, Renaissance humanism and the ideas attached to the English civil war were crucial watersheds in its emergence.

Renaissance concern for the natural, and learned, man who held many interests and responsibilities and represented the center of God's creation was an important step in conceptualizing the modern individual. Yet such a stage carried its limitations as well. Renaissance ideals looked backward to the ancients for wisdom and for model men and minds. And the communal demands of the Greek city-state, as well as the more hierarchical and militarily competitive Rome, would not seem fertile ground as incubators for the modern individual. Those embodying these ideals were for the most part "Renaissance gentlemen," so there are nagging doubts as to whether anything approximating a universal man was intended by humanists who had in mind a very specific group of men with important public, judicial, and familial roles to fill. Few men could have become this Renaissance gentleman, not simply for reasons of class, but also because most were excluded from the learning and the posts that would form and test the judgments prized by humanists.[4]

Thus the conflation of the adult male with qualities attached to citizenship and responsible adulthood laid the foundation for modern individualism and liberalism. Supposed "masculine" qualities (whether subsumed under sexual competitiveness, territorial propriety, rational discourse, stoic independence, or various aspects of male bonding) did not lead to the emergence of modern individualism or offer a useful lens to understand its nature. Nor can

4. Recent scholarship on Athenian politics has taken differing positions on the degree of democracy exhibited in ancient Athens. Josiah Ober, *Mass and Elite in Democratic Athens: Rhetoric, Ideology, and the Power of the People* (Princeton: Princeton University Press, 1989), and his *The Athenian Revolution: Essays on Ancient Democracy and Political Theory* (Princeton: Princeton University Press, 1996), argues for the broadly democratic nature of Athenian society. Arlene Saxonhouse, *Athenian Democracy: Modern Mythmakers and Ancient Theorists* (Notre Dame: University of Notre Dame Press, 1996), however, views the Athenians as more restricted in their political involvement, especially as regards the virtual exclusion of women from the public realm. Also, the majority of scholarship on the Renaissance especially as an event in intellectual history, continues to focus on the broad outline of an individualistic, human-centered universe tied to enhanced learning and a special interest in the languages and culture of the ancients. Anthony Grafton and Lisa Jardine, *From Humanism to the Humanities: Education and the Liberal Arts in Fifteenth- and Sixteenth-Century Europe* (Cambridge: Harvard University Press, 1986), discuss humanism's intellectual limitations. Ruth Kelso, *Doctrine for the Lady of the Renaissance* (Urbana-Champaign: University of Illinois Press, 1956), Joan Kelly Gadol, "Did Women Have a Renaissance," in *Becoming Visible: Women in European History,* ed. Renate Bridenthal and Claudia Koonz (Boston: Houghton Mifflin, 1977), 137–64, and my "Humanist Education and the Renaissance Concept of Woman," in *Women and Literature in Britain, 1500–1700,* ed. Helen Wilcox (Cambridge: Cambridge University Press, 1996), 9–29, discuss humanism's explicit gender limitations.

we learn about its nature through focusing on the absence of inherent characteristics of supposed "femininity," whether tied to a private/public divide or special qualities invested with emotional strength, cooperative instincts, and a particular morality. Rather, most instructive is the central fact that an adult male, whether tall or short, strong or weak, manly or effeminate, represents an independent individual and the qualities of the nation, through his training, society's evaluations of him, and the roles he fulfills, based solely on his sex.[5]

This work encompasses issues relating to the aging process and to class in order to develop a more inclusive picture of this independent individual or citizen. The phenomenon of "male maturation" has been central in creating the male individual who stands simultaneously as one and for the nation. In looking at educational treatises, guidelines for sons, advice literature, and regulations for apprentices, one discovers that their contents were gendered in precisely the same ways as discussions of citizenship. It is not that women did not age, and obviously they did get older, but that they simply did not advance through the stages of life that prepared an adult to represent his class, his region, or his nation. Thus the status, not the qualities, of the adult man made him beyond the reach of his female counterpart.[6]

5. While a number of scholars have raised questions about the overemphasis on femininity and masculinity, especially the ways in which using only feminine models to understand women's nature has led to an essentialist view, few have focused on the conflation of an adult man with a broad range of human activities. The psychologist Janet T. Spence has written most perceptively on the overemphasis on masculinity and femininity, arguing that strength, aggression, and the like are simply secondary characteristics and do not form the essential nature of men, nor are they accurate gauges for determining whether an individual man is representative of the qualities most characteristic of his sex. See J. T. Spence, R. L. Helmreich, and J. Stapp, "Ratings of Self and Peers on Sex-Role Attributes and Their Relations to Self-Esteem and Conceptions of Masculinity and Femininity," *Journal of Personality and Social Psychology* 32 (1975): 29–39. For a contrasting argument, see *The Making of Masculinities: The New Men's Studies*, ed. Harry Brod (Boston: Allen & Unwin, 1987). I do not intend to deny the importance of sexuality, sexual orientation, or physical appearance as ways society has categorized and discriminated against individuals. I simply contend that the modern individual is grounded most fundamentally in the independent male, no matter his other characteristics. For a discussion of physiological qualities, see *Deviant Bodies: Critical Perspectives on Difference in Science and Popular Culture*, ed. Jennifer Terry and Jacqueline Urla (Bloomington: Indiana University Press, 1995), and for a specific application in eighteenth-century England, see, for example, "Men About Town: Representations of Foppery and Masculinity in Early Eighteenth-Century Urban Society," in *Gender in Eighteenth-Century England: Roles, Representations, and Responsibilities*, ed. Hannah Barker and Elaine Chalus (London: Longman, 1997), 31–57.

6. There has been a great deal of scholarship among feminist philosophers, political theorists, and historians on the engendering of knowledge and of political status, but that work has focused overwhelmingly on gender differences rather than on the status of the adult male. "Masculine" and "feminine," "masculinity" and "femininity" are used when they seem to have no clear meaning beyond a simple identification of individuals or functions as male or female. For instance, "reason" is termed masculine not

Over the last decade several scholars have focused on problems inherent in tying universal qualities to a growing sense of nationhood and empire beginning with eighteenth-century England and highlighting especially the "rights of man" doctrine emerging from the French Revolution. But scholars have not sought the origins of this false universal in the political upheavals of seventeenth-century England. The greatest attention from feminist scholars (and others critical of a European and Enlightenment consensus) has concentrated on Enlightenment values and the limitations of the French Revolution. Feminist scholarship has highlighted how a greater sense of nation—particularly tied to concepts such as the brotherhood of man, the fundamental rights of the "people," and the growing importance of representative government—has hidden the fact that women, people of color, and propertyless men were excluded in theory and in practice from such a nation or set of values. Recently, these debates have been caught up in broader issues, such as whether the Enlightenment, or progressive values more broadly, should be discarded as ideas that were inherently false and thus harmful in establishing abstract principles that excluded the great majority of humanity.[7]

Joan W. Scott discusses the problems inherent in trying to hold on to the positive qualities of the French Revolution while deconstructing the language and actions of its leaders for their problematic universalism. Her concerns are twofold: that feminist historians have concentrated too much on an equality/

---

because women are incapable of it but because more men than women over the course of history have had access to higher education and been taught an academic regimen that stresses abstract thinking. But I would question whether that makes reason "masculine" or indicates that one needs to pursue the senses more closely as a source of epistemology in order to find a feminine source of knowledge or way of thinking. Such arguments can be found in Genevieve Lloyd, *The Man of Reason: "Male" and "Female" in Western Philosophy* (Minneapolis: University of Minnesota Press, 1984), Iris M. Young and Alison Jaggar, *A Companion to Feminist Philosophy* (Malden, Mass.: Blackwell, 1998), Iris M. Young, *Justice and the Politics of Difference*, and Christine Di Stefano, "Masculinity as Ideology in Political Theory: Hobbesian Man Considered," *Women's Studies International Forum* 6 (1983): 633–44.

7. For studies in the growth of a sense of nation in eighteenth-century Britain, see Linda Colley, *Britons: Forging the Nation, 1707–1837* (New Haven: Yale University Press, 1992), and Kathleen Wilson, *The Sense of the People: Politics, Culture, and Imperialism in England, 1715–1785* (Cambridge: Cambridge University Press, 1995). For the nature of feminism, see Karen Offen, *European Feminisms, 1700–1950: A Political History,* (Stanford: Stanford University Press, 2000), who critiques the overemphasis on "Anglo-American" or "equality" feminism that presses too strongly for women's equal nature and equal status with men in society. On women in the French Revolution and their absence from the central gains of revolutionary reforms, see, for example, Olwen Hufton, "Women in Revolution, 1789–96," *Past and Present* 53 (1971): 90–108, *Rebel Daughters: Women and the French Revolution,* ed. Sara E. Melzer (Oxford: Oxford University Press, 1992), and Harriet B. Applewhite and Darline Gay Levy, *Women and Politics in the Age of the Democratic Revolution* (Ann Arbor: University of Michigan Press, 1990) .

difference divide as an overly teleological way to analyze and assess the successes and failures of past feminist movements, and that they have not deconstructed sufficiently the contexts for past feminist efforts. This has encouraged feminist historians to take for granted that women were working to become a part of progressive and democratic movements that may have been neither. What is needed, she claims, is "reading the repetitions and conflicts of feminism as symptoms of contradictions in the political discourses that produced feminism and that it appealed to and challenged at the same time." She identifies such political discourses as "individualism, individual rights and social obligations" integral to establishing democracy and representative government.[8]

These debates have focused in recent years on the positive or negative influence of the Enlightenment on the nature of the French Revolution (and later liberal or democratic movements), its epistemological implications, and its relationship to current historical scholarship. Such debates encompass an ongoing discussion of the lack of fundamental change as a result of the revolution, the usefulness of postmodernism and the technique of deconstruction, and current intellectual trends. Recent scholarship has been less concerned about Enlightenment thought itself. And in many ways much of the dispute seems to be directed at false dichotomies, or at least straw men, on both sides. Surely one can appreciate the worth of pursuing objective knowledge while at the same time accepting its impossibility, and one can appreciate the values of individual fulfillment and social progress while also acknowledging that neither the Enlightenment nor the French Revolution came close to including all persons in such goals.[9]

8. Joan W. Scott, *Only Paradoxes to Offer: French Feminists and the Rights of Man* (Cambridge: Harvard University Press, 1996), 6.

9. The most important work to revive the worth of Enlightenment values and intellectual insights is *Telling the Truth about History*, ed. Joyce Appleby, Lynn Hunt, and Margaret Jacob (New York: W. W. Norton, 1994). Appleby, Hunt, and Jacob make clear their objective: "This book confronts head-on the present uncertainty about values and truth-seeking and addresses the current controversies about objective knowledge, cultural diversity, and the political imperatives of a democratic education." (3) What they offer is a strong defense of Enlightenment intellectual and political principles. Lynn Hunt, "Introduction," *The French Revolution and Human Rights: A Brief Documentary History* (Boston: Bedford Books, 1994), explicitly defends the centrality of the ideas of the French Revolution, linking them to the Declaration of Rights framed for the United Nations in 1948. While addressing the omission of women from revolutionary rhetoric, she ties the 1948 language of the "recognition of the inherent dignity and of the equal and inalienable rights of all members of the human family" with language from the Enlightenment's *Encyclopedia:* I am a man, and I have no other true, inalienable *natural rights* than those of humanity" (6). It is not Hunt's use of "man" that is key here, but the conflation of an individual man with the natural rights of humanity that raises questions and is the subject of this study.

Seventeenth-Century Contexts

The "freeborn Englishman" of the seventeenth century offers a different and prior model of the universal and is one that emphasizes the realities and historical groundedness of an Englishman rather than the more abstract nature of the rights of man. Justifications for his representing the nation, and the privileges and obligations tied to political standing, are continually situated in specific historical precedents from the past and specific social and political duties in the present. What he had been able to do in the past, and can continue to do during the 1600s, was crucial. The freeborn Englishman is portrayed both in the seventeenth century and later analyses as a situated being with privileges tied to Anglo-Saxon precedents, common law precedents, and the realities of office holding and public duties during the 1600s. While many of the arguments for precedent were either mythical or overblown, they were still framed in the language of actual events and efforts, not in the abstract language of the rights of man. With the recent advent of the "long eighteenth century" in the work of early modern scholars and the placement of the Enlightenment well back into the seventeenth century, the distinction between the more grounded qualities of the freeborn Englishman and the more abstract qualities of his eighteenth-century successor, both in England and France, has sometimes been lost.[10]

Carole Pateman questions traditional scholarship on the social contract, which dominated both seventeenth- and eighteenth-century theories of state formation. Although she has not analyzed the full range of documents emerging from seventeenth-century revolutions in England, she has critiqued the social contract as a construct that offered a supposed general agreement for the establishment of civil society (especially as exemplified in the writings of Hobbes and Locke) by pointing out that the agreement omitted women and at the same time required them to be part of a sexual contract that denied them the right to function as individuals within the state.[11]

10. J. G. A. Pocock, *The Ancient Constitution and the Feudal Law ... A Reissue with a Retrospect* (Cambridge: Cambridge University Press, 1987), remains the most definitive analysis of the precedents used by revolutionaries and reformers during the seventeenth century. *The Long Eighteenth Century: British Political and Social History, 1688–1832*, ed. Frank O'Gorman (New York: Arnold, 1997), captures the range of concepts and individuals integrated into Enlightenment efforts. When, as a number of scholars have done, Thomas Hobbes is considered an Enlightenment figure, not merely is the nature of Enlightenment thought expanded much beyond its core; but the scientific revolution and the Enlightenment become conflated in ways that obscure the nature of each.

11. While Pateman's argument is complex and deals with broad issues of political obligation and the nature of the state, it does revolve around the empowering of men in civil society at the direct expense of

While ideas attached to the English civil war, and the revolution of 1688–89, were expressed preponderantly by England's learned and politically active class, their writings represent a crucial advancement toward the concept of a universal man over the models of the earlier humanists. The ideal was not a Greek philosopher or Roman orator, but a "freeborn Englishman," one attached to a supposedly democratic early British society where a wide range of independent men held public sway. Men from a wider class range were expressing their views, and expressing them in a more democratic fashion, than had their predecessors of the sixteenth century. Here, at least, those on the left during the civil war highlighted independence and explicitly expanded the kinds of men who might be capable of it. And, whatever the true limitations of such expansion, enough commoners among the rank and file of the New Model Army, along the streets of London, and in separatist congregations believed the words were intended for them to alarm crown, Parliament, and military leaders. Yet such visions of an independent, political man, of whatever class, were not meant to include their sisters. Even so, the omission of women was seldom explicit, as was the omission of servants or tenants, and falsely universal language instead gave the appearance of their inclusion.[12]

Although we are most apt to think the greatest potential for excluding women is their simple omission, in reality, thought patterns and popular expressions that encourage the visual and linguistic linkage of men to the universal human condition are more significant. These include ideas about the goals to which all humans should strive, the evolution of "man" and the widespread linking of "brotherhood" to global ties among peoples. This linkage is often missed because it is so common, and therefore seemingly insignificant. While there are endless examples, an illustration from the cover of the *New*

their female counterparts. In fact, men's public status in many ways exists *as a result of* women's subordination within the family. As Pateman states, "What it means to be an 'individual,' a maker of contracts and civilly free, is revealed by the subjection of women in the private sphere" (*Sexual Contract*, 11).

12. Works on the nature of the English Civil War and the Glorious Revolution extend from G. P. Gooch, *Democratic Ideas of the Seventeenth Century,* 2nd ed. (Cambridge: Cambridge University Press, 1954), J. G. A. Pocock, *The Ancient Constitution and the Feudal Law* (Cambridge: Cambridge University Press, 1957), and a range of works by Christopher Hill, including *The Intellectual Origins of the English Revolution* (Oxford: Clarendon Press, 1965) and *The World Turned Upside Down: Radical Ideas During the English Revolution* (New York: Viking Press, 1972). Hill's revision of his 1965 *Intellectual Origins* continues to defend the civil war as revolution and the importance of its radical wing (Oxford: Clarendon Press, 1997, rev. pp. 285–400). While recent scholarship has tended to downplay the significance of the radical aspects of the civil war in contrast to the more moderate parliamentary maneuvering and compromise among Charles's supporters and opponents, David Underdown, *A Freeborn People: Politics and the Nation in Seventeenth-Century England* (New York: Oxford University Press, 1996), continues to argue for both the broad reach and radical implications of revolutionary ideas and actions.

York Times Book Review helped to clarify its simultaneous omnipresence and supposed insignificance. The illustration is for a review of works on evolution and portrays an early human figure metamorphosing into a contemporary man in a business suit. The visual image conveys that evolution culminates in a contemporary, white, middle-class adult male while the review's text discusses evolution of the species generally.[13]

Seemingly distant, but clearly parallel, is Prouse's case from 1635 that terms women "householders" and thus qualified for voting, taxation, and office, but denies them that right (or duty) in the particular and uses this denial to support a barrister's request to avoid service as well. The bulk of the case is devoted to the nature of householders and their public duties, clearly including women, but when making the explicit case for service as a collector of tithes, the decision reads: "it cannot be a good custom [for all to serve]; for then a woman being an inhabitant in one of the said houses, it may come to her in course to be constable, which the law will not permit." Such documents, and they are legion, acknowledge or recognize the existence and efforts of women as members of categories such as "inhabitant" possessing definable duties carried out by men, but do not recognize their right to do so as holders of such status.[14]

Somehow a woman can own land, hire a steward, or appoint a court leet, yet women are not landholders and have no legal standing (except those that delineate their relationships to individual men or sets of men). Further, women could be and were printers, brewers, engravers, clock makers, weavers, and the like, but they were never seen as embodying the occupation as were their male counterparts. They are seldom identified as a weaver or brewer, even though those were their occupations, but as a wife or widow with a descriptor indicating that she wove or owned a print shop. Women acting as individuals never seem to overcome or counteract a more powerful belief that women "can't" or "don't" act in various economic, legal, or political capacities. Perhaps the best-known phrase from the seventeenth century denoting women's perceived weakness and shared identity appears in *Lawes Resolutions of Womens Rights* (1632) when, in justifying women's inferior legal and political position, the author states that all women are considered "either as married or to be married," and thus all must suffer the legal disabilities of the *femme covert* whether or not they were in actuality married. The work continues

---

13. This color illustration, from a joint review of three works that focused on Neanderthals and the remains of early humans, portrays the sunglasses, white shirt, and tie of a middle-class man emerging from a Neanderthal skeleton. *New York Times Book Review*, July 4, 1993, sec. 7, p. 1.

14. "Prouse's Case," Croke, Car. 390. *English Reports*, vol. 79, 940.

by stating that marriage was never intended to be an equal relationship and compares the woman to a "little rivulet" and the husband to the Thames. Thus, just as the larger river encompasses the identity of the small stream as they merge, so the woman's legal identity vanishes upon marriage. Such values did not rule in every instance, and often individual cases allowed married women to own independent businesses and to operate economically independent from their husbands. Yet the exceptions seem only to have proved the rule, with popular opinion and legal commentators always returning to the legal disability of women as their starting point, if not their conclusion in every instance.[15]

Gender was not the only category that lent itself to a false universal in the early modern period; race also was incorporated into human experience without clear delineation. Yet for everyday English texts, gender difference and delineation of roles based on sex was central. Race, at least as it was linked to color, dealt overwhelmingly with discussions of foreign lands or the qualities of alien populations in England whose skins were of a darker hue.[16] But for women, the basic realities of birth, marriage, death, land transfer, and the determination of heirs meant their identity and the realities of their lives had to be considered either explicitly, or implicitly, through a false universal framework, encompassing fundamental aspects of life for early modern and, later, modern Britain. Those of another race or nationality were more apt to be subsumed under the heading of "other," rather than conflated with a male norm in a false universal. While this was sometimes the case for women as well, they were more apt to be hidden in falsely universal terms. The following example from the mid-seventeenth century incorporates race, gender, and the status of the alien. Such concerns over the nature of nation and empire become more prominent in the eighteenth century and will be discussed in Chapter 5, which treats the 1700s.

---

15. *The Lawes Resolutions of Womens Rights; or, The Lawes Provision for Woemen* (London: Printed by the Assignes of John More, 1632), 6–10. While there have been a great many works dealing with women's occupations during this period, a recent work that surveys both the varieties and definitions of women's work among working, middling, and elite women is Sara Mendelson and Patricia Crawford, *Women in Early Modern England, 1550–1720* (Oxford: Clarendon Press, 1998); see esp. chapters 5 and 6.

16. For a broad discussion of the role of race in early modern formations of identity, see *Race, Gender, and Rank: Early Modern Ideas of Humanity*, ed. Maryanne Cline Horowitz (Rochester: University of Rochester Press, 1992), which, as stated in the introduction, explores "particularity, difference, and hierarchy in Western ideas of human nature"; for an account of the use of racial imagery and non-European characters in sixteenth- and seventeenth-century drama, especially Shakespearean, see *Race, Ethnicity, and Power in the Renaissance*, ed. Joyce Green MacDonald (Madison, N.J.: Fairleigh Dickinson Press, 1997).

The Assembly-man, written by the royalist and Anglican John Birkenhead in 1647, but not printed until 1662, ridicules the Assembly of Divines by associating it with groups that feminist scholars (and others) have termed "the other," namely women, Jews, Africans, Turks, and Native Americans. The members of the Assembly, most commonly termed "Assemblers" by Birkenhead, were ridiculed for their ignorance, avarice, and presumption to claim standing and knowledge open only to seriously educated and legiti-mately appointed clergy. Birkenhead tied Assembly members to those of questionable character and learning, as the following excerpts illustrate:

> "but now their *Assembly* (as Philosophers think the World) consists of *Atoms;* petty small Levites, whose Parts are not *perceptible.*"

> "When they all meet, they shew [appear] Beasts in *Africk* [and] by promiscuous coupling ingender Monsters. Mr. Selden visits them (as Persians use) to see *Wild Asses* fight."

> "The onely difference 'twixt the *Assembler* and a *Turk,* is, that one plants Religion by the *power of the Sword,* and the other by the power of the *Cymetar.*"

> "Such might be expected because of their alliance with 'Ottoman Cromwell.'"

> "Their Divinity disputations are with Women or Lay-men."

> "His Prayer thus ended, he then look's round, to observe the Sex of his Congregation, and accordingly turn's the Apostle's *Men, Fathers, and Brethren* into *Dear Brethren and Sisters.* For, his usual Auditory is most part *Female.*"[17]

---

17. John Birkenhead, *The Assembly-man* (1647) (London: Printed for Richard Marriot, 1662–63), 5, 6–15. P. W. Thomas, *Sir John Berkenhead, 1617–1679: A Royalist Career in Politics and Polemics* (Oxford: Clarendon Press, 1969), terms *The Assembly-man* his "most substantial work of 1647" and notes that it was one of many satires against the Assembly of Divines, attacking especially its role in the "Visitation of Oxford University, begun in May." As a Laudian, Birkenhead, who Thomas argues was one of the most important innovators in royalist journalism during the 1640s and 1650s, was especially angry with members of the Assembly for their actions against Laud. For essays concentrating on those often left out of narratives of Stuart history, see Horowitz, ed., *Race, Gender, and Rank.*

Intellectual Frameworks

One of the most important intellectual schema organizing ideas in philosophical, religious, and social writings of the early modern period, tying human beings to a larger understanding of the universe, was the "Great Chain of Being." Here, all creatures fit within a universal chain of being in which the greatest to the smallest belonged somewhere along its expanse. At the apex, of course, was the deity. "Man" was the most important being on Earth, and all the plants and animals followed in order of their complexity and utility. This system incorporated all living beings and gave to each an appropriate and eternal place within God's (or the deist creator's) order of creation. All were there except for women; as one reads the discussion of the Great Chain, there is only one link in the chain for man, and that place is held by an individual with male characteristics, with intellectual qualities associated with the male, with judgments as to courage and character that were tied to men, and with offices and a life course followed by men. If women had a place, it was only to propagate the male man who would represent humans in the Great Chain of Being.[18]

The distinctions thinkers held concerning "man" as representing "human" and the nature of "woman" is made clear in the views of Immanuel Kant. Kant, in assessing God's greatness in creating a massive, integrated universe based on the principle of plentitude, seeks significance and design even among the lowest creatures, "For if a system has, in the long period of its existence, exhausted all the diversity of which its constitution is capable, and has thus become a superfluous member of the Chain of Being," then its extinction simply contributes to God's plan. As for the individual inhabiting the human link in the chain, Kant notes: "Human nature occupies as it were the middle rung of the Scale of Being, ... equally removed from the two extremes. If the contemplation of the most sublime classes of rational creatures, which inhabit Jupiter or Saturn, arouses his envy and humiliates him with a sense of his own

18. See Arthur Lovejoy, *The Great Chain of Being: A Study of the History of an Idea* (Cambridge: Harvard University Press, 1961), continually discusses the man at the middle of God's creation, his ability to reason, all of the creatures aligned beneath, and the heavenly creatures and God above. In describing his independence of judgment, his command of the lesser creatures and obedience to God, Lovejoy does raise questions of status—but they are questions based on social rank (servants are not to usurp the place of the master, and so on) or questions of species. Women are never mentioned, and the duties tied to man in the Great Chain conflict with the common characteristics of both the nature and duties assigned to women by some of the same authors (such as Pope and Kant) who write on the magnificent (if insecure) place man holds in the Great Chain. The Chain dominated discussions of human nature and the universe from the medieval period through the eighteenth century.

G.B. DELLA PORTA, "DE HUMANA PHYSIOGNOMONIA,"
MILAN 1586. BIBLIOTECA AMBROSIANA, MILAN.

Fig. 3 This representation of human physiognomy places a man at the center among
animals and various human ages and characteristics, conforming to the imagery
of the Great Chain of Being. Reprinted from André Chastel, *The Crisis of the
Renaissance, 1520–1600*, trans. Peter Price (Geneva: Editions d'art Albert Skira,
1968), 39.

inferiority, he may again find contentment and satisfaction by turning his gaze upon those lower grades which, in the planets Venus and Mercury, are far below the perfection of human nature."[19]

Yet women do not possess the qualities that distinguish this human nature from lesser beings. Kant terms women the "fair" and men the "noble" sex and ties such terms to women's inherent love of beauty and to men's greater vision and intellect. Of the "fair" sex, he notes: "there lie chiefly in the character of mind of this sex peculiar strokes, which clearly distinguish it from ours, and which principally tend to make it known by the criterion, *fair.*" The evidence of such qualities can be seen in women's strong attachment to beauty: "Already in youth they are willingly dressed and take a pleasure in being set off." In contrasting men's and women's abilities, he concludes, "The female sex have understanding, as well as the male, yet is it but a *fine understanding;* our understanding must be a *profound* one."[20] Thus that figure, who in Pope's words was "Plac'd in this isthmus of a middle state, / A being darkly wise and rudely great," while seemingly embodied qualities that could be termed human in reality represented the qualities early modern authors viewed as male.[21]

Such an intellectual system followed (and in some ways emulated) the "Seven Ages of Man," and was a well-known trope used in ballads, popular fiction, drama, even philosophy. Those seven ages included: infant, boyhood, student, soldier, jurist, pantaloon, and old age. Both in literary expression and in illustration, only males passed through those stages in the evolution of human existence, grew older, attended schools and learned how to be adults, tested their valor through battle, made judgments as local magistrates, tried to regain their young manhood as ridiculous pantaloons and ultimately declined into old age. Thus in the universal system of creation and human existence known as the Great Chain of Being and the "Seven Ages of Man," only males stood for human existence, and thus, again, the universal was more exclusive than the particular.[22]

19. Ibid., 193, 268.

20. Immanuel Kant, from *Observations on the Feeling of the Beautiful and Sublime* as quoted in *Woman in Western Thought*, ed. Martha Lee Osborne (New York: Random House, 1979), 154–55. Kant did not limit his critique of women's intellectual limitations to the abstract. He explicitly criticized contemporary women who were turning their minds to science and philosophy. "Women, who have their heads stuffed with Greek, like Mrs. Dacier, or carry on profound disputes about mechanics, like the Marchioness of Chastelet, might have a beard to boot; for this would perhaps express more remarkably the air of penetration, to which they aspire" (155).

21. *The Great Chain of Being*, 199.

22. The phrasing of William Shakespeare in *As You Like It* makes clear that only males go through the seven stages that he identifies as constituting human aging (William Shakespeare, *As You Like It*, as

Fig. 4 Hans Holbein the Younger's design of a clock for Sir Anthony
Denny which employs a male situated within broad temporal and
geographical methods of measuring. Reprinted from Arthur B.
Chamberlain, *Hans Holbein the Younger*, vol. 2 (London: George
Allen & Company, Ltd., 1913), pl. 43.

Spirituality and the False Universal

So much of the foundation for early modern intellectual and political concepts was grounded in religious terminology and spiritual imagery that it is
difficult to isolate issues of spirituality from the remainder of this work. Yet
the language of Christian faith and spiritual identity was consistently one
of equal standing and equal worth. Where, then, does it fit within a discussion
of the false universal? It fits easily, I would claim, because the abstract language of spiritual equality so often disappeared in the specificity of its human
embodiment. Whether in Anglican or Puritan sermons, funeral sermons and
eulogies written for those recently deceased, or the application of religious
principles to the political realm, specific examples of spiritual behavior were
overwhelmingly grounded in male qualities and existence.

It is true that when women devoted themselves to a spiritual life, they
personally identified with God and his broad goals for the human race. But
when they employed Scripture, and when others spoke of their devotion,
each turned to men as models to follow, and as representative of the qualities women were to pursue. Such realities reflect the absence of women from
leadership roles within established Christianity, and the use of the primitive
church—where male disciples were offered as models and Paul berated
women's unorthodox views and leadership—as a model for even the most
radical sectarian groups. Women who fell within the broad rubric of mystics,
or considered themselves prophets, were least apt to ascribe to institutional
restrictions. Still, even they used homocentric language and experience to
describe the ideal Christian.[23]

---

directed by John Hirsch and edited by Elliott Hayes and Michael Schonberg, Toronto: CBC Enterprises,
1983), 53–54.

    23. For the most complete discussion of women's religious experience during the seventeenth century,
see Phyllis Mack, *Visionary Women: Ecstatic Prophecy in Seventeenth-Century England* (Berkeley and Los
Angeles: University of California Press, 1992), and Patricia Crawford, *Women and Religion in England,
1500–1720* (London: Routledge, 1993). While both Mack and Crawford would argue for a greater female
agency among spiritual women during the 1600s, each notes the practical limitations on women prac-
ticing Christianity in the same manner as did their male counterparts. Phyllis Mack highlights the
importance of spirituality to women Quakers and prophets and sees it as possessing epistemological significance. Assurance in the soul beneath the skin mattered so much that "the woman or man who had
erased the self, or flesh, and exposed the soul ... was believed to speak a new, authentic language." And,
Mack claims, this was equivalent to "plead[ing] for the soul as a category of historical analysis" (7–8). Yet
this work contends that there is an irresolvable conflict when the soul as a category of analysis confronts
gender as a category of historical analysis. Works on radical Protestant women are most apt to point to
spirituality as central and where, according to *Profiles of Anabaptist Women,* ed. C. Arnold Snyder and
Linda A. Huebert Hecht (Waterloo, Ontario: Wilfrid Laurier University Press, 1996), the "calling of the

The writings of Christian women generally reflect an inherent conflict between an enhanced sense of power and personal worth through spirituality and the framing of such assessment in male-centered language and experience. Anne Halkett, in her *Meditations Upon the Seven Gifts of the Holy Spirit*, laments her inability to conform always to God's dictates in her life. She discusses her effort "to continue that Exercise, in which I have found so much Comfort, of employing my Morning Leisure, after my usual Devotion, upon some serious Meditation." Meditations dominated women's spiritual writings and reflected both their heartfelt devotion and their passive earthly role that little encouraged theological study or public commentary on a biblical text. In this instance, Halkett's work is based on Thomas Comber's *Discourse of Confirmation,* and is linked along with his work to translations of verses in Isaiah and Revelation that "describe the Gifts of the Holy Ghost by seven Spirits." She then proceeds to list those seven spirits that delineate good and evil, the spirit of devotion, "prudent managing [of] all our actions," and so on. The nature of each spirit is discussed in depth.[24]

Yet in these adumbrations upon texts relating to the Holy Ghost, Halkett situates her understanding within the potential spirituality of an individual man. She begins with the limitations of those lacking in spirituality; "the natural man receiveth not the things of the Spirit of God, for they are foolishness unto him, neither can he know them, for they are Spiritually discerned," and men are crafty and one must avoid their cunning ability to lead believers astray. In a section on the spirit of counsel, she pleads for spiritual prudence, and concludes: "And he who can thus prudently govern his Tongue, as not to offend in word, is a perfect Man, & able to bridle the whole Body." In phrasing her message and goals, not merely does she employ man as her model but ignores the strongly gendered discourse on controlling one's tongue, which had different significance for men and women (6–10).

Finally, Halkett adopted the language of the false universal in which men stand for human experience, and any distinctions among them are based on rank. "All," in her specific spiritual usage, as well as in general, is linked to economic standing: "This Spirit of Prudence is necessary for all, of all Ranks,

---

spirit" made the movement "radically egalitarian and personal." This meant that "Anabaptist women were persons called and empowered by the Spirit to a 'new life' of discipleship" (8). An alternative view of the role of gender in the Reformation in Germany can be found in Scott Hendrix, "Masculinity and Patriarchy in Reformation Germany," *Journal of the History of Ideas* 56 (1995): 177–93.

24. Anne Halkett, "The Occasion," in *Meditations Upon the Seven Gifts of the Holy Spirit, Mentioned in Isaiah XI. 2,3. As Also, Meditations upon Jabez his Request, 1 Chron. IV.10* . . . (Edinburgh: Printed by Mr. Andrew Sympson, and are to be sold by him and Mr. Henry Knox, 1702), preface, n.p.–5.

but especially for those that are in the highest Stations, whose actions are of great and publick Influence . . . who are no less accountable . . . than the poorest and meanest." This phraseology reflects falsely inclusive language and places spiritual affairs within men's earthly responsibilities. Such efforts to seem inclusive, while omitting women, are extraordinarily common in seventeenth-century writings. But their ubiquity does not limit their significance. She concludes that Christ adopted "our infirmities; For, for this end, he took on him our Nature, and became like to his Brethren, that he might be a mercifull and faithfull high Priest" (10–12). In highlighting the importance of counsel and prudence she discusses the complexities of human differences, and, while rather lengthy, it clearly reveals the exemplary language employed by women endeavoring to apply Christian values to their own lives:

> It's a great Blessing to a Nation to have Men of Counsel and Prudence endued with a Public Spirit, who may be capable for manageing publick affairs: But this Spirit of Counsel and Prudence, is also necessary for the meanest, for the right manageing all their privat affairs: It was this that instructed *Bezaleel* and *Aholiab,* and indued them with such skill in all maner of work-man-ship in Gold, Silver, Brass, and cuting of Stones: And it is this, that instructs the Husband man to discretion, and teaches him all the parts of his Husbandrie; . . . Yea, it is this Spirit of Counsel, that directs the meanest Servants to the prudent manageing of these affairs and offices, instructed to them; and *Solomon* tells us, that "a wise, discreet and prudent servant shal have rule over a Son that causeth shame," and shall have part of the inheritance among the Brethren. (12)

Such language and context confronted women who pursued spiritual lives at all turns. It was difficult to be a good Christian and live in imitation of Christ without remembering that religious teachers and the descriptors used in their teachings were of, and seemed designed for, men. Such realties often appear in the least likely places, such as in funeral sermons of women living during the second half of the seventeenth century. Although these sermons were presumably offered to recognize the accomplishments of their subjects, in reality they focused on men much more so than women. The sermon's text was most likely to focus on men, or alternatively, was based on the value of a loyal, pious, and obedient wife. The greatest numbers published between 1640 and 1700 were devoted to pastors' wives and normally mentioned the subject's life briefly near the end of the sermon, in platitudes that resembled directions found in domestic guidebooks. Examples include Daniel Burgess's 1694 sermon at the death of Sarah Bull, which devoted six of eighty pages to her life and noted that she focused on the hereafter, kept house well, was an excellent mother, and "reverenced [her husband] as her head," and Edward Reynold's five-page summary of Elizabeth Thomason's life (out of a sixty-eight-page sermon) that termed her young, solemn, meek-spirited, and industrious. Of the fifty-eight sermons published during this period which listed their female subject in the title, there is little distinction between Anglican and Dissenter in slighting the subject. Such is the case even when a woman such as Anne Skelton wrote her own works of meditation, which stressed enduring adversity. John Collinges's funeral sermon was included with Skelton's works in a 1649 publication, but it focused little on her life. Isaac Ambrose, in a sermon offered for Lady Margaret Houghton, praised her for her prayer, needlework, humility, patience, and her respect for ministers. Her death was even more precious, he claimed in the five pages devoted to her life out of a thirty-two-page sermon, because she so desired to be closer to Christ. While this could easily have reflected a full account of Houghton's nature, it is at least suspect that Ambrose, along with so many others, framed this praise on gender-restrictive qualities.[25]

No matter the subject, these sermons offered little concrete information about an individual's life. While one could assume such sermons would stress spirituality and eternity, still men's funeral sermons discussed how they had contributed to God's ends through their personal achievements. Women's sermons, though, reflected their contribution through relationships, seldom as individuals. One often gains the impression that a sermon was offered, and then published, not so much to honor the deceased but to acknowledge her relationship to husband or father. Certainly this is the case with *A Funeral Sermon on the Death of Mrs. Plaice, Late Wife of Mr. Joseph Plaice Merchant of Clapham*, which was dedicated to the widower, seldom mentioning the deceased, and when doing so praising her as patient, strong, prudent, discreet, and resigned to the will of God.[26]

25. Daniel Burgess, *A Funeral-Sermon Prech'd upon the Death of Mrs. Sarah Bull* (London: Printed and sold by A[ndre] Bell and J. Lansley, 1694), 78. Edward Reynolds, *Mary Magdalens Love to Christ. Opened in a sermon Preached at the funeral of Mistris Elizabeth Thomason* (London, 1659), 64–68. Anne Skelton, *Comforts Against the Fear of Death: Being some short meditations composed by that precious Gentlewoman, late of Norwich … A. Skelton* (London: Printed by J. M. for Nathaniel Brooks, 1649); Isaac Ambrose, *Redeeming the Time … A Sermon preached At Preston in Lancashire … at the Funeral of … the Lady Margaret Houghton* (London: Printed by T. C. for Nath. Webb and William Grantham, 1658).

26. W. B., *Sacred To the Precious Memory of Mris. Mary Boyleston, Daughter of Mr. Thomas Boyleston,*

Reading numbers of these records of women's spirituality, often the only records that remain of their spiritual lives, leads one to conclude that those offering women's funeral sermons never forgot their proper role as women. Clearly the women saw their spirituality as empowering in individualistic terms, but the language and examples available did not allow them to describe their spirituality outside the rhetoric of gender. There were exceptions among Quaker women and prophetic women such as Jane Lead, who spoke either of their direct service to God, or their embodiment of holy or spiritual qualities. Yet even these women used images that portrayed themselves as mothers, or as daughters, seldom representing all Christians in the faith and body of an individual woman, as did works on individual men.

Such realities are most stark when an author writes a strikingly different kind of work, as was the case with Nonconformist leader Richard Baxter, who in *A Breviate of the Life of Margaret, The Daughter of Francis Charlton ... and Wife of Richard Baxter*, though noting what a good and devoted wife Margaret had been, emphasized instead what harm had accrued to his wife through her continual sacrifices to his spiritual life. He notes that such sacrifices are seldom criticized for the harm they do to women. Works such as Baxter's reveal the stereotypically gendered and formulaic nature of the vast majority of funeral sermons, and their relationship to the false universal during the later 1600s.[27]

The Baxters were married for nineteen years before Margaret's death, and Richard Baxter was clearly distraught. This would, of course, make him a closer intimate of the deceased than most ministers offering funeral sermons. Yet families, and husbands in particular, regularly commissioned such sermons and their later publication. Perhaps Baxter's views were influenced by his

---

of Fan-Church Street, London (London: Printed for John Macock, 1657); Edmund Baston, *A Funeral Sermon on the Death of Mrs. Place, Late Wife of Mr. Joseph Plaice Merchant of Clapham* (London: Printed by Samuel Bridge, 1700).

27. Richard Baxter, *A Breviate of the Life of Margaret, The daughter of Francis Charlton ... and wife of Richard Baxter ... there is also published the character of her mother, truly described in her published funeral sermon, reprinted at her daughters request ...* (London: Printed for B. Simmons, 1681); quotations cited hereafter in the text. One of the more impressive attempts to create an explanation for women's relation to religion from the earliest times to the present is Rosemary Radford Ruether, *Women and Redemption: A Theological History* (Minneapolis: Fortress Press, 1998). Ruether discusses the means women employed to make Christianity their own. She focuses on the Wisdom tradition within Christianity, which through mystical ties allows one to take on God's wisdom, and the writings of Agrippa from the early 1500s and efforts of seventeenth-century Quaker women as part of a "major paradigm shift" which built upon the Wisdom tradition to grant women the same spiritual knowledge as male church leaders. She does, however, think that it had little effect on organized religion until the nineteenth and twentieth centuries (see her introduction, esp. 5).

wife's request in her will to print five hundred copies of her mother's funeral sermon which he had delivered in 1661, and to be buried next to her mother rather than by him upon his eventual death. He decides to write this brief history of Margaret's life to accompany the earlier account of his mother-in-law, and he states in a preface that it will be more directed to truth than similar works. In emerging from "melting Grief," this account of his wife was written "perhaps with the less prudent judgment; but not with the less, but the more Truth: For passionate Weakness poureth out all, which greater Prudence may conceal." The life is directed to the young in general, and to her nieces and nephews in particular, that they may improve their godliness through imitation of her. Yet, he fears, some will say he has simply given to his wife accomplishments that were more properly his. This he denies, and asks: "And must I needs bury the memory of them as hers, for fear of the sting of such Objectors? I have told them truly, It is not my own acts, but those that were properly hers, that I there mention."[28]

Perhaps his greater questioning of his own accomplishments, and his acknowledgment of his wife's, informs the personal and equitable nature of his narrative. The life begins: "We were born in the same County within three miles and an half of each other; but she of one of the chief Families in the County, and I but of a mean Freeholder (called a Gentleman for his Ancestors sake, but of a small Estate, though sufficient)." His future mother-in-law later moved to the neighborhood where Baxter was preaching, and lived by herself (although a widow with three children) until Margaret came from her brother's house to be with her mother. He notes she was seventeen or eighteen and describes her self-questioning path to Christ. He praises her language as a model, and respects her as an independent teacher for him and others (1, 6–8). After including her commentary on God's mercy in saving her from serious illness not long after she had become faithful, he notes: "Is not here in all these Papers (which I saw not till she was dead) a great deal of work for one day." He anticipates that there are those critics who will claim her statements of faith are familiar and should thus not be published. He differs: "It is not as matter of *knowledge,* but of *soul workings* toward God" that they are most impressive (22).

Baxter continues throughout this work to document Margaret's Christianity, but most impressive is his recognition that both her understanding and her support made it possible for him to be the important cleric that he was. Such

---

28. Baxter, *Breviate, preface,* irregular pagination; it is signed "July 23. 1681. Rich. Baxter."

recognition was absent from the greater numbers of funeral sermons omitting anything unique about their subjects. His work is so refreshing in its secular nature, which reveals their postnuptial agreement where he agreed to "have nothing that before our Marriage was hers," and she agreed that "she would so alter her affairs, that I might be intangled in no Law-suits" and "would expect none of my time which my Ministerial work should require" (47).

Richard Baxter continually praised his wife's spirituality, but in language that made her seem a real person, and he described the travails of marriage for both of them (but especially her) not simply as signs of Christian forbearance. She, who had come from a better family, had to endure his meager advancement due to his Presbyterian loyalties; and he was forced to move from post to post. She, he argues, had most of the burden: "First, we took a House in *Moorefields,* after at *Acton;* next that, another at *Acton;* and after that, we were put to remove to one of the former again; and after that, to divers others in another place and County; . . . and the women have most of that sort of trouble" (49).

There is much praise of her in this work: that she "could not endure to hear one give another any sowr, rough, or hasty word" and that she distributed books to the poor, whether "Conformist or Nonconformist . . . and many an hundred books hath she given to those ends." She joined him in prison, later lived in "part of a poor Farmers [house], where the Chimneys so extreamly smok't, as greatly annoyed her health . . . the Coal-smoak so filled the Room that we all day sate in, that it was as a cloud, and we were even suffocated with the stink." It was especially hard for his wife, who had weak lungs. Not merely did she not complain, but she paid for the landlady's son to be apprenticed, who later prospered. They ultimately moved to London, but it was there that she died. Baxter praised his wife unstintingly, but he also provided details, and spoke of his own misuse of her, in such a way that her religious devotion offers strong testimony to realities faced by ministers' wives during the late seventeenth century (49–55).

Seventeenth-Century Evolution of the False Universal

The manner in which the false universal operated within the social and political shifts of the seventeenth century is the core of this work. Here, I will simply introduce some broad-based questions that provide a framework for understanding the particulars of the false universal in the seventeenth century.

One such question was the linked development of modernity, the advent of revolution, and the market-based or republican-based evolution of the individual citizen. While scholars have focused little on the gendered nature of seventeenth-century politics, contemporaries did include such discussions in their works. Thomas Hobbes wrote about women's standing; he revealed his impatience with others' misunderstanding of women's role in the state. In defending himself against a charge of atheism, he notes that some are concerned by "his Attributing to the Civil Soverign all Power Sacredotal. But this perhaps may seem hard, when the Sovereignty is in a Queen: But it is because you are not subtle enough to perceive, that though Man may be male and female, Authority is not."[29]

Much scholarship is based upon a general belief, or underlying assumption, that seventeenth-century thinkers ignored gender as irrelevant to public standing and that it was unnecessary to treat gender inclusion or exclusion when discussing the nature of citizenship or the state. Yet such was not the case; although seventeenth-century thinkers were apt ultimately to come to the conclusion that women were excluded from political obligations, they did not accept such a view as timeless, essential, or universal. Rather, they used historically specific moments, or overt agreements and contractual arrangements, to argue that women either voluntarily gave up any political standing separate from their husbands, or that it was legally or contractually taken from them upon marriage. For instance, Thomas Hobbes is explicit in *De Cive* that far from being men's inferiors within a state of nature prior to civil society, women were their superiors. This superiority came from women's identity as mothers, which gave them the authority to determine paternity and to govern children, the only governable individuals within a state of nature. As Hobbes stated: "In the state of nature every woman that bears children, becomes both a *mother* and a *lord*."[30]

Hobbes grounded his arguments for denying any easy acceptance of male superiority in past and present military and governing realities: "the inequality of their natural forces is not so great, that the man could get the dominion over the woman without war," as both past and current traditions revealed. "Women namely Amazons, have in former times waged war against their adversaries, and disposed of their children at their own wills. And at this day,

29. Thomas Hobbes, *Considerations upon the Reputation, Loyalty, Manners & Religion, of Thomas Hobbes of Malmesbury, Written by Himself, by way of Letter to a Learned Person* (London: Printed for William Crooke, 1680), 40.

30. Thomas Hobbes, *De Cive,* the English Version, ed. Howard Warrender (Oxford: Clarendon Press, 1983), 122–26.

in diverse places women are invested with the principal authority; neither do their husbands dispose of their children, but themselves: which in truth they do by *right of nature*."[31] It was only after the establishment of the nuclear family within civil society that women gave up their superior standing by agreeing to protection through the contract of marriage. In Hobbes's analysis, the pattern of women agreeing to give up their superior natural state is similar to the subject giving up individual sovereignty to gain the protection of the monarch. However, it is unclear whether Hobbes allowed the same kind of individual resistance (similar to a subject's rights to resist acts that were personally threatening) to the wife to resist adverse use of her possessions or abuse of her body. For the purposes of this study, it is equally significant that the father's political standing emanates from his family role and from Hobbes's definition of the family as "a Father with Sons and Servants, grown into a civil person by virtue of his paternal jurisdiction," and that such a family structure now means that "the children are the father's." Thus it was not natural or essential that men were dominant or bested women in competition between the sexes; it was rather a result of the social construction of the early modern, nuclear family.[32]

John Locke, as well, does not take for granted that the modern individual could be identified with the position independent males held in the seventeenth century. His views emerge in the *First Treatise of Government* in which he attacked Filmer for denying obedience to the mother in his defense of patriarchalism, and, in his separate writings on education, where he stated that girls should be taught as boys and doubted easy assumptions about sexual difference. In *The First Treatise,* Locke asks rhetorically: "Can the Father, by this Sovereignty of his, discharge the Child from paying this Honour to his Mother? ... I think no Body will say a Child may withhold Honour from *her,* though his Father should command him to do so, no more than the Mother

31. *Leviathan; or, The Matter, Forme, and Power of a Commonwealth, Ecclesiastical and Civil,* ed. Michael Oakeshott (Oxford: Blackwell, 1947), 130–31.

32. While Pateman, *Sexual Contract,* 41–51, discusses this shift from natural equality (or superiority in the case of mothers) of women to men in the state of nature, she does not place it within an understanding of the false universal. While guaranteeing that women would lack status in the state, this shift just as significantly equated being a father with being a citizen. It defined the family as a *public,* not private, institution whose composition of a father and his male dependents justified as much the conflation of man and citizen as it did the exclusion of women from the state through a sexual contract. Making a public man distinct from his natural self, and from the nuclear family that was composed of father, mother, and children, was crucial in laying the groundwork for a false universal. This public construct of an adult male figure/citizen is central to Hobbes's vision, and at least as significant as an agreement between men and women that kept the latter relegated to a private family (*De Cive,* 122–26).

could dispense with him, for neglecting to Honor his Father."[33] Locke's problem with gender, however, was grounded in his understanding of the strong tie between property and the state, so that in the *Second Treatise,* he moves to limit his identification of competent citizens to a group of independent male householders. Here he states that "the great and *chief end* therefore, of Mens uniting into Commonwealths, and putting themselves under Government, *is the preservation of their Property.*"[34] Such a statement does not clarify what would be the case if the householder were independent but female. Yet Locke's emphasis on a propertied franchise has been used to explain the class-based nature of his political society, but less attention has been paid to its relevance to his treatment of gender.

The False Universal Beyond the Political

Locke had strong doubts about differences between the sexes as he noted in *Some Thoughts Concerning Education,* where he admitted that parts of a gentleman's education might be inappropriate for females, "though where the difference of Sex requires different Treatment, 'twill be no hard Matter to distinguish."[35] While skeptical as to how sexual difference should dictate distinct training, his reliance on the protection of property placed him in a different context when describing civil society. Land ownership was traditionally situated within the male line, and thus essential difference or similarity between the sexes was not the relevant factor for the origin of the state.

In establishing a framework to understand gender values that underlay so many of the classic and popular texts of the seventeenth century, it is essential to grasp the nature of a male maturation process that encouraged individuals of the 1600s to adopt a falsely universal language obscuring female experience within ostensibly nongendered (but experientially gendered) imagery and terms. And while the bulk of this work will focus on the evolution of, and impetus for, such universal language and imagery during the seventeenth century, many of these values and images continue today. Succeeding chapters of this work will follow such an evolution up through the liberal and radical

33. John Locke, *Two Treatises of Government,* ed. Peter Laslett (Cambridge: Cambridge University Press, 1988), *First Treatise,* 62, p. 186.
    34. Locke, *Second Treatise* 124, p. 350.
    35. John Locke, *Some Thoughts Concerning Education* (1705), in *The Educational Writings of John Locke,* ed. James L. Axtell (Cambridge: Cambridge University Press, 1968), 117.

theorists of the late eighteenth century (primarily in Britain, but touching on French thought and imagery) and into the first half of the nineteenth century; assess democratic views attached to the Reform Bill of 1832; and explore gender assumptions and the use of the false universal.

Recent scholarship on women's political status in early modern Europe, both among historians of women and feminist political theorists, has concentrated on women's lack of citizenship. The male maturation discussed above is prior to, and essential for, judgments concerning women's political standing; one cannot treat the public arena, or political writings and institutions, as distinct entities. Nor can scholars look only to discussions of women's political standing. Rather, we learn as much or more by analyzing how men became independent, political creatures because there we gain the fullest and clearest sense of the qualities conceived to be essential to political nature. Through these falsely universal discussions historians can discern how writers conflated qualities and life choices which were deemed possible only for men, with qualities taken to stand for all human beings.

Thus discussions of aging, manuals for training and education, and treatments of occupations, professions, and civic posts are the primary sources for this work. They will isolate the abilities, privileges, and responsibilities that were necessary for independence, whether as a guild member, a householder, a voter, or simply an adult man not dependent on another. Such qualities embody the false universal at the core of the modern individual. Thus, writings that concern preparation for, or deviation from, a public role tell us a great deal about underlying assumptions.

In examining how a process of male maturation underlay a false universal of human experience in early modern England, it is important first to look at the language of works that taught boys and young men (or their parents) the qualities needed for adulthood. While not exploring the gender distinctions of such early modern works, Philippe Arìes, in *Centuries of Childhood,* presented two important points underpinning this discussion. First, the early modern period constituted a crucial transition in altering the way in which children became adults; and, two, this transition was almost entirely restricted to males. According to Arìes, "boys were the first specialized children" with designated stages of growth that corresponded with attendance at public schools and was symbolized by clothing such as the change from short to long pants. Such an assessment is reflected in the minuscule attention Arìes gives to the education of girls. This reality was verified by Ruth Kelso in *The Doctrine for the Lady of the Renaissance* (1956), who noted, when speaking of humanist education, that "girls took a tiny step and boys a giant leap" with the expanding educational opportunities of grammar schools and universities during the 1500s in England.[36]

The falsely universal and gender-restricted language found in a range of mid-1600s Puritan works of educational reform and general educational guides tell us much about why a progressive sense of the modern individual was limited to males. In works such as Hezekiah Woodward's *Childe's Patrimony* (1640), Christopher Wase's *Considerations Concerning Free Schools as Settled in England* (1678), and Charles Hoole's *Children's Talk* (1697), the authors continually interchange the terms "children," "scholars," and "boys" as if they had identical meanings, or "men" and "parents" as denoting the same individuals. There is an implicit assumption in each of these works (and numerous others of a similar nature) that children grow up to be men. While universal terms are employed for males, gender-specific language and characteristics are attached to females. When speaking of girls' limited education, Wase, for example, never once uses the term "children," but informed his audience it was "girls" for whom a more restricted training was intended. And even Queen Elizabeth, who as the nation's monarch would have seemed to embody a nongendered position, was praised as "a tender Mother" for her support of grammar schools and colleges. While boys were obviously not the only children, yet were termed as such, Elizabeth was referred to as a mother while she clearly had never been one. A consistent pattern in these works is to universalize the language of male experience while engendering that of women's, even where circumstances would seem to dictate against it.[37]

Each of these works offers suggestions for the best educational, moral, and political training to accompany a child's progression or, in the words of William Gouge's introduction to Hezekiah Woodward's work, as he "goeth along from infancy to Childhood, thence to youth, and so on till he brings his childe to a growne, yea, an old man, full of dayes." These works did expand the social and educational spectrum of traditional training to a broader class of Englishmen and questioned the domination of the classics. Yet class elasticity was not accompanied by gender inclusion. In assessing John Milton's

---

36. Phillipe Ariès, *Centuries of Childhood: A Social History of Family Life* (New York: Vintage Books, 1962), 58; Ruth Kelso, *Doctrine for the Lady*, 58–77.

37. Hezekiah Woodward, *A Childes Patrimony Laid Out Upon the Good Culture of Tilling over His Whole Man* (London: J. Legatt, 1640); Christopher Wase, *Considerations Concerning Free Schools as Settled in England* (Oxford: Printed at the Theater in Oxford, 1678); Charles Hoole, *Childrens Talk, English and Latin* (London: Printed for the Company of Stationers, 1697).

Tractate of Education (1644) and John Dury's *The Reformed School* (1649), one discovers a hope for improving the access and quality of traditional grammar schools and universities. Of all of these works (and perhaps it reflects its civil war setting), Milton's is the most explicitly masculine, combining the need for effective citizens and soldiers with a hope for expanding the numbers who could receive quality classical and military training. His national educational scheme is structured around "manly and liberal exercises" that tie a solid training in the classics to educating the character of the child. He proposes that schools capable of teaching 150 pupils be organized throughout England.[38]

Wase and Milton share a sense of the scholar embodying the occupational place of learning in contrast with men of lesser occupations. Wase's *Considerations* recognizes the ties among scholars and other men and the formers' dependence on them: "the right bred scholar sees reason not to magnify himself against the industry of other honest laborers and Artists, since God hath char'gd his support in good measure on part of their labors." The scholar, then, was not simply a student but an individual who was becoming a man who lived off his studies. The male scholar was contrasted, both as student and master, with other male occupations, ruling out a place for females in proposed educational schemes from the 1640s and 1650s. Milton's educational proposal sought to produce "brave men and worthy patriots" who would "scorn all their childish and ill-taught qualities." While he doesn't mention mothers specifically (or women generally), one could assume some of the pupils' prior "childish" learning came from women as mothers and nurses. Milton scorned the empty learning of languages for their own sake. One should not be a parrot who spouts Latin. If a student knew "all the tongues" of the Earth but lacked solid grounding in them, he should no more "be esteemed a learned man as any yeoman or tradesman competently wise in his mother-dialect only."[39]

While expressing the humanist's (as well as the moderns') disdain for superficial classical knowledge, Milton lacked a positive view of women educating their children, as expressed more than a century before by Sir Thomas More: "Humanistic education is the chief, almost the sole reason why men come to Oxford; children can receive a good education at home from their

---

38. Woodward, "Preface," *Childe's Patrimony* [N.p., 1640]; John Milton, *Milton on Education: The Tractate of Education,* ed. Oliver Morley Ainsworth (New Haven: Yale University Press, 1928), 57–62 (the first edition in 1644 was titled simply *Of Education* and addressed to Samuel Hartlib); John Dury, *The Reformed School* (London: Printed by R. D. for Richard Wodnothe, [1647?]).

39. John Milton, *Of Education,* 3–5.

mothers." Finally, Milton explicitly outlines a graduated training built upon stages of maturation evident in the boy and young man. Pupils were to study those subjects that their abilities, and their future needs as citizens, dictated—from language preparation through history, geography, and religion, and finally tackling rhetoric, theology, and philosophy. All this was to produce the public man so familiar to students of humanism, but through a national educational program that would open school doors to a wider class of boys.[40]

In 1649, John Dury offered a plan for "Advancement of Universal Learning," inspired by the ideas of Comenius, a Czech reformer. He argued that expanded learning was crucial in a reformed commonwealth, and he stressed the importance of the teacher, or "the School-Master in a well-ordered Common-wealth," who took on similar significance in molding a citizen to the political and religious offices of magistrate and minister. He did make room for girls—if strictly limited—in this expansion, but no women (who could never be "free persons") were to be involved in any organizational efforts. In analyzing the gendered nature of Puritan educational reform, it is important to remember that it was not simply the fact that women could not become independent that prevented their education on the same terms as their brothers; also crucial was their inability to speak for themselves or others. Male maturation was an enclosed circle; only those who had standing could initiate it, and it prepared others like them for future independence.[41] Such training was tied to stages that occurred only among males, and that tied intellectual growth to physical maturity, imbuing the maturing process, and its ultimate product, the adult male, with admirable qualities absent in their sisters.

Such ideas were expressed clearly in a work mourning the death of a youth who was no longer a child, but had not yet reached manhood. In *A Handkercher for Parents' wet Eyes* (1630), the author describes an individual cut down in the midst of acquiring the qualities of maturity that made the adult male such an admirable representative of the human species: "arrived halfe way to the Solstice of his Age; Strong, active, well-shaped, well-graced, faire demeanoured, studious, of an honest and vertuous disposition, yeelding not onely the blossomes but the fruits of a good education." Not even the best among women was seen as possessing, or able to attain, such qualities. These universal standards—essential for defending the land, sustaining the nation's traditions, and understanding its intellectual principles and values—were

40. Ibid., 5–6; Thomas More, *St. Thomas More: Selected Letters,* ed. Elizabeth Frances Rogers (New Haven: Yale University Press, 1961), 95–100.

41. John Dury, *The Reformed School,* 3–5.

founded upon a male maturation process that was consistently placed in falsely universal language.[42]

This process was also grounded in an institutional setting that blended the personal and the political. For men, an early and easy combination of the personal and political led to success within their chosen occupation or profession. Such was not the case for women, in the past or more recently. During the early days of the contemporary women's liberation movement, women were criticized for discussing inappropriate, personal topics (sexual abuse, sharing of household chores, unequal power distribution in the home, issues of child care, and so on) and for arguing that the personal is political. Yet men's personal lives were often purposely integrated into the requirements for, and rewards of, their work. Avoidance of salary for gentlemen, professionals, and skilled artisans meant that such individuals eschewed cash payments and continued to be paid in kind, or in methods not thought of as straight salary (rents, fees, honorariums), so long as it was feasible. Universities continued high table, provided housing or mortgage subsidies for faculty; the church offered its clerics "livings"; gentlemen farmers (while clearly capitalists) worked to separate themselves from efforts seen as "money-grubbing" and hired overseers and conveyancers for such purposes. Guild members established a system to collect fees for nonbusiness activities, funerals, banquets, and the like, and turned over the setting of, and disputes over, fees to a governing body rather than handle such issues themselves, again isolating a man from individual enterprise.

Their institutions also incorporated personal, social, and ritualistic structures that symbolized who they were as significantly as the work they performed. Often the operations of these institutions were more indicative of the gendered nature of an occupation or profession, and were the reasons women were excluded from a trade rather than the actual labor involved. In the eighteenth century, lawyers, for instance, were forced to travel the six circuits to hear cases, and this took them from their family and social and professional networks in London. To overcome such hardships, the circuit established "the bar mess," which resembled the banquets and social gatherings carried out by a range of guilds, and, according to Daniel Duman, mostly involved with eating, entertainment, and drinking: such ties between the socialization of professional males and their economic status blurred personal and public life and created a system in which men came to hold a particular status and then reinscribed its nature and significance continually through the symbols and

42. J.C., *A Handkercher for Parents' Wet Eyes* (Printed by E[liz] A[llde] for M. Sparkes, 1630), 3.

institutions that supported it. Of the bar mess, Duman states: "In addition the messes acted as guardians of the professional conduct of the members and fostered a feeling of professional brotherhood and communal spirit among the barristers."[43] Thus, while modern feminists have been criticized for inappropriately inserting personal issues into public debates, the integrated personal and professional interests of men have not been equally scrutinized.

Conclusion

In trying to grapple with how the false universal actually operates in practice, I was drawn to an old joke I heard as a child. It is about the soldier whose mother has just died and whose sergeant cannot decide the best way to tell him. The sergeant then gives an order: "All of you men with plans to visit your mother this weekend, please step forward. . . . Not so fast, Private Jones." In many ways, I think this is close to how women are consciously or unconsciously omitted from language that they believe includes them. One reads in innumerable works the words "everyone" or "all" and assumes that one must belong to such inclusive terms. Then in reading on, one learns that what "everyone" is doing is taking a wife, or governing his household to protect the family (identified as wife and children), or has lost a job which makes it impossible to aid a mother or other siblings. If the reader is a woman, at that moment she is drawn up short and realizes that, no, while I thought the author meant me, he/she did not.

A good example of the latter moment appeared in a *Washington Post* story in the early 1980s; it was a time when traditional unemployment benefits were ending because of an extended period of high unemployment, and the State of Maryland had authorized an eight-week extension of benefits for the long-term unemployed. The story was about a young man who was unemployed, but still on his first set of benefits, and was having trouble helping out a mother who was close to using up her extended benefits and had two daughters to support. The story was about extended benefits, and surely a mother whose benefits were due to expire, with dependents, would have been more representative (and one would think more sympathetic) than a son who was simply having trouble assisting his mother. Yet the term "worker" without

---

43. For a fuller discussion of these arguments, see the introduction to *Women Writers and the Early Modern British Political Tradition*, ed. Hilda L. Smith (Cambridge: Cambridge University Press, 1998), 1–14.

woman or women in front of it is a false universal restricted to males, and thus an example about a man (whether totally relevant) was more appropriate than a woman outside that universal category. Such realities that are truly ubiquitous are missed because the arguments for more attention to male employment (such as their greater familial responsibilities) ignore the simple fact that being male is the most important criterion. In ferreting out such effects of the false universal one can look, for instance, at the distinct impact of the Great Depression or other economic crises on men and women. As we know, employers were discouraged from hiring married women, and single women were believed not to need employment because they worked for "pin money." Any available work needed to go to men with families. But, if this were the reason, why were there not similar policies for bachelors, also supposedly without family obligations?[44]

Finally, we need to read works more closely for their falsely universal language. Often, explanations for the inclusion of one sex or the other are based upon supposed characteristics or particular duties of one type of man or woman (for example, mother or father), but in reality are tied to the mere fact that an individual is a man or woman, girl or boy. That fact, which seems so obvious and without special relevance to the particular instance, is most often why a man or woman is described differently, encouraged to go in a particular direction, or restricted from membership in a wide range of social institutions.

The succeeding chapters of this work will explore the nature of such falsely universal constructions in works devoted to the young, the nature of citizenship, and the emerging focus on sensibility and consumerism during the eighteenth century. It will focus especially on the introductory sections of such works that include definitions of terms to be used later in the narrative, and those portions that set out broad goals the author hopes to achieve in the work, program, or institution being described. It will especially explore the ways in which authors discuss and define qualities associated with "human nature," "human," or "humanity" and those associated with "man" or "men," and then investigate how such discussions contrast with the same authors' discussion of "women," "the fair sex," or other descriptors tied to the female half of the human race. My contention is that the connection between the first two sets of qualities, in contrast with the distinctions associated with the last, most

---

44. For a discussion of the some of the definitional issues tied to the U.S. Social Security system, see Alice Kessler-Harris, "Designing Women and Old Fools: The Construction of the Social Security Amendments of 1939," in *U.S. History as Women's History: New Feminist Essays*, ed. Linda K. Kerber, Alice Kessler-Harris, and Kathryn Kish Sklar (Chapel Hill: University of North Carolina Press, 1995), 87–106.

clearly characterizes the false universal underpinning early modern gender values. Finally, this book will analyze where historians either create false universals or exacerbate their usage by employing terms that were understood by contemporaries to mean both women and men, but are later employed by scholars as inclusive nouns pointing only to males. Thus, the language of early modern England and the way later scholars have used it without gender-based interrogation are under scrutiny here.

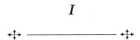

I

"Only of free Persons"

Male Maturation and the False Universal

An assumption central to the early modern false universal was that a process of male maturation lay at the heart of learning, social relationships, economic standing, and membership in the political realm. Men were portrayed as both individuals and as exemplars of the qualities that broadly characterized human existence. Women were discussed in much more specialized ways: normally in terms of sexual functions and relationships, in domestic roles, or as exceptions in public economic or political roles. A queen, although the most powerful political figure in the nation, did not symbolize women's political power (or generic political authority), while members of Parliament or magistrates were used to illustrate men's general political standing. A king did not merely symbolize male political authority but mutually reinforced the standing of the father as head of the family, while the father in turn embodied patriarchal authority on which the king's, as well as his own, leadership was grounded. And while women were responsible for a range of skilled and unskilled tasks, they did not inhabit an occupation in ways their male counterparts did, inscribe their sex with the abilities attached to that occupation, or define the standards of the trade through their skills. No matter how many carried out the trade, or what skill they displayed, women who held a post were still considered individual exceptions. Such was the case for those who held public office as well. Traditional accounts stressed that a woman held a public position because something out of the norm (usually a mishap) occurred in the nature of the trade or the state, or in the woman's own life, which led to her economic or political independence.[1]

Much has been written on the differences between the sexes articulated during the seventeenth century on religious, political, and economic principles, but less attention has been given to a gender-distinct aging process. While many scholars take for granted women's omission from the public and political world, few would deny that the female sex aged along with their male counterparts. Yet works on aging excluded women as surely from the stages of life as did those written about public offices. This chapter will explore that topic and will postulate the way in which Englishmen (and to a lesser extent women) visualized the distinct training and ultimate maturation of their sons and daughters, their students, apprentices and servants, and young people generally. While discussions of citizenship, appropriate religious roles for men and women, occupations suitable for each sex, or proper marital roles are crucial to an understanding of gender values in the mid-seventeenth century, they are more apt to feature application and outcome rather than basic nature. Thus, through a discussion of the aging and maturing of young males and females into adult men and women, we can grasp most thoroughly how the adults around them envisioned their essential natures, appropriate training, and adult lives.

To understand this seventeenth-century discussion we must grapple with its asymmetry. It was never a discussion of the nature, training and adult goals of two distinct sexes; rather, it was consistently grounded in a conflation of man and human in a large range of works directed to sons, apprentices, students, and so on. This was combined with a smaller body of works supporting specialized training for daughters, female servants, and girls. These realities become clear first quantitatively from an assessment of the number and types

---

1. Accounts of these claims abound, from the arguments of Robert Filmer and others who mapped the line of authority from Adam to fathers to male monarch, to the statements of various guilds that linked the standing of their members to the standing of freemen generally, to the many discussions (both pro and con) of Elizabeth's elevation to the throne as a particular act of God or nature, and from the claims of Leveller and sectarian tracts from the 1640s which tied their status to the "people" of England and the glorious past of the freeborn Englishman. Perhaps most significant, however, has been the general inattention to gender's place within these issues.

of works that appear under the heading "son" or "daughter" (and, alternatively, "young man" or "maid") in the electronic listing of works produced by the Library of Congress for the period 1625–1700. Among these, 624 works appear with the word "son" in the title, while only 187 appear with "daughter." Most significant, however, is not the number, but rather the distinct goals for each sex and the related distinctions in the type of works: those directed to sons are much more apt to be broad-based works preparing individuals to be responsible adults and citizens in English society generally, while official documents or private works referring to girls and women are more restricted.[2]

As noted earlier, William Shakespeare in *As You Like It* illustrates this process of maturation when he shifts his well-known portrayal of the world as a stage to the "Seven Ages of Man" in a manner conflating the identity of both sexes with the qualities of just one. Shakespeare does not merely use terms such as "schoolboy" and "soldier" to designate stages relevant only to men's lives, but he modifies gender neutral terms to ensure that they refer only to males. Terms such as "infant," "lover," and "old age" carry no gender-restricted qualities with them, but Shakespeare incorporates such qualities in his description of the aging process. The full text identifies the lover as directing his attention to his "mistress" and the pantaloon losing his "big manly voice." The seven ages of man was a common medieval trope,[3] and after

2. In perusing the Library of Congress's OCLC listing of works for English publications from 1625 to 1700 which included "son" or "daughter" in the title, the blurring of class lines is apparent as well as the greater social utility of adult males. If a sense of independence and individuation is tied to adulthood, then it is unclear whether women were considered capable of adult qualities. Care for others was stressed for both sexes, and seemed to represent the central quality for adult women, but any focus on individual development (except for areas of faith) was missing in discussions of female training. Even by the early nineteenth century women still lacked any clear stages of development. In an illustrated broadsheet entitled "The Life and Age of Woman: Stages of Woman's Life from Infancy to the brink of the Grave" (printed at Barre, Mass., by A. Alden, n.d.), the ages given are one, twelve, eighteen, thirty, fifty, seventy-five, and ninety. As might be expected from an 1840 work, the descriptions of these points in a woman's life emphasize feminine, romantic, and moral accomplishments. Even at year one, the description reads: "The strong attachment of the young which pervades the female sex is exhibited even at this tender age in the infant's grasping the doll as a favorite." Twelve seems to bring the greatest independence of character, with the girl being associated with the swiftness of the "antelope" and the spirit of a "lark." Eighteen is "considered the most critical age in the life of a female" as she seeks a proper husband, and at thirty she "may be considered at the zenith of her intellectual and physical powers." Now her attention is turned fully to her family. This continues at fifty, "where the time not spent providing for her household is devoted to counseling her children," whose success guarantees her own. By seventy-five her declining beauty remembers a life well spent, and at ninety (on the verge of death), she might still require some direction: "If the frail and constantly decaying state of the body is kept in view, it will lessen sensual pleasures and fix the affections where there is naught but beauty, light and time without end."

3. A useful overview of the concept of the ages of man during the medieval period can be found in J. A. Burrow, *The Ages of Man: A Study in Medieval Writing and Thought* (Oxford: Clarendon Press, 1986).

Shakespeare's comedy, it continued in use. The recent commentary on the comedy is instructive because scholars have given considerable attention to the class limitations of Shakespeare's stages of life without commenting on its gender exclusion.[4]

A mid-seventeenth-century work by Henry Cuffe, *The Differences of the Ages of Mans Life,* perpetuates the view that the aging process occurs only in men and argues that heat defines men's intellectual capacity and physical prowess. In making this argument, based on principles derived from Greek medicine, he links such heat to the stages of life and explicitly contrasts that progression with women and children, defining their natures as outside such a process of male maturation. Cuffe introduces the topic in a broad discussion of human nature and its place within the universe: "so the heart of man, the fountayne of *life* and *heat,* hath assigned to it by *Nature,* the middle part of our body for his habitation, from whence proceedeth *life* and *heat,* unto all the parts of the body, (as it were unto Rivers) whereby they be preserved and enabled to perform their naturall and proper functions." While heat may be the central characteristic of mankind, it is lacking in some people. Children who are "too ripe witted" when young either die young "or else toward their old age [become] most sottish" because "from the beginning they had but little moysture." In turning to Plato for an authoritative source, he concludes: "Plato doubted not to say, that looke how much moysture there is in us, so much also is our folly; and therefore it is as the same Plato observeth, that children and women are for the most part most foolish."[5] Thus this discussion

---

While Burrow makes clear the mutability of the "ages of man," sometimes being subsumed in three stages, other times in four, with less under Shakespeare's choice of seven, still he does not treat women's exclusion from the imagery or language of these stages. The introduction to his work begins: "As people grow up and grow old, they change. Individuals change in different ways, but there are held to be certain established norms in this matter." He, along with his predecessors, mingles "man," "a man," "people," and "person" as if they had overlapping meanings (1–3).

4. *The Seven Ages of Man,* ed. Robert R. Sears and S. Shirley Feldman (Los Altos: W. Kaufman, [1973]), vi. The most recent Variorum edition of *As You Like It* both makes clear the long antecedents for "the idea that human life may be divided into stages" and includes various authors' concerns over the inclusiveness and accuracy of Shakespeare's stages. Questions are raised about why there are no toys for infancy and "no playmates in boyhood; no hawking or jousting in youth," but no questions are raised about the conflation of "human life" with male maturation. (*A New Variorum Edition of Shakespeare: As You Like It,* ed. Richard Knowles with a survey of criticism by Evelyn Joseph Mattern [New York: Modern Language Association of America, 1977], 131–34).

5. Henry Cuffe, *The Differences of the Ages of Mans Life,* rev. ed. (London: Printed by T.H. and are to be sold by Nathaniel Buster, 1640), 3, 153–54. This massive work is mostly an attempt to show off the author's erudition and draws materials from a wide range of classical sources to comment on commonly accepted themes.

of the ages of man concludes with a familiar misogynist slur about women's moist nature making them foolish and confirming that they constitute a category along with children that removes them from an evolving rational nature.

Historians have written on the nature of youth and the training and education of both males and females, but they have given less attention to the linking of male education with human development and women's restricted education beyond such development. Ilana Krausman Ben-Amos's study of the nature of adolescence in sixteenth- and seventeenth-century England, *Adolescence and Youth in Early Modern England,* builds upon her earlier work on male and female apprentices in Bristol. A number of historians have discussed the subject of "masterless men" who are often associated with young men of the lower orders.[6] *The Experience of Authority in Early Modern England* devotes considerable attention to the socialization of young people, with a chapter treating women separately. The chapter most relevant to this work is Paul Griffiths's study of "masterless young people" in Norwich from 1560 to 1645. He concludes that women were treated differently from men and that independence, or being "at their own hand," was punishable only for women up to 1632, while 80 percent of those punished for being "out of service" were also women. While he expands the more common term from "masterless men" to "masterless young people," still the language of the relevant statute reinforces the broad status-based terminology for males and the more gender-specific language for females: "Whereas gret unconveye ys in this town in that senglewomen being unmarried be at ther owne hands and doe bake and brewe and use other trades to the great hurte of the poore inhabitants havinge wieffe and children."[7]

Even though Bernard Capp in the same collection points out that women constituted twenty percent of English householders in the early modern period, in the statute women are contrasted with inhabitants who are assumed

6. Ilana Krausman Ben-Amos, *Adolescence and Youth in Early Modern England* (New Haven: Yale University Press, 1994). Anthony Fletcher, *Gender, Sex and Subordination in England, 1500–1800* (New Haven: Yale University Press), includes chapters on educating boys and educating girls, and discusses their distinct patterns, but does not consistently link boys' training to broader human qualities (297–321, 364–75); for works incorporating an analysis of the nature of the term "masterless men," its importance in early modern English social policy, and its role in controlling the behavior and independence of the young, see A. L. Beier, *Masterless Men: The Vagrancy Problem in England, 1560–1640* (London: Methuen, 1985), and Paul Slack, *Poverty and Policy in Tudor and Stuart England* (London: Longman, 1988), as well as *Rebellion, Popular Protest, and the Social Order in Early Modern England,* ed. Paul Slack (Cambridge: Cambridge University Press, 1984).

7. Quoted in Paul Griffiths, "Masterless Young People in Norwich, 1560–1645," in *The Experience of Authority in Early Modern England,* ed. Paul Griffiths et al. (New York: St. Martin's Press, 1996), 152–53.

to have wives and children. Capp points out that women often had authority that early modern authors believed they lacked, and certainly this was the case. But it remains both true and crucial that the language of statutes and a massive range of social commentary continually conflated human and man, while categorizing women separately, no matter their actual status.[8]

A statute issued under Charles I offers a good example of the use of falsely inclusive language in one portion of an act, only to be clarified in another to exclude women. A law from 1630 is directed both to aiding the elderly poor and forcing the idle young and able-bodied adult to gainful labor: "For the training up of Youth in honest and profitable Trades and Mysteries, by putting them forth to be Apprentices, as also for the setting to worke of idle persons, who being of abilitie to worke, in some kinde or other, doe neverthelesse, refuse to labour, and either wander up and down the Citie and Countrey begging, or which is worse maintaine themselves by filching and stealing."[9] Directions for implementing the act followed and made clear that the term "persons" as used above meant only males, for in this section such persons were accompanied by women and children: "That no man harbour Rogues in their Barnes, or Outhouseings. And the Wandring persons with women and children, to give account to the Constable or Justice of Peace, where they were married, and where their Children were Christened; for these people live like Savages, neither marry nor bury nor Christen, which licentious libertie makes so many delight to be Rogues and Wanderers."[10] Such language obscures the fact that women were part of the broad-based status and occupational categories to which the legislation was addressed, and encouraged policies in which parish training and apprenticeship programs were reserved for men.

Ben-Amos's work is devoted throughout to males, except for chapter 6, "Women's Youth: The Autonomous Phase." While she offers a range of useful examples on the preparation for adulthood, and claims in her introduction that "this book is about young people, men and women in a broad spectrum of middling and lower groups of society, who, in the period between 1500 and 1700, spent at least part of their adolescence and youth away from their homes as farm servants, domestic servants, or apprentices," she does not adequately

8. Bernard Capp, "Separate Domains? Women and Authority in Early Modern England," in ibid., 117–45.

9. [Great Britain. Sovereigns. Charles I]. *Orders and Directions, Together with a Commission for the better Administration of Justice ... the reliefe of the Poore, the well ordering and training up of youth in Trades ...* (London: Printed by Robert Parker and by the Assignes of John Bill, 1630), 10.

10. Ibid., appendix, n.p.

differentiate the generalized instruction for boys and young men from the specialized teachings for girls and young women.[11] Her work makes clear, as well, the economic determination of childhood and adolescence, where employment and occupational training constituted the transition from childhood to adulthood for most children, in contrast to the classical education for upper-class boys and the emphasis on culture and social graces for elite girls educated at home or in finishing schools.

Ben-Amos begins her work with the seven ages, but fails to note their gender significance. Her materials, whether from prescriptive literature or the experiences of apprentices and servants, are drawn overwhelmingly from men. In chapter 6, she notes the special and more restricted directives for girls, but does not contrast them with males elsewhere standing for humans. In many ways, her treatment reflects the problem identified most prominently by Simone de Beauvoir in *The Second Sex,* and noted by innumerable later feminist theorists, that there are not two sexes but only one, with the second representing the "other" beyond the male norm.[12] Here, Ben-Amos emphasizes the more limited training and expectations parents held for daughters, but she also demonstrates that such expectations and prescriptions often did not conform to reality.

Rather than adulthood, adolescence, Ben-Amos claims, offered women "a measure of autonomy and independence," when they both "learnt and performed a host of agricultural tasks and skills" in the countryside and "a range of skills and competencies acquired through formal and informal apprenticeships" in towns. She points to the difficulty of assessing women's acquiring skills on the same terms as men. They were more apt to undergo informal apprenticeships or to gain skills as domestic servants. When women assumed management of shops as widows, "it was clear that they had gained the skill to manage the craft," but unclear how and when they obtained such skills. Their place was recognized more as a partnership: "Married women in Bristol were normally considered formal parties to apprenticeship contracts, and in the Register of Apprentices their names appeared almost as a rule alongside those of their husbands, indicating that the apprentice was subject to their discipline and supervision as well." But because we have so few institutional and legal documents tracing women's lives from childhood onward, we tend to find them in records only as secondary figures or as participants in transitional

11. Ben-Amos, *Adolescence and Youth,* 2.

12. Simone de Beauvoir, *The Second Sex,* trans. and ed. H. M. Parshley (1952; reprint, New York: Vintage Books, 1989).

moments of male maturation. As Ben-Amos notes, "the informal nature of such learning makes it difficult to gauge its precise dimensions," and thus makes it virtually impossible to contrast the specialized (and often obscured) direction women pursued to adulthood in opposition to the general, recorded, and public route taken by men.[13]

As is clear in Ben-Amos's discussion of adolescence during the early modern period, training for adulthood was determined by rank, especially for males. While women from the upper and lower ranks were given distinct training based on whether they were being prepared to serve in another's home or to supervise their own servants, the domestic skills taught differed less than did the preparation of gentlemen from those lower on the social scale. The former learned to manage the family estate, prepare for public office or for a profession while the sons of yeomen, artisans, and cottagers, whose highest sights were normally an apprenticeship, more likely received little training and ended up as agricultural laborers or performing service in a local household.

These realities make it more difficult, therefore, to identify stages of development for women than for men. *Lawes Resolutions* was one of the few works to include a chapter on divisions in women's lives beyond the much used, but seldom commented on, "maid, wife and widow." Here the stages vary greatly from Shakespeare's seven ages. The stages of a woman's life are: at age seven a father can seek money contributions to the costs of a wedding agreement from his tenants to marry a daughter, at age nine she qualifies for dower, at twelve she can consent to marriage, at sixteen she is past the age the lord can select a husband for her, and at twenty-one she is able to "make a feoffement." With the exception of feoffement, this was a passive progression tied wholly to decisions concerning marriage. While it was common to reduce the category "woman" to the legal and domestic standing of "wife," the author made clear the problems inherent in having "wife" stand for all women. In the portion of *Lawes Resolutions* treating single women, the anonymous author asks the reader to focus on the standing of virgins, for here "the Law differeth little or not much from the common form apperteyning unto males." Finally, to determine women's legal and political disabilities, the author notes that one could turn to patrilineal naming (along with biblical and legal restrictions) for more evidence: "Let us speake of heires, and see a little in what cases a woman shall inherit. It is knowne to all, that because women lose the name of their

13. Ben-Amos, *Adolescence and Youth*, 134, 146–47.

ancestors, and by marriage usually they are transferred in *alienam familiam,* they participate seldome in heirship with males."[14] There was little concern over confusion of cause and effect, or awareness of circular reasoning. Surely women taking their husbands' names must have been a result rather than an indicator of their lack of legal or political standing. Thus, a pastiche of biblical commentary, legal precedent, and linguistic explanations was offered to explain fundamental issues of women's failure to evolve into independent adulthood. As will be discussed in Chapter 5, this alters dramatically after 1700 when ideas associated with the values tied to sensibility and the "fair sex" influenced much that was written about women.

Programs of Educational Reform

The parameters of this process of male maturation are found in educational treatises and guides for behavior directed at sons and young men generally. While one would assume works written by men and addressed to other males would employ gender-specific attributes, in reality they were more apt to stress presumably human qualities attached to adulthood, independence, morality, and personal responsibility. Discussions of schools, curricula, and the best ways to mold an adult male were continually intermingled with discussions on human aging and the qualities associated with the best of human nature. While a classical curriculum underlay the education offered by grammar schools and universities, by the mid-seventeenth century more authors (especially those associated with religious reform) were envisioning additional diverse training opened to a wider class of individuals. This effort in many ways built upon the humanist program for a "New Learning" that had influenced educational leaders from the early sixteenth century. But, by the mid-1600s, educational reformers sought to integrate reformed Christianity with a more practical curriculum. This does not mean, though, that reformers were moving to displace the classical curriculum based upon Latin (and to a lesser extent, Greek) grammar and literature. Puritan educational reformers intended to keep the classical basis of such training; they simply wanted to extend the training to involve more practical subjects and to expand the student body beyond the gentle classes. These works reveal a pattern of male

---

14. *The Lawes Resolutions of Womens Rights; or, The Lawes Provision for Woemen* (London: Printed by the Assignes of John More, 1632), 7.

maturation that was denied to women, allowing the one sex to develop qualities and gain status not open to the other.[15]

Such Puritan educational reform tracts emerged in the late 1640s and advocated extending educational opportunities to a greater proportion of England's population. Even though the term "Puritan" has been questioned over the last few decades, there were still English individuals who wanted to reform institutional education in order to ensure a more godly population. Closely aligned with Continental reformers, they believed the main goal of education was to instill a set of beliefs that underlay personal acts of social and political responsibility.[16]

The ideas of Czech reformer John Comenius and the English educator and Polish immigrant Samuel Hartlib were central to the values that characterized these works. Comenius (1592–1670) had an enormous influence on Protestants seeking to reform educational practice during the seventeenth century. As an early seventeenth-century thinker, Comenius blended an interest in the new science with a strong reliance on his reformed faith. While Comenius offered a program to improve instruction in Latin, he saw its value not in itself, but as a second language that would allow scholars to communicate with those beyond their mother tongue. He favored direct instruction on a common model that could overcome the limitations of individual teachers. And he pushed for both universal schooling and for a focus on content over language

---

15. Charles Webster, *The Great Instauration: Science, Medicine, and Reform, 1626–1660* (New York: Holmes and Meier, 1975); Robert F. Young, *Comenius in England* (Oxford: Oxford University Press, 1932). For Puritan influences on university education, see *Seventeenth-Century Oxford*, vol. 4, *History of the University of Oxford*, ed. Nicholas Tyacke (Oxford: Clarendon Press,1997), and for its prominence at Cambridge University, see Arthur Gray, *Cambridge University: An Episodical History*, esp. chapter 9 on John Milton and the Interregnum period (Cambridge: W. Heffer & Sons, 1926), and Elisabeth Leedham-Green, *A Concise History of the University of Cambridge* (Cambridge; Cambridge University Press, 1996), 66–107.

16. The term "Puritan" has become suspect as historians have abandoned the older phrase "Puritan Revolution" to describe both the origins and nature of the English civil war. A range of scholars have raised questions, some believing the term has a more secure meaning than others, about clear distinctions between Anglicans and Puritans and the degree to which the beliefs and actions of the latter were fundamental to events in England from 1640 to 1660. For these discussions, see Patrick Collinson, "Wars of Religion," in his *The Birthpangs of Protestant England* (New York: St. Martin's Press, 1988), 127–55, and his *Godly People* (London: Hambledon Press, 1983); Peter Lake, *Anglicans and Puritans? Presbyterianism and English Conformist Thought from Whitgift to Hooker* (London: Unwin Hyman, 1988), offers a nuanced definition of "Puritan" that reflects the more careful recent use of the term: "The term 'Puritan' is used to refer to a broader span of opinion, encompassing those advanced protestants who regard themselves as 'the godly', a minority of genuinely true believers in an otherwise lukewarm or corrupt mass" (7). On a separate role for religion in the mid-century revolution, see John Morrill, *The Nature of the English Revolution* (London: Longman, 1993), 45–90.

so that knowledge rather than grammatical purity could form the basis of instruction. The goals for his reforms were an improved method of teaching Latin and a survey of knowledge offering universal education. Samuel Hartlib became familiar with Comenius's work through two foreign students studying at Cambridge, and he persuaded Comenius to come to England in 1641. Hartlib and others encouraged the establishment of a college teaching his universal system, or panosophy, but the oncoming civil war prevented its founding and led to his departure within nine months of his arrival in England.[17]

Comenius was impressed with English interest in reforming education but somewhat put off by their emphasis on social hierarchy and dress. In a letter to his colleagues in Poland he noted that people attended services in great numbers, English men and youths took notes on sermons in shorthand, the country had enormous numbers of books readily available, and "They are eagerly debating on the reform of schools in the whole kingdom in a manner similar to that to which my wishes tend, namely that all young people should be instructed, none neglected."[18]

Samuel Hartlib, Comenius's most important English disciple, was the son of a Polish merchant who had married an English woman from a wealthy merchant family doing business in Danzig. He emigrated to England in 1628 and in later life became a friend of John Milton. Hartlib's interests were quite broad, but the two that directed much of his life were a concern to improve the nature of English education and its agriculture. He received a pension from Parliament in 1646 for his works on husbandry, and his most famous work on educational reform was *A Reformation of Schooles, designed in six excellent Treatises* (1646), which was a translation of a 1642 work by Comenius. He tried throughout his life to reform English education on the model set forth by Comenius.[19]

English authors who allied with these two reformers included John Dury and Milton. While the English were eager to expand schooling, they did not adopt the principles set forth by Comenius as regards including all children in their reforms. Comenius laid out his principles in a work that appeared in English in 1657, and differed fundamentally from the educational reform

---

17. *Comenius,* ed. John Sadler (London: Macmillan, 1969), 5–7; this book, which is in a series on educational thinkers, introduces Comenius, analyzes his educational program, and includes excerpts from Comenius's proposals. *Samuel Hartlib and the Advancement of Learning,* ed. Charles Webster (Cambridge: Cambridge University Press, 1970), 27–39.

18. Sadler, ed., *Comenius,* 1–17.

19. Webster, ed., *Samuel Hartlib,* 27–39.

efforts put forth earlier by Dury and Milton. While his English followers showed less inclination to concern themselves with girls' education, Comenius wrote that education should not be for "the children of the rich or the powerful only, but of all alike, boys and girls, both noble and ignoble, rich and poor, in all cities and towns, villages and hamlets." And in pushing for a universal system of education, Comenius reiterated his desire that women be included in his scheme. Anticipating his critics, he responded, "If any ask, 'What will be the result if artisans, rustics, porters, and even women become lettered?' I answer, 'If this universal instruction of youth be brought about by the proper means, none of these will lack the material for thinking, choosing, following and doing good things.'"[20] In this statement, Comenius stresses two points relevant to the prominence of the false universal: first, he makes clear from the phrase "and even" that women were the most problematic group to include, even more so than rustics or porters. Second, he uses the categorization that I will discuss in greater detail in Chapter 3, the tendency for authors to contrast a particular economic status of men with women as a whole. Such usage confirms the mutually exclusive categories of age, condition, and sex in which condition was a category separate from sex, and thus could be contrasted with women, just as if they were a group outside of rank, occupation, or economic standing.

Milton made clear that his educational scheme was never intended to include women, and although Dury makes some space for girls in his reformed schools, they were intended for boys' training. Women's lack of individual freedom hampered their educational role. In *The Reformed School*, Dury's educationally democratic effort was not intended equally for both sexes. Its primary goal was to reach the young while they were still not corrupt, through "training up Reformed School-Masters." He saw schools as especially important in a politically reformed society, and he noted that "the School-Master in a well-ordered Common-wealth, is no lesse considerable then either the Minister or the Magistrate." Preparation for a male public life permeates his program. Although including girls in the school would seem to entail a need for women in its planning, Dury made clear this was not intended for the association that would organize the schools. "The Association should be only of free Persons; therefore we shall not consent to joyn with any (specially with women) but such as are free to dispose of themselves." In this, and three other

20. Quoted in *Education in Tudor and Stuart England*, ed. David Cressy (New York: St. Martin's Press, 1976), 101–2.

works seeking similar reformation of education and religion, all printed in 1649 and 1650, Dury revealed little interest in including women in his plans for a Comenius-inspired "Advancement of Universal Learning." Women were simply not the independent, public individuals responsible for a nation's educational, religious or moral qualities. Never attaining independent adulthood, they were incapable of urging or belonging to a more broadly representative society.[21]

Contrasting the works concerning boys and girls' education is not a simple task, given their distinct nature and audience. The works directed to boys' education, in contrast to occupational or professional training, focused on a broad-based curriculum and employed universal language addressed to and embodying the qualities inherent for successful development of the nation. In addition to such works, there were guides to individual sons written overwhelmingly by members of the peerage and gentry, and by fathers rather than mothers. Works addressed to apprentices, and to a lesser degree servants, incorporated both the skills needed for the intended tasks, but also qualities attached to being a successful human being; such works will be discussed primarily in Chapter 3.

The works addressed to girls were largely works of advice to daughters, normally penned by fathers. Women left advice for children, *The Mothers Legacy* being the most famous early seventeenth-century example, but they were written more for the needs of younger children and did not distinguish subjects or recipients by gender. Another early seventeenth-century work, *The Mother's Blessing*, written by Dorothy Leigh, is a plea to those who would watch over her children in case of her death and is also a strongly religious work.[22]

21. Quotation from John Dury, *The Reformed School* (London: Printed by R. D. for Richard Wodnothe, 1649), 13–14. See also John Dury, *The Reformed Librarie-Keeper with a Supplement to the Reformed School* . . . (London: Printed by William Du-Gard, and are to be sold by Rob. Littleberrie, 1650); and John Dury, *A Seasonable Discourse* . . . *What the Grounds and Method of Our Reformation Ought to Be in Religion and Learning* . . . (London: Printed for R. Wodnothe, 1649).

22. Elizabeth (Brooke) Joceline, *The Mothers Legacy, to her Unborne Child* (1624) (Oxford: Printed and sold by Jo. Wilmot, 1684), was written by a woman who died in childbirth instructing her unborn child (if female) to learn the Bible and prepare for a traditional female adulthood; Dorothy Leigh, *The Mother's Blessing, Being Several Godley Admonitions Given by a Mother unto her Children upon her Death-bed* ([London]: Printed by I. M. for I. Clarke, W. Thackery, and T. Passinger, 1685). For a discussion of English women's writings during the second half of the seventeenth century, see Elaine Hobby, *Virtue of Necessity: English Women's Writing, 1646–1688* (Ann Arbor: University of Michigan Press, 1989). Phyllis Mack, *Visionary Women: Ecstatic Prophecy in Seventeenth-Century England* (Berkeley and Los Angeles: University of California Press, 1992), 305–50, outlines Quaker women's sense of maternal concern and spiritual oversight for children. For both their own children and apprentices and servants placed in their care, Quaker mothers displayed a harsh regimen that focused most heavily on spiritual purity.

Most of the literature focusing on expanding educational opportunities was directed at those families who could afford to forgo the labor of children for a lengthy training period, and this severely restricted the numbers who could qualify. Yet, while the plans for educational expansion were clearly limited to a small minority of the population, the reach of their rhetoric was much greater than their realities. Such plans for educational reform were strongly tied to the political and religious values of the mid 1600s; they stressed the same emphasis on inclusion, on the evils of hierarchy, on the artificiality and impracticality of traditional classical education as did the "moderns" in the debates between "ancients and moderns," anti-episcopal Puritan tracts, and the Leveller attacks on the current social and political system. Thus the language of these works stressed their falsely universal nature, giving the impression that all would be included when in reality all women and most men were excluded.[23]

This chapter concentrates on the guides directed to sons and other young men that conflate qualities surrounding aging with those of citizenship and national identity, while including works addressed to daughters primarily as contrast. Such discussions were found only in those works discussing males. Milton's *Tractate* concentrated on how to construct a competent, independent adult who could simultaneously pursue his own interests while overseeing those of family, locality, and country. Thus the key to understanding the values of these works addressed to students, apprentices, and the sons of merchants, gentry, and nobility is their continual integration of broad physical and cognitive stages with a life pattern laid out for men of their rank or for those aspiring to its membership. While seldom explicitly detailed as such, divisions left to women were based on sexual activity, marriage, childbearing,

---

23. Richard Foster Jones, *Ancients and Moderns: A Study of the Rise of the Scientific Movement in Seventeenth-Century England*, 2nd ed. (St Louis: Washington University Press, 1961); a brief overview of attitudes toward education, and the realities of educational expansion during the Tudor and Stuart periods, can be found in the introduction to *Education in Tudor and Stuart England*, ed. David Cressy (New York: St. Martin's Press, 1976), although I disagree that either prescriptively or in reality women were included in the reformers' plans as Cressy contends: "Universal schooling, of women as well as men, in English rather than Latin, and with a pious and practical curriculum was to usher in a new social order" (10). He does note that these plans were proposed rather than implemented, but still they constituted plans overwhelmingly restricted to boys. Works on individual reformers continue to ignore their omission of women, such as *Arenas of Conflict: Milton and the Unfettered Mind*, ed. Kristin Pruitt McColgan and Charles W. Durham (Selinsgrove: Susquehanna University Press, 1997). Two works that discuss Comenius and Hartlib are G. H. Turnbull, *Hartlib, Dury, and Comenius: Gleanings from Hartlib's Papers* (Liverpool: University Press of Liverpool, 1947), and *Samuel Hartlib and Universal Reformation: Studies in Intellectual Communication*, ed. Mark Greengrass et al. (Cambridge: Cambridge University Press, 1994).

or, for others, spinsterhood, childlessness, or menopause as factors that distinguished their life stages and set goals for instruction.[24]

Milton in his rather brief *Tractate* offers only one of the many guides to boys' training that encompass a range of choices presumably human. His is an integrated program incorporating educational, military, political, and religious goals for pupils. It has a Baconian ring to it, criticizing current classical training in favor of a more practical one with a wider social reach. The work opens with a letter addressed to Samuel Hartlib and demonstrates Milton's sense of the importance of the project and the honor due a reformer such as Hartlib. Milton believes, even though he has not concentrated on it, that reforming education is "one of the greatest and noblest designes, that can be thought of, and for the want whereof this nation perishes," but Hartlib has done so, which has given him "the esteem of a person sent hither by some good providence . . . to be the occasion and the incitement of great good to this Island."[25]

By 1644, John Milton was proposing a system of schooling where each town would "finde a spatious house and ground about it" for an "Academy big enough to lodge a hundred and fifty persons" and there establish a school for its young, but only its male young, to pursue a more rigorous, applied, and militarily useful curriculum than that taught in grammar schools and universities. It was to have twenty "attendants" who administered the school under the control "of one." Milton's universal and inclusive language would have seemed by necessity to include the interests of girls, but for him the way to achieve those universal goals was by the teaching of "manly and liberal Exercises" to boys. In following Shakespeare's model, he agreed that the process of aging was key to understanding the nature of human (male) experience.[26]

Milton follows the physical description of the house intended for a school with the evolution of education from its earliest stages through its highest: "This place should be at once both school and University, not needing a remove to any other house of Schollership, except it be some peculiar Colledge of Law, or physick, where they mean to be practitioners." He next outlines the universal themes that drive his work: "The end then of learning, is to

24. For a general discussion of women's younger years, see Mendelson and Crawford, *Women in Early Modern England*, 75–123.

25. John Milton, *Of Education. To Master Samuel Hartlib* (London: Thomas Underhill, 1641), 1. Hereafter cited in the text by page number.

26. Milton, *Of Education*. By 1673, the work was known as the *Tractate of Education*, and was reprinted a number of times from the seventeenth century through a Harvard Classics edition of 1913. See vol. 3, *Harvard Classics*, ed. Charles W. Eliot (New York: P. F. Collier, [1910–ca. 1937]) .

repaire the ruins of our first parents by regaining to know God alright." While knowing languages was commendable, to master only "the words and lexicons" did not move one beyond "any yeoman or tradesman competently wise in his mother dialect only." Yet, while claiming universal goals, references to producing a "learned man" and to yeomen and tradesmen make clear that only males were required or were capable to "repaire the ruins of our first parents." Reflecting the views of Thomas More as much as Francis Bacon, he bemoans the "seven or eight yeers [spent] meerly in scraping together so much miserable Latin, and Greek, as might be learnt otherwise easily and delightfully in one year." Yet Milton's more democratic and efficient curriculum presumes a highly motivated and gifted student body; his "Plan of Studies" would challenge the most intrepid scholar, such as when he claims one can learn Italian "at any odde hour" (7–8).

Milton's heavily packed curriculum sped up classical language training while including more practical skills, and these additions to the classical curriculum included bringing in outsiders to gain the "helpfull experiences of Hunters, fowlers, fishermen, Shepherds, Gardiners, Apothecaries; and in the other sciences, Architects, Engineers, Mariners, Anatomists." Thus his universal religious and educational goals were intertwined with a range of male occupations. Learning from men who have displayed success in these areas offered models for the boys who were being taught. But even more fundamental to his confusion of the stages of life for all with the training and goals for males, is his justification for teaching different subjects based on stages of physical and cognitive development. Following their language training, and by ages ten to twelve, "yeers and good general precepts will have furnisht them more distinctly with ... reason ... [or] judgement contemplate" to prepare them to study ethics. Next, following a sense of "personall duty," it is time to "begin the study of Economies." Following the study of economics, as pupils move closer to the end of adolescence, they could "dive into the grounds of law, and legal justice." Near the end of this "Plan of Studies," and after reading Aristotle's *Poetics*, "will be the right season of forming them to be able writers and composers in every excellent matter, when they shall be thus fraught with an universall insight into things." Whether, "in Parliament or counsell, honour and attention would be waiting on their lips" (3–5).

Milton's program was not simply one built upon the stages of life that prepared men for their broad-based duties in English society. It was also organized as an organic whole that encompassed human aging, the best training, and the contributions a worthy man should make to his country, in which "methodicall course it is so suppos'd they must proceed by the steddy pace of learning onward, as at convenient times for memories sake to retire back into the middleward, and sometimes into the rear of what they have been taught, untill they have confirm'd, and solidly united the whole body of their perfected knowledge, like the last embattelling of a Romane legion" (6). While Milton's was the clearest military imagery in such educational theory and understanding of male development, other works used training and careers open only to men to conflate human aging with male experience.

An earlier substantial work, preceding Puritan educational reform efforts that emerged during the late 1640s, was Ezekiah Woodward's *Childes Patrimony Laid out upon the good Culture or Tilling over his Whole man* (1640). It presents in many ways both the lengthiest and most thorough attempt to set out an ideal education. In the dedication, Woodward claims he treats "an old and ordinary subject . . . , but newly handled, and in no ordinary way." As a member of a younger son's household who had fallen on hard times, Woodward dedicates this work to Sir Robert Pye who had provided him with some financial assistance and was, in standard effusive dedicatory prose, a supreme example of Christian charity.[27]

The dedication is followed by "to the Reader," signed by the well-known Puritan author of domestic guides, William Gouge, who highly complimented the work and also made clear the supposed universal inclusion and intent of such educational treatises: "This *Treatise* tendeth to the erecting of faire *Edifices* to the Lord, which are the *children of men.*" In praising Woodward as a religiously grounded educational reformer who builds a solid foundation for his pupils, Gouge places his accomplishments in familiar male stages of development: "[Woodward] layes his foundation very deep, even in the mothers wombe: and goeth along from *infancy* to *childhood,* thence to *youth,* and so on, till he brings his childe to a *growne, yea, an old man,* full of dayes, going to the grave in a full age; like as *a sheafe of corne come in, in his season.*"[28]

Gouge continues his summary of Woodward's work, which links parents (fathers) to others responsible for the child's (boy's) progress. Woodward's directions were to "Parents, Guardians, Schoole-masters, Tutors, Governours,"

27. [Woodward, Ezekiah]. *Childes Patrimony Laid out upon the good Culture or Tilling over his Whole man. The first Part, Respecting a Childe in his first and second Age. . . .* (London: Printed by I. Legatt, 1640), *Epistle Dedicatory to Sir Robert Pye,* n.p. Hereafter cited in the text by page number.
28. William Gouge, "To the Reader," in ibid., n.p. The source for the final sentence of the quotation is Job 9:26. William Gouge wrote *Of Domesticall Duties: Eight Treatises* (London: Printed by John Haviland for William Bladen, 1622).

and also ministers. In this work, and elsewhere, the use of the terms "parents" or "parent" varied as to whether they meant fathers or fathers and mothers. When linking the parent to other male authority figures, it was most apt to mean only the father, but when tied to general duties regarding a child (especially when quite young), then it normally included both mothers and fathers. Determinations as to when it was employed as a false universal are discernible through descriptive and exemplary materials, such as when the parent's experience at university or occupation was used as a guide for directing the child's development. As so often with the false universal, the author never indicated when the terms "parents" or "parent" referred only to males or when it included both men and women.

Gouge next follows this statement with a description that is remarkable for its inclusion of virtually every aspect of aging, while at the same time clarifying that this universal progression refers only to men: "[Woodward's work] concerns the mothers care of the childe in her *wombe,* or after in the *infancy,* or both Parents care about a new birth, or initiating it in pietie, good manners, good literature at *home,* at *schoole,* at *University,* or any other good *Seminary;* . . . Yea also about *calling, marriage, carryage* to Parents, to their superious, equalls, and inferiours, in all ages, times, and places." Gouge concludes his positive assessment of the work with its broad utility: "This Author hath more punctually and pertinently, handled all kinde of duties from ones first entrance into this world, to his going out thereof, then any of the fore-named Authors, or any other that have written of the like subject" (n.p.). His reference to "fore-named" authors, which includes a range of classical and Christian authors, is to Woodward's sources. Of those, only one—Saint Jerome's epistle to Laeta concerning the education of her daughter Paula—has any relevance to girls' education, and it has no influence on the nature of Woodward's treatise itself.

The first ten chapters of the work treat childhood from birth to preparation of the adolescent boy for an occupation. It pays great attention to determining the stages of life and includes sections such as "Child-hood and youth; how they differ." The work itself has a strongly Puritan flavor with advice against parents' overly great fondness for the child, the sin of pride, the evils of idleness, and so on. Those with the child's charge must urge him to useful employment, but it should not be extraordinarily difficult; "labour, how naturall to a man," means the task was a simple one. The work encourages wholesome habits, both in interacting with others and in eating, exercise, and the like. Woodward focuses on nature and what a child could learn from observing. Finally, while pointing a student to a future career, he wants him to have a chance to grow generally and criticizes parents in the section entitled "The designing a Childe to a Calling. Parents too early and preposterous therein" ("Table of Contents"). A process of male maturation is evident throughout Woodward's work. He continually interchanges stages and qualities attached to childhood with nouns, adjectives, and pronouns referring only to males. If parents discipline a child well they will find that he will "with Gods blessing, outgrow *Childishnesse,* and then, *Child-hood;* and as it may be neglected, you may know that by its Childishnesse, it is a *Boy* still" (10–11).

The symbolism of the seasons appears quite frequently in works on boys' education, but virtually not at all in those addressed to girls' training—again stressing that the process through which males mature has no counterpart for their sisters. In language similar to Milton's, Woodward ties educational stages to the seasons of nature. While earlier in his work Woodward includes women in the term "parents," here it clearly refers only to fathers as the individuals who make decisions concerning students' lives:[29] "The childe had, anciently amongst the Romanes, three set over him, the *master* to instruct; the *governour* to correct; the *parent* to do both, or to see carefully that both were done. So the *parent* was principall, and his work the chiefe: Now it is otherwise; the *parent* commonly doth just nothing, the *Master* must do all, look to the childs book, and manners both." In utilizing his seasonal metaphor, Woodward ties the efforts of fathers and teachers to the maturation process of the child: "We [parent and teacher] must account *childehood* and *youth* our *seedtime,* so these ages are; we must not let slip our season, we must not sleep, nor let our hand hang down; we must know that our harvest, which but the reaping of hopes, . . . depends upon our care and diligence in this ploughing and *sowing season*" (16–19).

One of the other important genres that outlined general guides for young men, beyond tracts of educational reform and school curriculum, were those works addressed to sons. The guides of Lord Burghley and Sir Walter Raleigh are probably best well known, but there were many written by fathers from both the middling and gentle classes. Two less well-known works are *The dutifull Advice of a loving Sonne To his aged Father* (1632) and Francis Osborne's *Advice to a Son or Directions for [the] most Important Encounters of This Life* (1656). Burghley's work was written around 1584 and Raleigh's not printed until 1632.[30]

29. In his second chapter on time, Burrow, *Ages of Man,* also stresses the importance of the seasons as a means to show the progress of a man through the stages of life (55–79).
30. *The dutifull Advice of a loving Sonne To his aged Father* (London: Printed for Benjamin Fisher,

Burghley's brief work stresses religious faith and a life of responsibility and good habits. Other than commending regular prayer to his son, he urges him to adopt clean habits before setting out for his business. Learning and travel should prepare him for adulthood, and he places him in the care of a well-trusted friend, "Thomas Windebank ... for the opinion that I have received of his Honesty and of his ability to travel by reason of his language, ... you do follow his advice and counsel in all proceedings ... [and] if you will not therein conform yourself I shall revoke you with some shame."[31] He lays out directions for his son to find a suitable wife; he urges against marrying one who is poor, "a dwarf or a fool," and to take into consideration both the nature of one's own estate as well as one's intended: "If thy estate be good, match near home and at leisure; if weak, then far off and quickly." In his advice concerning his son's prospective offspring, he distinguishes between children and daughters; in the former he encourages patience, respect, and preparation for responsibility; for daughters he recommends: "Marry thy daughters in time, lest they marry themselves." As for sons, he advises against widespread travel "beyond the Alps," which would result only in pride, and he urges against raising them for soldiers, "for war is of itself unjust unless the good cause may make it just." While Burghley might have wanted the same Christian qualities to be exhibited in sons and daughters, still he saw only sons moving through a progression of learning and travel to adulthood.

Raleigh's work is more typically Machiavellian, urging his son to calculate the qualities he wanted in friends and to avoid relationships that lacked personal reward. Most important was one's choice of friends, "for by them thou shalt be judged what thou art." Raleigh urges against him forming ties with "the poore and needy," for even though he might assist them many times, if he fails to do so once, "such men will become thy mortall Enemies."[32] Raleigh's directions to his son regarding a wife and marriage mirror the more calculated visions offered during the early seventeenth century and echoed by James I— remember who's in charge and marry for estate, competence, and sufficient beauty to ensure "comeliness" in one's children. Raleigh's advice for providing for a widow reveals his assessment of women and their place within the family:

1632); Sir Walter Raleigh, *Sir Walter Raleigh's Instructions to his Sonne: and to Posterity,* 4th ed. (London: Printed for Benjamin Fisher, 1633). A modern edition of three of these works appears as *Advice to a Son: Precepts of Lord Burghley, Sir Walter Raleigh, and Francis Osborne,* ed. Louis B. Wright (Ithaca: Cornell University Press for the Folger Shakespeare Library, 1962).

31. Burghley, *Certain Precepts for the Well Ordering of a Man's Life,* in Wright, ed., *Advice to a Son,* 5–6, 9–11.

32. Raleigh, *Instructions,* 1–3. Hereafter cited in the text by page number.

"[L]eave thy Wife no more than of necessitie thou must, but onelie during her widdowhood ... To conclude, Wives were ordained to continue the generations of Men, not to transferre them, and diminish them, either in continuance, or abilities; and therefore thy house and estate which liveth in thy sonne, and not in thy Wife, is to be preferred" (24–27).

While *The Dutiful Advice of a Loving Son* was a work from a son directed to an aging father, it reflects the same values of male maturation in comparison to the passive and nonevolutionary path designated for women. The work discusses the need to seek salvation and to pursue a worthy life before it is too late. It both acknowledges the qualities of various stages of life and points to the problems old men face when they did not use those ages appropriately to mature both as Christians and as human beings.

He characterizes the ages of man as follows: "The prerogative of Infancie is innocencie; of Childhood, reverence; of Manhood, maturity; and of old age, wisedome." But men, such as his father, who waited until the end of life to seek God and to justify the use of their days, were bound to find sorrow: "No, no, they that will loyter in seedtime, and begin to sow when others reape; they that will ryot their health, and beginne to cast their accounts when they are scarce able to speake ... let them blame their owne folly if they dye in debt and be eternall beggers, and fall headlong into the lap of endlesse perdition."[33]

While Francis Osborne wrote a longer work that focused on the range of activities his son would face over his lifetime—studies, love and marriage, travel, government, and religion—the values offered parallel the works discussed above. He wanted his son to learn at school rather than at home because youth was best characterized by "patience and obedience," and it was the most opportune time for skilled masters to have total control over the child's time. He offers useful advice in his section on schooling, such as "a few books well studied and thoroughly digested nourish the understanding more than hundreds but gargled in the mouth as ordinary students use." While much of the work's first section treats issues of learning, he considers the sensible judgments required as one reaches young adulthood. His discussion of marriage carries warnings about selecting an unworthy wife and blames such difficulties on Eve's failings. A wife's failings were tied to those of her sex, "being foundered by the heat of lust and pride and unable to bear the weight of so much of our reputation as religion and custom hath loaded them

33. *Dutiful Advice*, 6, 55–57.

withal," and such weaknesses have grave consequences that "diffuseth itself like a leprosy over posterity" because of the mother's role in the family.[34]

After broad-based advice on proper behavior while traveling, Osborne turns to government. Here he encourages wise and considered judgment, urges against joining with the multitude until one is sure its view will carry the day, advises opening government and society to new families, suggests avoiding letting one's conscience too strongly dictate one's view of the state, and so on. While this section has a variety of advice, it can be most centrally characterized in the following statement: "If authority exacts an acknowledgment from you, give it with all readiness, it being the highest frenzy to dispute your innocency with those who are able to convert the greatest into a fault" (87). His final section on religion returns to some of the broader qualities required of men as the responsible adults in society. In urging a middle route between lack of principle and a too tender conscience, Osborne urges his son not to allow his conscience to "baffle your wit out of the bounds of discretion" and to "keep reason always in your eye." While conscience must be a guide, it should never lead us "to betray our well-being" (102).

Osborne, along with others offering advice to sons, presents judgments that appear appropriate for human beings generally; but in metaphorical phrases that contrast the thoughtful route sons should take with the qualities of women, or in sections that warn about prospective wives, it is clear that these broad principles were not intended for, and would not fit, the female half of the population. For example, Osborne, when making a point about how society assesses issues of honesty, places it in the following rhetorical context: "Hypocrisy, though looked upon by the church, the spouse of Christ, as a gaudy and painted adulteress, yet if she passeth undiscovered the result is not so dangerous as that of open profaneness." Tying general guidance for male maturation to comments that both malign women's character and deny them basic human qualities continually reinforces the association between human nature and males in contrast to women's particular nature (97–98).

Specialized Works for Girls' Education

Contrasting the works concerning boys and girls' education is not a simple task, given their distinct nature and audience, since these works omit the broad-based curriculum and universal language just discussed. Writings addressed to

---

34. Osborne, *Advice to a Son*, 42–44, 62–64. Hereafter cited in the text by page number.

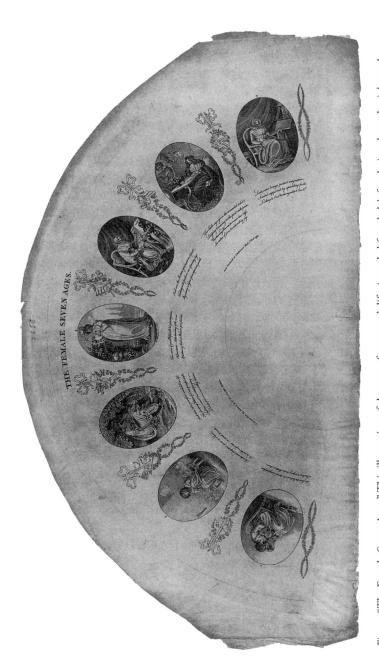

Fig. 5 "The Female Seven Ages." This illustration of the ages of a woman's life, intended for a lady's fan during the early eighteenth century, verifies the sexual and maternal nature of such progression, ignoring even those occupations traditionally female. Reprinted from The Folger Shakespeare Library Collections.

girls were largely works of advice to daughters, normally written by fathers. Women's advice for children, as noted earlier, was most prominently penned upon imminent death.[35]

Works that treat the subject of preparing young people for adulthood were clearly divided along lines of gender during the sixteenth and seventeenth centuries. Those directed to girls were more apt to be written to individuals, and they stressed creating a woman who would both fulfill the roles intended for her and enhance the family from which she came and the one she would eventually join. There was no broad calling or set of social responsibilities that directed her education.

Thus the education for boys created a norm not found in the more personal and specialized works directed to their sisters. The only exceptions to the latter are a handful of educational works that are grounded in feminist ideology and argue polemically for the serious need to educate girls. Other works that purport to treat women's education are much more apt to discuss issues of social behavior and human relationships, with only a small portion devoted to an academic curriculum.[36] The plan for a female academy written by Edward Chamberlain (Chamberlayne) seems a precursor to Mary Astell's later proposal of a college for single women, but its curriculum was significantly more limited. Guided by its "Lady Governess, and grave Society of Widdows and Virgins," Chamberlain's academy was supposedly based on Protestant colleges in Germany. The school was needed, he claimed, because women before the civil war had been noted for "Reverence, Obedience, Faithfulness" to their husbands, but this pious type of matron had faded in recent decades. Because of the spread of sects and licentiousness, an education was needed "to reduce (if possible) the Female Sex of *England* to their Pristine Vertues."[37]

35. Leigh, *The Mother's Blessing,* and Joceline, *The Mothers Legacy,* are the two most well-known titles.

36. Few recent works have appeared on women's education in early modern England. Traditional treatments include Dorothy Gardiner, *English Girlhood at School: A Study of Women's Education Through Twelve Centuries* (Oxford: Oxford University Press, 1929); Josephine Kamm, *Hope Deferred: Girls' Education in English History* (London: Methuen, [1965]); and Phyllis Stock, *Better Than Rubies: A History of Women's Education* (New York: Putnam, 1978). While there are no recent full-length studies, much information on the topic can be found in Merry Wiesner, *Women and Gender in Early Modern Europe,* 2nd ed. (Cambridge: Cambridge University Press, 2000), in Fletcher, *Gender, Sex, and Subordination,* and in Mendelson and Crawford, *Women in Early-Modern England.*

37. [Edward Chamberlayne], *An Academy or College: wherein Young Ladies ... may be ... instructed in the true Protestant Religion* ([London]: Printed by Tho. Newcomb, 1671), 2–3. The Chamberlain family (sometimes spelled Chamberlayne) took great interest in women's training; along with their well-known efforts on behalf of forceps being employed during birth, both Hugh and Peter Chamberlain offered their guidance, and the latter proposed establishing a college for midwives. See Peter Chamberlen, *A Voice in Rhama; or, The Crie of Women and Children* (London: Printed by William Bentley for John Marshall, 1647).

The goal was not only to instill piety in young women but style as well: "Deportment, which usually sets off, and recommends young Ladies to good Husbands" was essential. To make up for the decline in Anglican institutions, parents had often been forced to send daughters to Catholic schools abroad or Dissenting academies at home, and this had led to unorthodox beliefs. Unlike the more academic and numerous schools proposed by Dury and Milton, Chamberlain proposed one school near London. His lengthy description incorporated preparation for marriage and slighted any advancing abilities that might call for specialized training as women matured:

> These are therefore to give notice, to all whom it may any way con-
> cern, that near *London,* in a pleasant healthy Soil and Air, there is for
> both the purposes above-mentioned, proposed a large House, with a
> Chappel, fair Hall, many commodious Lodgings, . . . all encompassed
> and well secured with strong high Walls: Also there is a Reverend,
> Learned, and Pious Divine in the same Parish, ready to officiate daily
> Morning and Evening as Chaplain; a grave discreet Lady to be Gov-
> erness, with divers other Matrons . . . are to assist in the Government
> of the Colledge, without expecting any gain, profit, or emolument
> for themselves; . . . Moreover, there will come at due times the best and
> ablest Teachers in *London* for Singing, Dancing, Musical Instruments,
> Writing, French Tongue, Fashionable Dresses, all sorts of Needle
> Works; for Confectionery, Cookery, Pastery; for Distilling of Waters,
> making Perfumes, making of some sort of Physical and Chyrurgical
> Medicins and Salves for the Poor.[38]

36. Few recent works have appeared on women's education in early modern England. Traditional treatments include Dorothy Gardiner, *English Girlhood at School: A Study of Women's Education Through Twelve Centuries* (Oxford: Oxford University Press, 1929); Josephine Kamm, *Hope Deferred: Girls' Education in English History* (London: Methuen, [1965]); and Phyllis Stock, *Better Than Rubies: A History of Women's Education* (New York: Putnam, 1978). While there are no recent full-length studies, much information on the topic can be found in Merry Wiesner, *Women and Gender in Early Modern Europe,* 2nd ed. (Cambridge: Cambridge University Press, 2000), and in Fletcher, *Gender, Sex, and Subordination,* and in Mendelson and Crawford, *Women in Early-Modern England.*

37. [Edward Chamberlayne], *An Academy or College: wherein Young Ladies . . . may be . . . instructed in the true Protestant Religion* ([London]: Printed by Tho. Newcomb, 1671), 2–3. The Chamberlain family (sometimes spelled Chamberlayne) took great interest in women's training; along with their well-known efforts on behalf of forceps being employed during birth, both Hugh and Peter Chamberlain offered their guidance, and the latter proposed establishing a college for midwives. See Peter Chamberlen, *A Voice in Rhama; or, The Crie of Women and Children* (London: Printed by William Bentley for John Marshall, 1647).

38. Chamberlayne, *An Academy,* 5–9. The plan was to operate by informing fathers and guardians of its existence, allowing subscribers to pay money to the Mercers' Company to support a young lady's study;

In contrast, Bathsua Makin's proposed school at Tottenham High Court was to be a serious education for gentlewomen. While it included needlework, artistic skills, and conversational French, Makin also offered advanced training in history, geography, mathematics, and, because of her own extensive knowledge, a range of languages. Students could learn French and Latin, and for those who showed an interest and aptitude they could pursue Greek, Hebrew, Italian, and Spanish, "in all which (this Gentlewoman) hath a competent knowledge." She took her first pupils at age eight or nine after they had learned to read well and began teaching them foreign languages. She also taught the natures of plants and minerals. Her knowledge was widespread, and she was one of a very few English women who taught boys in a grammar school run by her father, a minister.[39]

As noted in the discussion of Hezekiah Woodward's *Childes Patrimony,* Saint Jerome's instruction to Laeta was identified as a work that influenced Woodward, even though girls had scant presence in his educational schemes. Laeta was a Roman aristocrat who Jerome advised on how to educate her daughter Paula (grandaughter to one of Jerome's strongest allies in the church, also Paula, a powerful churchwoman who had built Jerome his own monastery). Jerome's instructions in the form of a letter established an extensive education for Paula, a much more ambitious program than that put forth by the majority of seventeenth-century authors. While Saint Jerome is considered one of the more misogynistic among church fathers, it is interesting to note what a strongly academic and broad-based education he proposed for this girl intended for the church by her mother. It contrasts so starkly with the educational treatises written for girls in the seventeenth century, except for the handful of works such as Bathsua Makin's, which were written as feminist pleas to offer advanced training to adolescent girls.[40]

Jerome's lengthy letter to Laeta makes clear that it is lack of vocation, and omission of women from the general human goals of learning and advancement,

and the names of six stationers were listed as contacts for those interested in the school. Another interesting element to the work was a postscript that noted plans for a college for "Old Men, either Batchelors or Widdowers," verifying the need for their maintenance and again contrasting the categories of sex and age with the norm of male maturation.

39. Bathsua Makin, *An Essay to Revive the Antient Education of Gentlewomen, in Religion Manners, Art, and Tongues* (London: Printed by J.D. to be sold by Tho. Parkhurst), 41–43. For a discussion of her life, see the introduction to Frances Teague, *Bathsua Makin, Woman of Learning* (Lewisburg: Bucknell University Press, 1997).

40. [Saint Jerome], *Certaine Selected Epistles of S. Hierome as also the lives of Saint Paul The First Hermite ... Translated into English* ([Saint-Omer: Printed at the English College Press]) (Permissu Superiorum, MDCXXX).

that most determined their limited training during the early modern period. This patristic author, who wrote harshly against women's nature (especially their sexual allurements), outlined an intellectually ambitious program for Paula, emphasizing the need especially for those who taught her to respect her and her projected future role within the church. It confirms as well the large amount of scholarship that documents the important standing of women religious and the advantages emanating from their training and their institutional governance.[41]

Key to Paula's importance was her mother's faith, in contrast to her unbelieving father, and the dedication of the child to the church. Jerome's instructions were directed to "a Mother," and they [were] "to teach you how you are to instruct our *Paula,* who was consecrated to Christ before she was borne; and whome you conceived in your vowes, before you did it in your wombe."[42] His instructions began with the typical admonitions against her reading "unclean" works or spending time with "waiting maides" who might lead her astray. She should also not learn contemporary songs, but only "sweet Psalmes." His advice stressed her earliest steps of learning, that she should learn the alphabet but not alone "by roat, but by use." It is in many ways a progressive regimen, urging that she receive small presents upon the completion of certain tasks and warning that "if she be slowe of wit, let her not be chidden." Above all, in her early life she should "be not brought to mislike learning" (114–15).

Following his discussion of her earliest training, Jerome continued with the requirements for her appropriate instruction if she were to be an important leader in the church. A master should be brought to teach her, and his nature clarifies Jerome's sense of her importance: "And I hope a learned man will not thinke much, to do that in the behalfe of a noble virgin, which *Aristotle* did for the sonne of *Phillip,* who tooke the office of clarckes or booke wrighters away, by teaching him first to reade." He discouraged her from using informal language and remaining in the company of ill-educated and uncultured women.

41. For an older biography of Jerome that gives some attention to his relationship with women religious, and Paula in particular, see J. N. D. Kelly, *Jerome: His Life, Writings, and Controversies* (London: Duckworth, 1975), and for the best treatment of the standing of nuns within the church and society more broadly, as well as specific discussions of Jerome and Paula, see Jo Ann Kay McNamara, *Sisters in Arms: Catholic Nuns Through Two Millennia* (Cambridge: Harvard University Press, 1996).

42. Saint Jerome, *Certaine Selected Epistles,* 113–14. Hereafter cited in the text by page number. Her faith led Jerome to address his instructions to Laeta and not to her husband, who was an important, well-educated man, but not a Christian. Jerome's assessment of him is clear in the phrase, "a man, I confesse, most illustrious, and most learned; but yet walking hitherto in darkness."

He next employed a military metaphor to describe her future religious vocation: "Let her quickly be told, what her other grandmother, and aunt she hath; and for the service of what Emperour, and for what Army she is brought up, though yet she be but a green souldier." And, "Her very habite, and cloathing, must tell her to whom she is promised. Take heed you bore not through her eares, & that you paynt not that face, which is consecreated to Christ, either with white or red, nor oppresse her necke with gold, & pearle, nor load her head with gemmes; nor make her haire yellow, and bespeake not by that meanes, a part of hell-fyer for her" (118–21).

It is clear that Jerome held clear distinctions between men and women, both in terms of the greater worth of the former and the particular route to worthiness for the latter: "It is written of woman, that she shall be saved by the bringing forth of children; if they remayne in faith, and charity, and sanctification, with chastity." But it was not his affection or admiration for women (of which he had scant) that led Jerome to argue for the importance of Paula's training, but because she fell within a calling that required it. That calling led her to follow in Christ's footsteps: "When she beginnes to be a little growne, and to *encrease in wisedome, age, and grace, both with God and man,* after the example of her spowse, let her go to the Temple of her true father, with her parents; but let her not depart with them out of the Temple" (121–23).

Finally, her training was similar to that of a man drawn to the church (or of early modern models for men intended for the professions and public service), and ultimately her calling overcame the weaknesses of her sex in Jerome's eyes and made her education essential. That education was to include a "certain number of Greeke verses" followed by "the teaching of the Latin tongue." While concentrating on the Scripture and Christian authors, she was also allowed the best of classical authors. Unlike the education suggested for seventeenth-century girls, she was to avoid finishing school touches, and, he directed, "Let her be deafe to musicall instruments, and not know why the *Pipe,* the *Lyra,* and the *Harpe* were made." Her training was to be placed in the hands of her aunt and grandmother, who were "two pious women" (122–26).

While this was a strongly religious regimen, discouraging either much mirth or cultural pursuits, still it seems an education not so different from one Jerome might have suggested to parents of a young boy destined for the church. His concluding sentence makes clear his personal interest in her proper preparation: "I will carry her upon my shoulders; and though I be an old man, I will by imitation of stammering frame wordes fit for a Philosopher of the world; I, who shall not be instructing that Macedonian King, who was to be destroyed by poison; but a hand-maid and spouse of Christ our Lord, to be prepared for his celestiall kingdome" (126).

The works of the seventeenth century addressed to daughters, in contrast, were much more apt to be gender-restricted and not tied to any future vocation, except for marriage. Works directed to women and girls were overwhelmingly guides on getting along with others (whether one's own family or one's husband and his family), how to behave in public, and the domestic skills required of a good wife. While domestic management required as wide a range of skills as many positions held by men, little attention was given to the management or the financial skills crucial to running a successful household. The greatest attention was directed toward fancy sewing and embroidery, relations among individuals within the household, interaction between servants and mistresses, moral and religious principles, and social and cultural graces tied to being a lady (or a middle-class wife with social ambitions). For the most part, formal education constituted a minute proportion of these works, and even there it was education tied overwhelmingly to religion and piety.[43]

Works with "daughter" or "daughters" in the title were most apt to be addressed to particular individuals, with the single largest number being funeral sermons for those dying young, or those identified in the title not only as "wife of," but also as "daughter of" at the time of death. Among the guides for daughters' future lives, the most well known is Lord Halifax's *The Lady's New-years Gift: or, Advice to a Daughter* (1688), and while more general and lengthy than other such treatments, it represents standard concerns; namely, the training of a young female to fit within a family framework, and pleasing husband and other family members while maintaining one's basic moral and religious core.[44] The second largest number of works with "daughter" in the title were more religious allegory than guides for a daughter. They are discussions of a young woman who was seduced by members of another religious faith (usually Catholic), revealing both her trustful nature and innocence, but

43. For works that focus on the training of wives and their lives following marriage, see Margaret J. Ezell, *The Patriarch's Wife: Literary Evidence and the History of the Family* (Chapel Hill: University of North Carolina Press, 1987), Susan Dwyer Amussen, *An Ordered Society: Gender and Class in Early Modern England* (Oxford: Basil Blackwell, 1988), and Mendelson and Crawford, *Women in Early-Modern England*, 126–64.

44. [George Savile, Lord Halifax], *The Lady's New-years Gift; or, Advice to a Daughter* (London: Printed and are to be sold by Randal Taylor, 1688). Hereafter cited in the text by page number. *Advice* went through numerous printings before 1700. It was written to his daughter Elizabeth when she was only twelve, but even so had only four years to grasp its lessons before she married at the age of sixteen. For a brief discussion of the context for its writing, see *The Works of George Savile Marquis of Halifax,* ed. Mark N. Brown (Oxford: Clarendon Press, 1989), 2:335–38.

also her inability to judge religious arguments well or to read Scriptures with care. The remainder were primarily romances and ballads, usually telling tales of sexual seduction.

These guides for daughters were patterned on the medieval mirror for good behavior and religious faith. They tend to be formulaic, as are many of the works addressed to sons, but at least Halifax acknowledged the uneven playing field experienced by the two sexes during the late 1600s. In his advice to his daughter, Halifax, perhaps recognizing the increase in learned women and especially women writers after 1640, felt some obligation to justify his rather harsh words: "You must take it well to be prun'd by so kind a Hand as that of a Father.... Some inward resistance there will be, where Power and not Choice maketh us move; but where a Father layeth aside his Authority, and persuadeth only by his Kindness, you will never answer to Good Nature, if it hath not weight with you." He begins with the need for serious education to buttress one's Christian faith; however, reflecting the increasing role of rational Christianity, he favors a faith grounded in reason and not superstition. For his daughter's education, he maintains that "the first thing to be consider'd is Religion; it must be the chief Object of your Thoughts." Religion must be adopted and cherished before other distractions dilute its appeal, but it must be religion for an adult: "Religion doth not consist in believing the Legends of the Nursery, where Children with their Milk are fed with the Tales of Witches, Hobgoblins, Prophecies and Miracles." Also, reflecting the values of "the Trimmer," he favors toleration: "It is not true Devotion, to put on our angry zeal against those who may be of a different Persuasion" (6–10).

Halifax's advice stresses the importance of tolerance and rationality, but it lacks serious intellectual content. Rather, he is more concerned with social custom in preparing his daughter for her responsibilities as an adult and devotes the bulk of his 134-page treatise to relations between husband and wife. The work seeks a pleasant, almost rarefied, mix of reason and faith and uses both practical language and romantic imagery. In defining the nature of religion, Halifax offers this combination: "Religion is exalted Reason, refin'd and fitted from the grosser part of it: It dwelleth in the Upper Region of the Mind, where there are few Clouds and Mists to darken or offend it" (16). While the language reveals the greater commercialization of the late seventeenth century and its attraction to science, the role he outlines for his daughter's married life remains clearly restricted (16–23).

Sometimes he sounds very much like Juan Luis Vives, who 150 years earlier had written the most important humanist work intended for an English audience on the topic of women's education. As Vives urged women's education only to prevent pernicious ignorance and to steer them away from abstract and philosophical works, so Halifax also saw a limited reach to women's training. They should follow their minds to faith, but should judge belief less critically, "for your Sex . . . in respect that the Voluminous Enquiries into the Truth, by Reading, are less expected of you."[45]

Women's educational or occupational training was restricted on two related grounds: either they lacked the ability to pursue advanced training (and this was not stated by the majority of authors), or their lives did not require such training, and such training would subvert the goals they should be seeking. Halifax explicitly links these two elements, however: "You must first lay it down for a foundation in general, that, there is inequality in sexes, and that for the better economy of the world; the Men, who were to be the law givers, had the larger share of reason bestow'ed upon them; by which means your sex is the better prepar'd for the compliance that is necessary for the performance of those duties which seem'd to be most properly assign'd to it" (25–26). While he does allow for some flexibility for those exceptional women who "nature is so kind as to raise them above the level of their own Sex," the typical woman was to set the standard for women's training and the parameters of their adult lives (30).

In three other works addressed to daughters, similar themes were evident: Hugh Peter's *A Dying Fathers Last Legacy to an Onely Child* (1660), a broadside entitled *A Directory for the Female Sex: Being a Father's Advice to his Daughter* (1684), and *Instructions to a Nobleman's Daughter concerning Religion . . . now Directed to all of that Rank . . . , and others of that Sex* (1700). Each work heavily stresses religion and none acknowledge emerging abilities that might direct women to advanced skills as they move toward adulthood. Certainly women, in addition to Christian attributes, were to learn the domestic and social skills of the household, but there was no suggestion that these required intellectual abilities beyond those present during childhood. Peters, a Puritan minister executed as a regicide in 1660, composed his legacy for his daughter while awaiting trial and execution. It possesses the poignancy and directness often found in works linked to imminent death. A strong religious bent (with a more active Christianity than that of Halifax) dominated Peter's work, with secondary attention paid to marriage. He advised her to "Hear the Best Men,

---

45. Juan Luis Vives, *The Instruction of a Christian Woman,* in *Vives and the Renascence Education of Women,* ed. Foster Watson (New York: Longmans, Green & Co., 1912); Halifax, 22.

Keep the best Company, Read the best Books, especially make the Grounds of Religion your own." But his Puritan message did invite her "to Content in a low Condition," and adopt a "Meekness of Spirit," a message carrying different meanings for men and women. Peters also recommends John Brinsley's *A Looking-Glasse for Good Women*, a work harshly critical of women which continues for pages about Eve's transgression and its negative impact on the sex.[46] The "two very great Turns in mans Life" are "a lawful Calling" and "Marriage," but Peters addresses the latter, "because of your sex," as an institution where she must match her husband's "love, teaching, providing, honouring" with "subjection." After defending his loyalty to the state, and, after claiming he was only seeking a kingdom suitable for good men, Peters returns to her. He plans to appoint a friend to watch out for her following his death and encourages his daughter to "serve in some Godly Family" until marriage.[47]

The broadside in verse, *A Directory for the Female Sex*, has a strange phrase identifying its audience, "all Young Ones (especially those of that Sex)," which illustrates the pattern of early modern writers to make age, condition, and sex exclusive categories. The term "young" was restricted to males, but the message here was for daughters, so the author had to modify "young" with "especially those of that Sex," even though the phrase "Advice to his Daughter" would certainly seem to make such clarification unnecessary. This brief work also stressed religion—"Give first to God the flower of thy Youth"—and the fact that she should focus on the everlasting and "scorn this deluding World." The author urged her toward prayer, meditation, and a godly husband, discouraged envy of neighbors and attention to worldly things. He neared his conclusion with the verse: "The Grace of Meekness is a Womans Crown. / Be loving, Patient, Courteous and Kind."[48] John Prevoste wrote *Instructions to a Nobleman's Daughter* for the use of a noble family, but extended its utility first to others of that rank and then to women generally. Religion dominated the first lesson to be learned: "Let the Catechism never be forgotten." He

46. Hugh Peters, *A Dying Fathers Last Legacy to an Onely Child; or, Mr. Hugh Peter's Advice to his Daughter* (London: Printed for G. Calvert, 1660), 4, 12, 24, 27. John Brinsley, *A Looking Glasse for Good Women, . . . and Advice to such of that Sex . . . led away to . . . Separation* (London: Printed by John Field for Ralph Smith, 1645), 1–48. Brinsley is a fine example of those works that are so obvious and heavy-handed in their castigation of women that they form their own satire; after going on for pages, and with many more to come concerning Eve's transgression and her responsibility for mankind's ills, he includes the following: "As it was at the first, so now, (it cannot be hid) The woman, the woman, she is deceived" (7).

47. Peters, *A Dying Fathers*, 43–45, 110–16.

48. *A Directory for the Female Sex: Being A Father's Advice to his Daughter* (London: Printed by George Larkin, 1684).

does make some provision for rational advancement. "Religion begins thus in Childhood; ... [yet] much more in our Age of Understanding it is to be continued, and to be improved."[49]

Yet, when speaking about actual stages, he reverts to male pronouns and experience: "All that we did, and learn'd in the more serious Undertakings of our Childhood was only designed for Discipline and Method to dispose us for the doing and learning more hereafter, as he can never be Rich, who keeps not that which he has gain'd, and he can never be Skilful in any Art or Science, who forgets the first Notions of it he once was taught" (5). The remainder of the work concentrates on religious and moral development, especially as situated in noble birth, but in illustrating the seemingly unbreakable link between males and stages of aging, in a work establishing standards for the lives of women, he ties the natural progression of the seasons to male evolution: "[God] who has fixt the times for Night and Day, for Summer and Winter, and for everything, who has those Creatures Order which know little else: ... [and Solomon wisely carried forward God's plan with] ... every Man under his Vine, ... his Wisdom also appeared in the Order of his private Business, that of his Family, ... as well as in greater Things." It concludes with sample prayers suggested for a lady (58–61, 110–20).[50]

The major problem with so much of the material on aging and education discussed in this chapter is that both the type of sources, and the assumptions

---

49. John Prevost, M.A. *Instructions to a Nobleman's Daughter Concerning Religion At first designed for One, now ... all of that Rank, ... and others of that Sex* (London: Printed by W.R. for D. Brown and L. Stokey, 1700), 2–3. The dedication is to an anonymous lady, but the individual whose catechism is being discussed is identified on page 9 as "The Lady Catherine Manners, afterwards Marchioness of Buckingham." Hereafter cited in the text by page number.

50. One of the numerous sermons preached on the occasion of a female death, *A Sermon Preacht Upon the Death of Mrs Anne Barnardiston, ... at the Age of Seventeen* (London: Printed by J. A. for Benjamin Alsop and John Dunton, 1682), illuminates their formulaic nature and the secondary importance of the recently deceased individual. The first thirty pages of the sermon is a typical call for congregational repentance; it then returns to the deceased. As with all such sermons, which heavily concentrate on the wives of ministers or Christians dying young, the person's dying moment was used to instill guilt and to further belief in its hearers. Barnardiston was described as a pious, believing Christian who kept faith to the last, and within a few hours of death "she was very desirous that a worthy Minister whom she named, might immediately be sent for." In addition, an hour before her death, "she was heard to Say, Be gone, Satan! Be gone! Thou Art a Lyar from the Beginning, and the Father of Lyes. O come Lord Jesus." The message the congregation was to take away: "the great difference between the Death of the Holy and the Unholy, of the Righteous and the Sinner" (31–38). While funeral sermons generally were used as lessons for the audience, those for women consistently stressed three themes: a significant amount of her life spent in piety and devotions, her dedication to domestic concerns and concern for the poor, and her lack of interest in the things of this world. They reinforce the notion that women were to find fulfillment only in domestic settings and through religious ties.

surrounding them, are so different for males and females that they are hardly comparable. Because educating boys was a public act that related to the religious and political establishment of the nation, laws were passed and records were kept, in grammar schools and universities, both as regards their training and the characteristics of those who trained them. But girls' education lacked a public and official role, and while individual parents devoted their attention to it, and some authors wrote about it, an institutional record is lacking for comparison. With girls educated at home, as servants, through informal apprenticeships, or in isolated boarding schools that did not prepare for advanced training afterward, their education was a private and unrecorded affair. Yet, it was not only that boys' education had an official function that girls did not, but that their education was *the* education of children and youth and characterized the male maturation process leading to the only true adulthood articulated for seventeenth-century England.

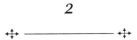

"Citizens of the same City ... Brethren and Sisters"

Gender and Early Modern English Guilds

Little synthetic work has recently been done on the history of guilds and women's role within them during the late medieval and early modern periods. Yet historians continue to emphasize three themes when discussing the role of women in the evolution of guilds as institutions, or crafts as occupations, in the early modern period: the limitations of women's place in guild history, the prominence of widows in any such involvement, and a decline of women's numbers and status during the sixteenth and seventeenth centuries. This chapter will contend that this interrelated analysis is incomplete, and in some instances inaccurate, and will concentrate on the importance of deconstructing the falsely universal language used in guild documents, as well as current scholars' failure to deconstruct gender-based language when it appears—and the complex impact such language had on both male and female guild members.[1]

1. Current scholars assume that guild members were overwhelmingly men, and women tend to be treated only when they are the explicit subject, not in general histories of guilds or in an account of a single guild or trade. And virtually no one treats the gendered qualities of male guild members, taking that membership to be the norm and thus not influenced by the qualities attached to the sex constituting such

Apprenticeship was not simply a step in preparation for a future occupation, but an important stage in the process of male maturation. While women were members of guilds and displayed a range of skills often identical to men's, the guild operated as an organization that facilitated and recognized male stages of advancement. This process undercut the real accomplishments of women and even their presence as apprentices, mistresses, and wearers of livery (or other symbols of guild membership). In many ways it seems as if the symbols, rewards, and public ceremonies attached to advancement have been seen as more important indicators of a craftsman's skill and standing than the knowledge and demonstration of the craft itself. And when historians analyze guild membership and the history of guilds, they have not always made distinctions between this symbolic material and the identity and nature of guild-based work.[2]

Women were involved in both religious and craft guilds most heavily during the late medieval period but continued with some force through the

---

membership. Historians are as apt (if not more so) to employ falsely universal language as the documents on which their studies are based. For example, Joseph P. Ward, *Metropolitan Communities: Trade Guilds, Identity, and Change in Early Modern London* (Stanford: Stanford University Press, 1997), opens his book with "Modern attempts to classify forms of human affiliation have ancient roots" while excluding women from the organizational structure of his study. After including some ancient references, he turns to early modern London, and then makes a number of distinctions regarding guild membership: native versus immigrant status, city versus suburb for the degree of well-controlled alliances, and conflicts between rank-and-file members and the guilds' governors. While he notes that women could be members, they have little impact on his analysis, and neither "gender" nor "women" appears in the index to the work.

2. Scholars such as Steve Rappaport, *Worlds Within Worlds: Structures of Life in Sixteenth-Century London* (Cambridge: Cambridge University Press, 1989), focus on the topics of social mobility, the class background of individuals who became apprentices, and the proportion of those who were able to advance to journeymen or the status of master. Yet social mobility is presented as a male phenomenon in the early modern period, with measurements of men advancing beyond (or not) the occupation or status held by their fathers. Women's advancement (if mentioned at all) is tied to the occupation of their husbands and whether it exceeds their fathers' status. Thus, using social mobility as the primary lens through which to assess the career of individual guild members (or the nature of guilds as a whole) by necessity focuses on a process of male maturation. But in the case of Rappaport and other historians, there is no recognition that such a focus skews their analysis toward men or requires them to view this career progression in a broader context of men's private and public training, and mobility generally, in early modern England.

While Paul S. Seaver, *Wallington's World: A Puritan Artisan in Seventeenth-Century London* (Stanford: Stanford University Press, 1985), focuses on a single seventeenth-century craftsman, Nehemiah Wallington, he also analyzes Wallington's life as if the male life cycle were the norm. Seaver begins with his subject, sketching "the events of his childhood and young manhood." His deceased mother is used as a lesson in Puritan steadfastness. In Seaver's words: "What Nehemiah made of her long illness, her agonizing death, or of her loss, he does not say." While Seaver's subject was obviously an individual man, there is little treatment of how his sex influenced his life, allowing him to devote years to introspective Puritan commentaries while the women in the family operated more as the "Artisan[s]" of the work's title than did he (27–28). Some gender context for understanding his choices and life pattern would have been useful.

early seventeenth century. Their presence is documented by inclusion in guild charters and as apprentices or as individuals performing functions guild governing bodies recognized and often worked to prevent. The process of male maturation clearly dominated the language and structure of guild efforts, and this dominance is evident in the conflated status of economic skill and success and the public designations attached to such skills. Much recent scholarship has focused on the viewpoints and actions of aldermanic courts and the evidence drawn from them that spotlights the public and governmental nature of guild service, more so than its economic aspect.

Individual crafts appear more male and more a mark of urban citizenship when portrayed through some men's service as aldermen and through the decisions set down by aldermanic bodies than when observed through the day-to-day productive life of guild members. Thus, by stressing the importance of the aldermen over rank-and-file members and their function as governors of their fellow craftpersons, scholars have placed the public role of male leaders in the forefront. They have done so without acknowledging such an approach, and certainly without acknowledging its gender implications. Such efforts have led to women being overlooked as guild members, encouraged readers to read gender-neutral terms as ones tied only to men, and to focus on a process of male maturation at the center of guild structure leading from boyhood to apprenticeship to journeyman to master to alderman as being emblematic of the path followed by all early modern guild members. Yet women were excluded from public posts, and few men successfully advanced along such a continuum. But all were involved with making products that defined them as fundamentally as this maturation process that was successful for only a few.

Scholars need to rethink women's roles in guild history, and, as a part of that process, to reconsider the nature of guilds generally. Most important to this general reassessment are the gender assumptions that accompanied judgments undertaken by guild, craft, and merchant organizations in the early modern period. That rethinking should include specialization among historians today, a rereading of guild charters and patterns of their enforcement, as well as a reassessment of the relation of the guild to other urban institutions and values.

Quantitative Analysis of Women in Guilds

Records of the guilds of weavers, clockmakers, and printers document women's involvement as daughters, wives, or single women, and raise doubts about the overwhelming emphasis by historians on widows as the only group of women allowed into guild membership. They reveal that women took boys as apprentices as well as girls, and that women were termed "citizens" along with their male counterparts through the mid 1700s. In the case of the weavers, the records also raise some questions about women's withdrawing from active employment outside the home by the 1750s because fathers identified as "gentlemen" continued to pay for their daughters to pursue apprenticeships.

Lists of apprentices and those made free of the Company of London Weavers exist for the second half of the seventeenth century through the mid-eighteenth century. While records do continue into the nineteenth century, my analysis will end with the eighteenth, given the topic of this work and the changing nature of guild structure and significance beyond the early modern period. Individual records contain information about apprentices, including their number and the nature of their indenture, or about those admitted to the freedom. Alternatively, information about individuals that lists dates both for apprenticeship and for admission to the freedom is also included. Thus I was able to gain totals for women who were apprenticed as weavers and for a smaller group that was made free of the company. In addition, I surveyed the numbers of women who trained apprentices, both male and female, and assessed the proportion who gained the freedom through apprenticeship (or servitude), patrimony, redemption (purchase), or by designation of the board of aldermen. One such document, the freedom record from October 17, 1737, to December, 15, 1766, lists eighteen women who were made free. The first five entries lack detailed information, but of those with fuller biographical materials, nine were free by patrimony, one by redemption, and three by servitude. As noted in the following entries, "apprenticeship," "servitude," and "service" were used interchangeably to designate one's years of training. Such terminology is made clear in the following two examples: "Elizabeth Milner, 3rd July, 1749, Daughter of the Reverend Dr. John Milner living in Fenchurch Street Milliner bound Apprentice the 24th of June 1742 to Thomas Durm Citizen and Weaver of London is made free by Servitude on the Testimony of this said Master," or "Alice Evans, 17th July, 1749, living in Mile End old town in the Parish of Stepney Parile bound Apprentice 5th July 1742 to Samuel Ogle Citizen & Weaver of London is made free by Servitude." In these records and elsewhere, women were also designated as "citizen and weaver," and their guarantee of an individual's qualifying for the freedom is also acknowledged. An example is Mary Gabell, who became free on August 6, 1749, through patrimony upon the testimony of her sister Sarah Pawlett, "Citizen and Weaver, and John Stanley Citizen and Weaver of London."[3]

The names of apprentices and those admitted to the freedom are contained in two separate listings. The first for 1661 includes thirty-five women whose names end in A through K and were apprenticed as weavers, of whom six were designated as "free." This list has limited detail, with individuals being identified by their date of apprenticeship, the number of years they were apprenticed, and those who were made free. The latter were either simply termed "free," or in the cases of Mary Anne Bearstow and Sarah Heslopp, designated as "free by patrimony." Of the thirty-five apprenticed female weavers, eighteen were apprenticed to a couple with both husband and wife named, nine were apprenticed to men and six to women. Of those apprenticed to women, only two were apprenticed to widows. In two instances, the apprentice was turned over to another master or mistress during her training; in one she moved from a couple to a woman and in the other from one man to another.[4]

This pattern continues with those from the second half of the alphabet, except more apprentices were made free, the great majority by redemption upon order of the court of aldermen. Of the thirty-two women who were listed, twenty-six were apprenticed with two of those being granted the freedom, while six others were made free either through patrimony or redemption. Among those apprenticed, ten were apprenticed to a couple, eleven to men, and four to women, with two others being transferred to mistresses during the course of their apprenticeships. Again, most were not apprenticed to women. Among those designated as free, the majority gained this status through patrimony or redemption—the latter overwhelming through the action of the board of aldermen. Again the majority being admitted to the freedom or taking in apprentices were not widows, and the following entry reminds us that women gained standing as individuals: "Jane Sutton, 23 Nov. 1668, spinster, Admitted a freewoman on order of Ct of Aldermen."[5]

Another listing covers weavers for the years 1709–21 where girls were apprenticed overwhelmingly to men, and those who gained the freedom did

3. Guildhall Ms. 4656/7. The manuscript listings of apprentices and those admitted to the freedom are divided into a number of different record books, with varying levels of detail. Some simply list name and date of apprenticeship, years of apprenticeship (normally seven but sometimes eight or even nine years), and the date and nature of attaining the freedom. I am concerned with records from 1660 to 1750 and have attempted to extract information about female apprentices and mistresses and to pinpoint those few who were admitted to the freedom.

4. Guildhall Ms. 4657A, vol. 1, pt. 1.

5. Guildhall Ms. 4657A, vol. 1, pt. 2.

so mostly through patrimony. Of the twenty-four women listed, four gained the freedom through patrimony and two on report of a master or mistress. Of the twenty apprenticed, sixteen were apprenticed to men and four to women. The training of one woman led to her taking her own apprentice, as in the case of Alice Mead who was apprenticed to Susanna Shorter on September 8, 1712, and then took Ann Mead (likely her sister) as an apprentice later that month. Alice is listed as free, but Ann is not. Mary Sankey, who was apprenticed to a widow, is listed as "Free on rept. of Widow Glew." Other than documenting the continuing number of women who were apprenticed as weavers into the eighteenth century, the number apprenticed to men greatly expanded.[6]

As one advances further into the eighteenth century, women who are listed as free of the company, and some of those who are apprenticed, have some prior occupation, simply seeking the freedom through the aegis of the weavers. Most likely they had little actual training or experience as weavers. Beyond the first half of the seventeenth century, many individuals appear to have used the freedom more as a standing to operate a business than as a designation of skill in a particular craft. The last record in this group lists both apprenticeships and freedoms from September 5, 1737, to March 18, 1765. Forty-one women are listed; it is one of the most interesting of the records because so many women are identified according to a separate occupation beyond weaving, and their fathers come from a wide range of ranks.

Of the women listed as apprenticed, fourteen were apprenticed to men and fourteen to women, with none apprenticed to a couple. Fifteen are admitted to the freedom, with all but two gaining that status through patrimony. A number appear to enter the freedom as adults because they are identified by occupation, including fanmaker, pawnbroker, and two milliners. Among those who were apprenticed, fathers' occupations include yeoman, butcher, plainmaker, apothecary, barber, weaver, merchant, mariner, lapidary, baker, carpenter, linen draper, cleric, cane-chair maker, brazier, tailor, surgeon, brewer, gunstock maker, and two identified as gentlemen. While one might expect craftsmen to apprentice their daughters to a trade other than their own—although most historians have argued such preparation for independent employment had vastly declined by the eighteenth century—it is remarkable for merchants, drapers, gentlemen, and high-ranking clerics to be doing so.[7]

6. Guildhall Ms. 4657A, pt. 1: A–VA; pt. 2: VE–Y.

7. While economic historians, and historians of women in particular, argue that middle-class women became less active economically by the second half of the eighteenth century, Leonore Davidoff and

Examples of the latter include "Elizabeth Milner, 21 June 1742, dau. Of Rev. John Milner, D.D. of Pelham, Surrey, Apr. to Elizabeth Forward, spinster, weaver of London, £60. 7 yrs., 2 May 1748, t[urn] o[over] to Ann Aitner, citizen and salter, 3 July 1749, of Fredrick St., milliner." Not merely did John Milner apprentice his daughter to a female weaver, but he also paid a substantial fee for her training. The two gentlemen who apprenticed their daughters to London weavers in December 1753 were David Griffith and Robert Stamper of Chicester. Henrietta Griffith was apprenticed to Sarah Gavell, "citizen and weaver" and Jane Stamper to Emblen Stamper (likely a relative), also designated as a citizen and weaver. Mary King, whose father was a linen draper, was apprenticed to Isaac Oake, and Ann Gibson's father, identified as "John of Wellclose Square, merchant," was apprenticed to Sarah Oak, a citizen and weaver. Among those women who are listed as having apprentices, thirteen are termed "citizen and weaver." In one instance, a girl is listed as apprenticed to the husband while the training was to come from the wife: "Susan Walker, 5 June, 1758, dau. Of William late of The Minories, gunstock maker, dec'd, apr. John Robinson cit. & weaver husband of Isabella of Lambeth Lace merchant—to be instructed in lace trade. £42. 7 yrs."[8]

A sampling of male weavers taken from the A through K listing for 1661 and the list for 1709–21 reveals, as one would expect, a much larger number of male apprentices (averaging twenty-six to thirty on each page sampled), but a fairly comparable number to women who advanced from apprenticeship to the freedom. An average to 7.15 male apprentices advanced to the freedom from this sample taken from the later seventeenth century record. The numbers increase between 1709 and 1721 with thirty to thirty-three being apprenticed each year, but with fewer admitted to the freedom: an average of 6.03. In addition, those free by patrimony averaged around two for the earlier period, with one being the most common figure, with only one sample producing five and another three; there is little change for the later period, and if at all, the number is smaller. The number of women attaining the freedom through patrimony increased significantly as the listings advance from the seventeenth to

---

Catherine Hall, *Family Fortunes: Men and Women of the English Middle Class, 1780–1850,* remains the most influential treatment of this topic (Chicago: University of Chicago Press, 1987), esp. 272–316.

8. Guildhall Ms. 4657A/4. This listing has much more information than the earlier ones about the occupations of women who are apprenticed, as well as the backgrounds of their fathers. Given the much larger numbers of male apprentices, I sampled their listing on every tenth page and compared it with the total numbers for women as to the nature of their apprenticeship and the proportion of their admissions to the freedom.

the mid-eighteenth century, perhaps signaling fathers' greater concern over the security of their daughters' economic standing as the 1700s progressed.

Evidence from printed guides to various companies of clock makers also reveal that women continued as apprentices and members of the companies into the eighteenth century. Among clock makers in Exeter from 1631 to 1732, thirteen women are listed as members of the company, but none as masters, wardens, or assistants. The numbers hold fairly steady for the late seventeenth and eighteenth century, but with women members appearing most heavily near the end of the 1600s and into the 1700s. Five women became members in the 1690s, with only two during the 1680s and none earlier in the seventeenth century. Six were made members in the eighteenth century from 1706 to 1730.[9]

For the clock makers in London, there is a printed register of apprentices from 1621 to 1921. In reviewing this listing both for women who were apprenticed and for women who took in apprentices themselves, one discovers that women were apprenticed in the trade through the mid-eighteenth century; and significant numbers were mistresses to others learning the trade. Widows for the most part took both boys and girls to train. Sixty-seven women are listed as apprenticed from the mid-seventeenth until the late eighteenth century. They follow patterns similar to the London weavers, except that the number of girls apprenticed to couples remains steady rather than peaking during the seventeenth century; a significant number were apprenticed to men, and others to women, the majority of whom were identified as widows. Of the thirty-one girls who were apprenticed to couples, eleven were apprenticed in the late seventeenth century, seven more from 1700 to 1715, and the remainder through the 1740s. There were twenty girls apprenticed to men with no significantly higher percentage for any period within the span of 1680–1770. Of girls apprenticed to women, thirteen were to those not identified as widows, and four apprenticed to widows. Boys were much more apt to be apprenticed to widows than girls. Of the boys apprenticed to women, forty-nine were apprenticed to widows and thirty to women who were not widows.[10]

---

9. Octavius Morgan, *List of Members of the Clockmakers' Company: From the Period of their Incorporation in 1631 to the Year 1732* (Exeter: William Pollard, 1883), reprint from the *Archaeological Journal* 40 (1883): 193.

10. *Register of Apprentices of the Worshipful company of Clockmakers of the City of London from its Incorporation in 1621 to its Tercentenary in 1931*. Compiled from the Records of the Company by Charles Edward Atkins ([London]: Privately printed for the Company, [1931]). While there is some variation in the information given for individuals, each entry normally includes the name, the date of apprenticeship, the master or mistress, and the years of service. If the individual became free of the company, then that date is given. Sometimes the father's or mother's name and occupation are listed, but other times not.

Among the London clock makers, both boys and girls were apprenticed to one individual and then turned over to another; there is no pattern, though, as to whether they were more apt to be turned over to a member of one sex or the other, or whether girls would ultimately end up with women and boys with men. For the boys, the largest percentage of those who gained the freedom were apprenticed to widows. Two of the most prolific mistresses were Elinor Mosely and Joanna May, both of whom had a number of girls and boys as apprentices. Near the conclusion of this listing, some men are identified as "Some of the more eminent Clockmakers and their Apprentices," but except for Thomas Tompion, who had twenty-three apprentices between 1673 and 1699, both Mosely and May had more apprentices than men on the list, but neither they nor any other women are included in the group of "eminent" clock makers. Finally, in a sampling of every tenth page, the numbers of male apprentices who attained the freedom varies from six or seven out of twenty-two to twenty-five apprentices, with nine instances in which more than ten individuals reached the freedom. This means that a greater proportion of these clock makers gained the freedom than the London weavers sampled above. Women gained the freedom in smaller proportions than did their brothers, and those men who had apprenticed with widows were most successful.[11]

Some of the more interesting entries were those such as George Edwards, in which he was listed as apprenticed "to Christopher (or Jane) Saxbey," where most individuals were apprenticed either to a couple or to a specific man or woman; Daniel Fletcher was apprenticed in 1664 to William Godbed "in favour of the widow Smith, his mother"; Isaac Jefferies was apprenticed in 1760 "to Mary Fish, cit. and Draper" and became free of the clock makers company on November 2, 1767. One indication that girls were apprenticed to men routinely was the case of Faith Leake, who was apprenticed to John White and then turned over to Daniel Quare; she was admitted to the freedom in September 1693. Evidence that women sought social mobility for their sons is offered in the case of John Nichols, who was apprenticed in 1738; his mother Lydia from Hackney is identified as a "laundry-woman," yet she apprenticed him to a watch maker, and he ultimately attained the freedom.[12]

Finally, two girls were apprenticed to married women to learn their trade. Ruth Smith was apprenticed in 1674 to "Thomas Birch, and Jane, his wife, to

11. Ibid.
12. Each apprentice is listed alphabetically without reference to chronological order. As one moves beyond 1750, the numbers decline dramatically, but the numbers of women do not reduce in greater proportion than men.

learn the art the said Jane useth," while in 1747 Susanna Smith, the daughter of a bookseller, was apprenticed to Hanna Wilson, the wife of James Wilson. Both boys and girls were apprenticed to fathers and mothers, with girls being apprenticed to fathers and boys to mothers in comparable numbers. It is interesting to note that in 1698 Anne Webster was apprenticed to her father, as was her brother George, but only her brother was made free in July 1703.

Women are included in other guild documents, such as those listing loans that allowed the Bristol Company of Weavers to construct a guildhall; women provided substantial portions of these loans. In Exeter, women were asked to contribute to revenue efforts, and they received death benefits. But women in Exeter and elsewhere did not gain from the educational schemes and fellowships established by guilds. In Exeter, the weavers' guild authorized a school in 1675, but its pupils were not to include girls; rather, a John Laskey was to "Keepe a Free Schoole in ye under hall for teaching thirty boys, poor Freeman's sons of the Corporation, such as shall be approved by the Master and Wardens. Ye said boys to be taught to read write and cypher gratis." While the author does not remark on the absence of girls from the school, he does note that widows were members of the company who were called upon to provide financial support. A "widow Morris" provided funds to repair the chapel window in 1610, and Elizabeth Clarke had a number of apprentices in 1620. Either through apprenticeship, patrimony, or inheritance as widows, women could be free of the company and were expected to contribute to its costs, but had more limited access to its benefits than their male counterparts. They were effectively denied positions as officers and lacked access to educational subsidies provided by the guild.[13]

Women also had an important presence among printers and are included in Plomer's dictionary of booksellers and printers operating in Britain from 1641 to 1667. Thirty-eight women are listed either as booksellers or printers or both. Most are identified as widows, and they were most apt to print religious works. Most of the women listed did not print a substantial amount of publications, and only a few published political pamphlets or books. But many published controversial or significant works. Anne Griffen published a work on the popish mass, was criticized by William Laud, and later testified against him. Martha Harrison received a warrant from the Council of State for printing a libelous tract in 1649 and also printed Agrippa, and Alice Norton printed

13. Beatrix F. Cresswell, *A Short History of the Worshipful Company of Weavers, Fullers and Shearmen of the City and County of Exeter* (Exeter: William Pollard & Co., 1930), 30–31.

political broadsides and pamphlets. While most of these women ran small establishments, those of Anne Maxwell and especially Mary Simmons were more substantial. In a 1668 survey, Maxwell is "returned as having two presses, no apprentices, three compositors and three pressmen," while Simmons "is returned [in 1666] as having thirteen hearths, a greater number than any other printer on the roll."[14]

Plomer also produced a listing of printers and booksellers from 1726 to 1775. The majority of the fifty-five women listed came from London, but they represent a larger geographical reach than the seventeenth-century listing, with a number from Bristol, Birmingham, and Nottingham. The list contains examples of women actively managing their business, not simply acting as caretakers for their deceased husbands. Elizabeth Craighton from Ipswich, 1728–76, held an interest in the *Ipswich Journal* with her brother; she then become co-printer with a nephew following her brother's death, but when he became bankrupt she made a partnership with another nephew and continued to manage the *Journal*. An Anne Dodd was listed as a pamphlet seller who owned three shops in London from 1726 to 1743. When she came under attack for unfair political satires, she claimed she was left with many children to support. Her husband was not listed as either a printer or a seller. Mary Hinde, printer and bookseller in London from 1767 to 1774, produced a forty-page list of her publications. Finally, Anne Ward, a printer in York from 1759 to 1789 and the widow of Caesar Ward, was the first printer to publish *Tristam Shandy*, and she published the *York Courant* for thirty years following her husband's death. He had gone bankrupt in 1745. Ward demonstrates the difficulty with designating a woman a widow and in so doing suggest that she was simply temporarily taking over her husband's craft or business. She not merely kept the business going much longer than he, but also more successfully.[15]

This sampling of women as skilled craft and business people in the seventeenth and eighteenth centuries suggests that some characterizations of women's roles in guilds have been incomplete. Not all women, and in many situations not the majority of them, trained in a particular craft or admitted to the freedom under the aegis of a particular guild did so as widows. They were

14. Henry R. Plomer, *A Dictionary of the Booksellers and Printers who were at Work in England, Scotland and Ireland from 1641 to 1667* (London: Printed for the Bibliographical Society by Blades, East & Blades, 1907). Cornelius Agrippa was a sixteenth-century author who is noted for his works on the excellence of the female sex.

15. H. R. Plomer et al., *A Dictionary of the Printers and Booksellers who were at Work in England, Scotland and Ireland from 1726–1775*. ([Oxford]: For the bibliographical society, Oxford University Press, 1932 [1930]).

more apt to be listed as citizens, to be included in guilds as spinsters, and to train with men as often as with women than has often been thought the case. Women appear to have functioned as individuals rather than as members of families, or as caretakers of family establishments. In addition, there is evidence that fathers continued to pay for their daughters' training in various crafts up to the mid-eighteenth century, and that perhaps middle-class women did not disappear so readily into the household and family businesses as historians have usually assumed. While certainly only a limited sample, this group of women should lead historians to look more closely at women's economic roles in early modern England. Sara Mendelson and Patricia Crawford, while speaking of women's independent labor, still focus on women's unskilled, lowly paid work (under Olwen Hufton's rubric of "makeshift"), and while this was true for the great majority of women, it is clear that substantial numbers continued to gain training and function as successful individuals in the early modern economy as late as 1750.[16]

Historical Scholarship on Women, Gender, and Guilds

The greatest outpouring of interest in guilds occurred between 1880 and 1930, with most of their histories being written by clerks of various companies and many by amateur and general historians before the profession took on its current structure of professional training and specialization. Most of these works, especially accounts of an independent company or guild, were privately printed works that are most commonly held at the British Library or the Guildhall Library. There is a treasure trove of information in these accounts, and they have been widely used by historians. They do lack, however, a systematic analysis of a particular body of archival materials. Exemplary materials are used throughout, so one can find tantalizing bits of information that are quite fascinating, but not the quantification or precision of contemporary social, economic, or urban historians.

Yet what these accounts lose in analysis they make up for in breadth and context. We understand the history of a single guild, the guilds of London, or those of another locality, within the context of the area and the economic and political developments of the age often more clearly than we do

---

16. Mendelson and Crawford, *Women in Early-Modern England,* esp. 256–300. In their discussion of women in guilds they concentrate on the role of widows but also point to women gaining more independent employment as craftpersons by the 1690s in London (327–36).

in contemporary work—especially the specialized article directed at probing a specific topic concerning a single guild or region. And, except for recent studies specifically concerning women's past, we learn much more about women's place in guild history than we do from present-day urban and economic historians. There are between two hundred and three hundred national, regional, city, or individual guild histories circa 1880–1930; lesser numbers by nonprofessional historians continue up to the present. In reviewing the major surveys of guild history such as Joshua Toulmin Smith's *English Guilds;* William Herbert's *The History of the Twelve Great Livery Companies of London* (1887), and George Unwin's *The Gilds and Companies of London* (1908), we find much evidence of women's place in guild history. Equally important was H. F. Westlake's *The Parish Guilds of Medieval England* (1919), which questioned Toulmin Smith's assessment of the basic secular nature of the late medieval religious guild. Somewhat later, and less well known, but equally sweeping, is Stella Kramer's *The English Craft Guilds,* published in 1927, but based upon her Columbia University dissertation of 1905.[17] From these works we discover that the division between craft and merchant guilds and religious guilds in late medieval towns was much less clear and secure than is often thought. Women were members of a wide range of guilds, were admitted to the freedom and wore livery along with men, and wardens and aldermen were to be elected from their number, explicitly from both "brethren and sistern." These sisters were single and married women as well as widows. Sixteenth-century charters emphasized both religious and political duties of craft guilds along with the economic oversight they performed for their craft. Such realities have, for the most part, been known by those working in urban, labor, and economic history, but have generated slight discussion of gender issues.[18]

17. Joshua Toulmin Smith, Esq., *English Gilds: . . . From Original MSS. of the Fourteenth and Fifteenth Centuries* (London: Early English Text Society, 1892), was written earlier but edited by his daughter Lucy Toulmin Smith following his death and published in 1892 with reproductions of documents for the Early English Text Society; William Herbert, *The History of the Twelve Great Livery Companies of London* (London: Corporation of London, 1887); George Unwin, *The Gilds and Companies of London,* ed. William F. Kahl (London: Frank Cass & Co., 1963); H. F. Westlake, *The Parish Gilds of Medieval England* (London: Society for Promoting Christian Knowledge, 1919); Stella Kramer, *The English Craft Gilds* (New York: Columbia University Press, 1927).

18. Few current historians are doing institutional histories of livery companies generally or individual guilds, but Steve Rappaport, *Worlds Within Worlds,* devotes little attention to women and does not grapple with their presence in the charters and their absence from apprentice rolls as he discusses social mobility in Tudor London; Tim Harris, *London Crowds in the Reign of Charles II* (Cambridge: Cambridge University Press, 1987), places guild political institutions at the heart of urban and much royal politics, but gives little attention to women belonging to the freedom. Eric Kerridge, *Textile Manufactures in Early Modern England* (Manchester: Manchester University Press, 1985), indexes women under "womenfolk" and does

Accounts focusing directly on women's participation in the guilds have consistently emphasized the negative.[19]

Contemporary studies reflect the specialization of the historical profession so that economic historians pay little attention to the religious aspects of their guild's charters and operations, and those treating the political development of towns and cities give slight attention to women's roles within guilds when linking guild structure to the nature of urban citizenship. Such specialization has limited our ability to gain an understanding of the nature of guilds as a whole, the link between religious and economic guilds, the place of women in guild history, and the shift in guild structures and priorities from the late medieval to the early modern period.

Definitional Issues Relevant to Guild Membership

While the numbers of sources for the false universal are massive, certainly the most authoritative is Scripture, with sermons and religious commentary coming in second. The religious foundation underlying so many economic and political documents make clear the centrality of religious values to social and political policy in early modern England. The confusion and conflation of craft and religious guilds build upon the interlocking pillars of religion and politics forming the values that were both taught and sought in apprentices. Thus, to divide the qualities of the citizen and the honest and responsible tradesman from the qualities of "man" as embodied in Adam and his descendants leads to distinctions that would not have been made by authors during

---

not provide a serious analysis of their crucial role in the area. Joan Lane, *Apprenticeship in England, 1600–1914* (Boulder, Colo.: Westview Press, 1996), has only four references to women, all as masters.

19. Merry Wiesner, "Spinning Out Capital: Women's Work in the Early Modern Economy," in *Becoming Visible: Women in European History,* 2nd ed., ed. Claudia Koonz and Renate Bridenthal (New York, 1989), 221–50, and "Early Modern Midwifery: A Case Study," in *Women and Work in Preindustrial Europe,* ed. Barbara Hanawalt (Bloomington: Indiana University Press, 1986), argues for the displacement of women in sixteenth-century crafts as craft membership came to be associated more with citizenship. Grethe Jacobsen, "Law and Reality: Conflicting or Integrated Determinants of Women's Role in the Crafts" (paper presented at Vienna, November 1992), finds a similar pattern for Danish guilds. Diane Willen, "Women in the Public Sphere in Early Modern England: The Case of the Urban Working Poor," *Sixteenth Century Journal* 19 (1988): 559–75, assesses women's public role among poor women who held social duties, and Ilana K. Ben-Amos, "Women Apprentices in the Trade and Crafts of Early Modern Bristol," in *Continuity and Change* (1991), discusses the place of town women in economic terms and looks for explanations for women's status.

the 1600s. While specialized works focused on the qualities attached to a particular trade or office, still the moral and socially responsible traits associated with them were integrally linked to Christian values.

The conflation of these values, and the false universal of "man" embodying "human," is exemplified in two seventeenth-century works, the anonymous *A Moral Essay Upon the Soul of Man* and John Stoughton's *Choice Sermons Preached Upon Selected Occasions.*[20] In addition to embodying a false universal, they offer the religious base for works addressed to economic issues. *A Moral Essay* contrasts men with beasts but uses examples that clarify that the moral principles outlined are intended only for men. The work is divided into three parts, and the second part, which lays out the specifics of those duties human beings owe to God, draws specific examples only from the lives of men. The work's third part, which ties the duties incumbent upon this life with the requirements of eternity, also omits women. This does not mean, of course, that women were not expected to be either good or responsible, simply that they were not expected to be so as an independent adult.

In Stoughton's fourth sermon, "The Magistrates Commission; or, Wisedom justified: Before the Judges," he identifies God's plan with "man" and those resistant to that plan with a witch. He uses Psalms 2:10–12 as his scriptural text, which begins, "Bee wise now ... O yee Kings." Kings must govern wisely to ensure the victory of religion and morality, and the enemy to such government in the world is in the form of a witch: "The World is a Witch, the proofe is certaine by her Familiar, the Spirit of Rebellion against God; which haunts and possesses those that doate upon her" (135).

Stoughton advances from this contest between God's rulers on Earth and its wicked nature to realities attached to the rule of Hebrew kings. Maintaining order was key to linking the power of God and the authority and wisdom of his rulers, with "the many hands of the multitude which must receive information from these, and direction; and what condition soever." Stoughton did not simply link male rulers with God's will and wisdom; rather, he exemplified the false universal pattern of linking "all" to the "condition" of men. Disorder came from women's ignorance, in contrast with the truth pursued by God's earthly governors. The Earth "can have but one God, and God will approve but of one Religion" (140). But misinformation was apt to arise from women,

---

20. *A Moral Essay Upon the Soul of Man* (London: For A.F., 1648), n.p.; John Stoughton, *Choice Sermons Preached Upon Selected Occasions.* Both works will be hereafter cited in the text by page number.

who should be ignored: "the Christian Religion is the true Religion, and let it trouble no man that hee heares two women laying claime eyther to the living childe, so ambiguously that the controversie cannot be decided, ... The woman is indeede in scarlet *Revel.* But her Scarlet is dyed red in the blood of the Saints, shee that would have the living child divided" (160).[21] Such divisions led Stoughton, along with other seventeenth-century authors, to term men "Nursing-Fathers to this Son" (160).

While such a religious discussion may seem far removed from the nature of guilds and apprenticeship, it is not. Religion played a dominant role in the language of guild charters, the punishment meted out to guild members by aldermanic courts, and the directives for and petitions and actions of seventeenth-century apprentices. Apprentices were to gain independence not simply to demonstrate skill in a craft, or even to obtain the privileges of the freedom, but above all to do God's will and to interact with their fellow members, and people generally, on Christian principles.[22]

21. Stoughton's work, and that of others who vilified women to press the case for religious orthodoxy, has been interpreted as a work of political and religious import without serious gender implications. Yet the continual practice of Puritans, Anglicans, Independents, and Presbyterians in linking their opponents to the supposed irreligious, immoral, and ignorant qualities of women did indeed have significant impact on women's being seen as outside the parameters of these institutional boundaries. And such boundaries often seemed to incorporate the category "human" as well.

22. The emphasis on religious and political principle is demonstrated most prominently in documents emerging from groups of apprentices, and works directed to them, from 1640 to 1660, and again during the 1680s. These documents exemplify the Puritan and Dissenter views that were so prominent among artisans in London and other English cities at the time. It is difficult, then, to separate the massive Christian literature that conflates "man" and "human" from the literature which associates guild members with God's minions on earth and politically with the people of England. Works from the 1680s are often brief, and while apprenticeship literature was always subject to sexual and satirical qualities, the following political tracts are quite brief and some have humorous language grounding political debate: *A Friendly dialogue between two London-apprentices, the one a Whigg, and the other a Tory* (London: Printed for Richard Janeway, 1681), which frames the dispute in stereotypes of the slothful Tory and the Whig anxious for his next brew and any easy handouts; the broadside, *A Letter of Advice to the Petitioning Apprentices* (London: Printed by N. Thompson, 1681), reproves them for their organized roar that was able to produce nothing but a mouse, but is more serious in their "aspersions upon Authority, and [efforts to] vilifie the very Throne of Justice"; and the last by J. M., identified as a London apprentice who defends his fellows against charges of disloyalty and compares the actions of 1641 against the measured goals of 1681. In 1641, "London youth" pressured Charles I to seek a different abode than Whitehall, "among a more peaceable and civilized part of his Subjects," but the loyal apprentices of 1681 are "in abhorrence of such wicked Principles" and offer up themselves "to the Service of so gracious a Prince"; see *A Vindication of the Loyal London-Apprentices: against the false and scandalous aspersions of Richard Janeway* ([London: s.n., 1681]). As in the case of these brief tracts and broadsides, it is difficult to pin down apprentices' genuine voices, as their political enemies were so often placing remarks in their mouths.

Moral and Social Parameters of Apprenticeship

Instructions for apprentices strongly emphasized their need for personal morality and religious belief. Many were associated with one side in a political dispute, with apprentices sometimes being encouraged to support Independents, other times Presbyterians, and at other points the established church against its critics. Of the large number of petitions emerging from apprentices, many had religion as their primary topic. In other instances, they combined concern for religion with demands for political involvement and respect for their views and standing. An example of the language common in apprentice petitions appeared in one from 1681 which assured the apprentices' (five thousand in all) loyalty to the king and thanked him for his "Promises to maintain the true Protestant Religion by Law established, by which we have been taught, that to Fear God and Honour the King is the chief Character of a true Christian."[23] This comment was followed by an assurance of loyalty to the crown and a willingness to fight to preserve the king's sovereignty and the Anglican Church.

Works directed to apprentices and their masters integrated religious, political, social, and moral values. They focused much less on issues of an economic or occupational nature than on the status of apprentices within English society generally and the qualities they hoped to instill in the young. In a 1674 work, *The Cities great Concern, . . . whether Apprentiship Extinguisheth Gentry,* the author treats each of these questions. Larger numbers of those joining guilds were from the gentry than had been previously thought, and this tract highlights the social issues inherent in that reality.[24] The "Booksellers Report" sought to highlight the work's importance; the seller notes the great interest shown in the status of apprentices over the previous fifty years and the important contribution this work makes to that discussion: "the general good of this famous City and Citizens, and particularly of some of us, who claim an Interest of Birth herein, whether it be Bond or Free."

A subsequent preface following "The Booksellers Report" points to the importance of trade and places it within the traditional biblical language of

---

23. Quoted in Harris, *London Crowds,* 174.

24. Edmund Bolton, *The Cities great Concern, . . . whether Apprentiship Extinguisheth Gentry* (London: Printed by William Godbid, 1674), (which was printed originally in Latin in 1607 and in English in 1610). For a succinct discussion of the recent scholarship on the class makeup and role of apprentices in early modern London, see Ward, *Metropolitan Communities,* 1–6, 50–57, 115–20; for a discussion of the concern expressed in this tract, see Paul S. Seaver, "Declining Status in an Aspiring Age: The Problem of the Gentle Apprentice in Seventeenth-Century London," in *Court, Country and Culture: Essays on Early Modern British History in Honor of Perez Zagorin* (Rochester: Rochester University Press, 1992), 129–48.

a male-centered progression. While God had provided great abundance, it still required concerted effort for all to gain: "which the Offspring of *Adam* doth now enjoy. As therefore the World it self was too great a Patrimony for one man, had not God been pleased to have given him a large and numerous *issue* to enjoy and improve it ... had not *Commerce* and *Traffick*, heightened by the ingenuity and industry of man unlocked these *hidden* Mines and secret Treasures, and by an easie yet speedy passage brought them to our very doors."[25]

This work, along with so many others, conflated labor with citizenship and assumed that men's productivity led to their status as citizens: "By these it is we come to be as it were *Citizens* of the *World*, and to have correspondence and intercourse with the remotest Countries." Trade had the effect of making the whole world "a common *Mart*" and was the way that Englishmen exhibited their economic prowess; it served as a "*spur* to labour and Industry." Trade proved the superiority of such a nation and meant that "most *Isles* and Maritime places exceed all In-land Cities and Countries in Riches, and variety of plenty."

The preface to *Cities Great Concern* ties the growing commercialization of England during the second half of the seventeenth century to Christian goals; an individual man who encompassed Christian, national, and economic qualities identified himself as an Englishman. In focusing again on the centrality of trade, the author asks: "for what has been the Propagation of the Gospel, but a kind of a *Religious Commerce*, whereby the *souls* as well as the *Bodies* of Mankind might be supplied with necessaries for a better life." Christ's teachings moved only in piecemeal fashion when carried by individual apostles, and as Christ realized this, he turned to fishermen whose nets reached wider audiences: "Hence is it, our *Saviour* made choice of *fishermen*, who were to pass as it were through the *Zodiac*, and disperse his precepts; their *calling* and *Trade* rendring them skilful in *Navigation*, and bold in adventuring, and the blessed *Master* inspiring them with Gifts and Parts to improve it to the inlargement of his Doctrine and Kingdom." Thus Christianity spread through the care of heaven "and the indefatigable Industry of *Man*" ("Preface"). Finally, not only was trade essential to the spread of Christianity, institutions of learning were also commercial centers and tied to the occupational goals in training young men for adulthood: "Nay, the *Universities* themselves are but as it were a

---

25. "Booksellers Note" and "Preface," in Bolton, *The Cities great Concern*, n.p. The author directs his book "only to such Masters or Citizens as are generously disposed, and worthily qualified Men" and to young men who see the city as a citadel, "the body and the head of Man." Hereafter cited in the text by section and/or page number.

learned Corporation, and *Society,* each several *Art* and *Science* therein not much unlike our several *Companies,* and inferior Schools, which fit *Youth* for those places, but as *shops,* wherein young men are initiated *Apprentices,* and afterwards commence *Masters*" ("Preface").

Following the work's lengthy preface, Bolton justifies in great detail the importance of crafts and commerce and argues that gaining one's standing through trade was at least as honorable as gaining it through the sword or the gown. His greatest aim was to undercut those authors who have "lodge[d] upon the hopeful and honest estate of Apprenticeship the odious Note of Bondage, and the barbarous penalty of loss of Gentry." Those who made such charges were ill-informed about England's past, for its policy "did ever leave the Gates of Honour open to City-Arts, and to the mystery of honest Gain, as fundamental in Common-weals" ("To the Reader"). In addition, the apprentice is compared later in the work to the wife as regards the dowry she brought to marriage. The author notes the dual contractual relationship involved, with the apprentice agreeing to offer service and the master "to teach him his Art to the utmost." The importance of this agreement was such that "Which Master's part is grown to such estimation, as that Apprentices now come commonly like Wives, with treble more portions than formerly to the Masters" (48).

The Cities great Concern is divided into four parts and traces the links between apprenticeship and gentility from the Romans through Elizabethan England. Bolton argues that only in Turkey was such a link denied. While this work, and others like it, have been analyzed as evidence for the growing importance of commercial values, and the relative gain in status of London merchants and masters of various crafts, it is also important for its focus on a male progression grounded in Christian, political, and economic values. Such a blending of the authoritative discourses and dominant institutions of early modern England in a work simply arguing the importance of trade and the exalted status of the apprentice reaffirms the centrality of male maturation to such arguments. Scholars concerned with only one aspect of this integrated discourse have failed to point out its gender implications, which could easily have been as important and long lasting as the particular arguments related to the nature of apprentices.

In addition, another range of works conflates economic, political, and religious themes while utilizing confused gender identities, and perpetuating a false universal with men embodying each as a single individual. One of the more interesting of such works is *The Standard of Equality, in subsidiary Taxes and Payments; or, A just and strong Preserver of Publick Liberty.*[26] This work, one of the economically democratic writings coming from Levellers and other critics of the crown during the late 1640s, supported a more equitable tax structure. Its author argues "that all rates and taxes fall intolerably heavy on the middle sort of people, contrary to their birth-right, liberty, and the rules of all equality and justice" (113). This tract, which was reproduced in the *Harleian Miscellany,* argues strongly against the economic advantages of the aristocracy and for a fair tax policy toward artisans and merchants. But in doing so, the author employs falsely universal language that places women outside of his demands and conflates individual men with the interests of the middling sort. The work is directed against those who underpaid excises and "presume to cheat and deceive the public" (116).

England's elite gained most from its public institutions and only through charity were a deserving few others housed at colleges and hospitals. Even so, taxes were taken from those who could least afford them, thus "the poor labourer, who hath threshed all day for a livelihood, should himself be threshed at night with unconscionable payment for things tending to the bare support of Nature." He opposed an excessive tax on labor and "that men be not made to pay excise for the dropping of their own sweat" (116).

The overall structure of the work encourages a four-part tax system based on lands, houses, goods, and money at interest (116–19). His work sought "a just and impartial dividing of all taxes, according to men's several estates" (116). This interesting and broad-based proposal for a more equitable system of taxation, intended to remove tax burdens from the poor and encourage trade, made clear that women were not included in the economic categories being discussed. His model to judge a proposed tax system employed the following language: "And surely, as parents presume with uncontroulable confidence more sharply and severely to correct their own children (then the sons of strangers) as having a peculiar reference to, and proper dominion over them, so the commonwealth may be bold to lay a round tax on use money, a son, a creature of their own; owing its birth and being to the courtesy and sole subsistence, to the connivance and toleration of the state" (118).

---

26. *The Standard of Equality, in subsidiary Taxes and Payments; or, A just and strong Preserver of Publick Liberty* (London: Printed by D. H., 1647). The author expressly identifies with the middle classes: "Whereas if any condition of people may pretend to more favor due unto them, the middle rank of men seem best to deserve it, because, I may say, they lie in continual service, and their labour so beneficial to the commonwealth, ought to be countenanced, and instead of these unreasonable weights, wings of encouragement should be given to their industry" (114). Hereafter cited in the text by page number. The work is signed "Philo Dicaeus."

His program would ensure social mobility, in language that implies general inclusion, but with examples only from men. The "equality" of his program "will inspirit all trades with a vigorous cheerfulness," and he specifically mentions that "the spinsters wheel would merrily turn round" (120). The author employs particularly inclusive language when he assures his readers that "None will regret at the payment of taxes, when equally proportioned amongst all persons, on all commodities" (120). But when justifying his program and the good it will bring to the commonwealth, he conflates this universal language with men's ambitions and realities. First, his concern is personal—that someone else will take, and receive credit, for his ideas and his labor because "many men when they have conquered an hard invention, another is crowned with all the credit thereof." He believes this happens especially when "some great person, stepping in by force or favour, ejects the true owner ... of what his industry acquired" (120). Finally, his assessment of the broad impact of this program again makes clear the gender-restricted meaning of "all" and the specific significance of this tax reform for men: "This will publish and clear the several conditions and values of men, as they are estated and entrusted in possessions, that so, if the ability of their minds and civility of their behaviour be answerable to their means, they may be suited accordingly with places of power and trust in the commonwealth" (121).

Gender Controversies Surrounding Early Modern Guilds

Developing a generalized picture of women's role within early modern guilds is not an easy task, given the idiosyncratic and unsystematic nature of the evidence; yet, as discussed earlier, we can gain a general sense of their place through apprentice lists and records of those gaining the freedom. There is evidence in a range of guild histories that charters explicitly included women as members, as eligible for the freedom of the town and as wearers of the company's livery.

A 1648 edition of *The Charter of the Company of Clothworkers of London* and an 1881 volume of *The Ordinances of the Cloth-workers' Company, together with ... Fullers & Shearmen of the City of London* document the inclusion of women in the guild's membership. The 1648 account notes that James I, when renewing an Elizabethan charter, drew freely from Elizabeth's language. This language mentions both brothers and sisters, but employs sex-specific terminology such as "fraternity," "brotherhood," or "freemen" to denote the

membership as a whole. Elizabeth turned to precedent, relying on the authority of Edward IV, who granted the right to three of his "liegemen" to establish
a "Fraternity or perpetuall Guilde" of fullers composed of "the men of the
Mistery or Art of Fullers then inhabiting or thenceforward to inhabit within
His City of London, or Suburbes of the same, of the Brethren and Sisters, of
the free persons of the same Mistery or Art, and of others who out of their
devotion will be of the same Fraternity or Guilde."[27] She then refers to a
charter of Henry VII allowing the shearmen to establish their separate standing, and a charter of 1531 in which Henry VIII combined both guilds into the
company of clothworkers. Other than the inclusion of women, perhaps most
significant is the religious nature of the charge given to the shearmen by
Henry VII and continued in their title under his son. Such reality documents
the close ties between religious and craft guilds. In the medieval period, members of craft and religious guilds took part in religious ceremonies and processions jointly. In the late fourteenth century, the dean and canons, for instance,
of Saint Martin-le-Grand admitted the saddlers to all the benefits of their
masses and prayers, while in addition "also granted the gild two masses a
week, one for the living and the other for the dead."[28]

Henry VII called the guild "the fraternity of the Assumption of the Blessed
Virgin Mary of Sheermen of the City of London" and said his goal was to
"erect and establish a guild or fraternity in honour of the same Virgin, of the
men of the Mistery aforesaid and others." When Henry VIII combined the
shearmen and fullers, he took the shearmen's title and called the new guild
"the Gild or Fraternity of the Assumption of the Blessed Virgin Mary of the
Cloth-workers in the City of London." While honoring the Virgin, this guild
had authority to elect its officers and to oversee the quality of production;
it, as its counterparts, combined religious, community, political, and economic
efforts. This Henrician charter states that the master and wardens should
"make and have among the Citizens of the same City, being then Brethren
and Sisters of the same Fraternity of Cloathworkers and the most sufficient
thereunto, one Livery or Robe" to "use as often, and whensoever they please.
And that they might hold and keepe their Feast or Banquet" at a convenient

27. *The Charter of the Company of Clothworkers of London* (London: N.p., 1648), 1–4; *The Ordinances
of the Clothworkers' Company, together with ... fullers & Shearmen of the City of London. Transcribed from
the Originals ...* (London: Privately printed, 1881), 20–22.

28. Westlake, *Parish Gilds,* 7. In addition, Westlake states that craft and religious guilds had overlapping memberships, and women might be members in one portion of the guild but not another: "On the
religious side the craft-gilds included in many cases the wives of their members and frequently men who
were not of the same 'mystery'" (21–23).

date around the assumption of the Virgin Mary. The 1881 translation of Henry VIII's charter, and earlier documents pertaining to fullers and shearmen, clarifies that "freemen" served as an inclusive term with "brothers" and "sisters" together composing the guild's freemen, when granting rights to the master and wardens and to the commonalty or "the Brethrene and Susters of the Freemen of the same Misterie or Crafte."[29] Another ordinance of the guild of shearmen as noted under Henry VI reveals the range of women's involvement in guild records and governance. It designates that a chest should be kept in the company's hall for the use of all to keep valuables, "and that there be in the same cheste a register booke for to engroce theryn the names of the brethren and sustren." The compilers of records for an 1890 *Annals of the Barber-Surgeons of London* note that "from the earliest times the custom has prevailed to admit women to the freedom, mostly by apprenticeship, but also by patrimony, and these freewomen bound their apprentices, both boys and girls, at the Hall."[30] Although these materials concern the origins of the London guild, there are charters for other regions as well, and a guild from Lincoln established in 1369, as did others, the equal application to female members of guild charity or fines for lack of conformity to rules. For example, "if any brother or sister of this guild fall into poverty or sickness ... this guild shall give to him 6d. per annum," and "if any brother or sister, ... shall not come when he be summoned," he shall be fined.

Other evidence, especially from the history of the merchant guild of Exeter, documents that sons could gain membership in a guild through patrimony by way of either mother or father: "that the eldest sone of every ffreeman or ffreewoman of this Societie after his deathe shall have the pryvelege of the freedome of this Companye according to the auncient liberties of the Citie," and a similar rule operated for apprentices where "the Apprentice of every ffreeman or ffreewoman of this Companye shall be admytted to the freedome," after completing his or her time and paying initiation fees. Corroborating evidence comes from a history of Preston, in which a guild office could be inherited from either the mother or the father. Within the guild merchant, a mayor of Preston in 1411, Henry de Hoghton, was the son of Roger de Ethelstone who had married Margaret, a co-heir with her brother, "and whose son John held Brocholes in right of his mother." In this instance, as was

29. Materials in this paragraph are from *Charter of the Company of Clothworkers*, 13, and *Ordinances of the Clothworkers' Company*, 20.

30. *The Annals of the Barber-Surgeons of London*, 2 vols. (London: Blades, East and West, 1890), 260, 577–79.

generally the case, the guild merchant overlapped in membership and function with the town government, and thus officers were noted as the mayor and
aldermen of the guild.[31]

This revised analysis and chronology of women as active members in guilds
in the medieval period, continuing into the sixteenth and early seventeenth
century, declines during the decades of the civil war and Restoration and in-
creases again by the 1690s, offers a reassessment of current scholarship. It also
ties the role of women in guilds to concurrent economic and political trends
that could have contributed to this pattern. The early eighteenth century saw
a dual recognition of women's involvement in the crafts and an effort on the
part of some, especially stationers, to restrict their employment. Materials
from the clock makers' company document two points being made here: the
small recognition of women in guild documents during the mid- and later seventeenth century and their reappearance in the early eighteenth century. A
1631 charter makes no mention of women as members of the guild except
for a reference to widows who are noted as exceptions to the exclusion of
all those who have not served a seven-year apprenticeship, "unless such as be
the Clockmakers' widows of the city of London ... for so long time only
as they shall so continue widows."[32] However this, and similar studies of
restraints against women's labor, can be read either as documenting the large
numbers of women workers in that area, the particular bias or fear of women
workers by the guild in question, or the inability of women to pursue their
occupation.[33]

Guilds that received their original charters under Charles II were much less
apt to include women among those eligible for membership than those with
charters granted through the early Stuarts, which used earlier precedents.

31. Taken from a charter granted by Queen Elizabeth in 1560; quoted in William Cotton, *An Elizabethan Guild of the City of Exeter ... the Society of Merchant Adventurers* [Exeter: N.p., 1873], 14–18. The
material on Preston comes from William Dobson and John Harland, *A History of Preston Guild; the
Ordinances of various Guilds Merchant. The Charters to the borough, the incorporated companies* (Preston:
W. and J. Dobson, [1862]), 23.

32. Margaret Hunt, "Hawkers, Bawlers, and Mercuries: Women and the London Press in the Early
Enlightenment," *Women and the Enlightenment, Women & History* (New York: Institute for Research in
History, Haworth Press, 1984), 41–68, contends that the stationers worked to keep women from hawking
almanacs and other popular publications on the streets.

33. *Some Account of the Worshipful Company of Clockmakers of the City of London,* Compiled
principally by Samuel Elliott Atkins and William Henry Overall ([London]: Privately printed, 1881),
31, 155. The authors served, respectively, as clerk of the company and librarian to the corporation of
London.

Women are not mentioned in the charter of 1677 of the coachmakers and coach harness-makers of London.[34] However, the clock workers' history, written in 1881, notes that: "In the year 1715, it appears that the Company recognized and sanctioned the taking of Female Apprentices," and lists "among numerous other instances" Mariane Viet (1715), Rebeckah Fisher (1715), Charlotte Hubert (1725), Catherine Cext (1730), Anna Maria Shaw (1733), Elizabeth Askell (1734), and Susanna Smith (1747). These female apprentices were bound to men, to husbands and wives, and, in one instance, the apprentice Elizabeth Askell to Elinor Mosely, who was not identified as a wife as were the other mistresses.[35]

It is difficult to determine a pattern as to which guilds were more receptive to women and which least; but given the limited evidence, guilds most closely tied to women's traditional occupations seem least apt to include them as apprentices or freewomen and to bring charges against male members for employing women. The charter of innkeepers mentions nothing of women, even though women were heavily engaged in keeping inns. Richard Y. Hawkin, in his 1955 history of York, notes that although one-fourth of weavers were women, "only six women appear in the freemens roll and not a weaver amongst them" over a fifty-year period in the fourteenth century.[36] Alfred Plummer's *The London Weavers' Company, 1600–1970,* notes the harsh penalties brought against any member allowing women to weave in his establishment: in 1649, a member was fined 20s for having women working on two of his six looms; in 1653 John Hogg had to fire an unmarried woman who had been employed for a year and to pay £5 if she were ever to weave for him again; one member defended himself by saying he had employed a woman "out of Charity her husband having beaten her, but she is now returned [to him] who is a freeman." Another weaver termed the court of wardens "a company of

34. See *A History of the Worshipful Company of Coachmakers and coach harness-makers of London,* Compiled by direction of the Lord Iliffe, Master (London: Privately printed, 1937), 84–94. Women are also omitted in a charter of Charles II in George Elkington, *The Coopers: Company and Craft* (London: Sampson, Low, Marston & Co., [1932]), 121–23.

35. *Some Account of the . . . Clockmakers* (1881), 155. Charlotte Carmichael Stopes, *British Freewomen, Their Historical Privilege* (London: S. Sonneschein, 1894), also documents women's guild membership and notes that, "The Clockworkers Company, although only founded in 1632, had female apprentices sanctioned by the company as late as 1715, 1725, 1730, 1733, 1734, 1747" (81).

36. Richard Y. Hawkin, *A History of the Freemen of the City of York* ([City of York Gild of Freemen], 1955). P. J. P Goldberg, *Women, Work, and Life Cycle in a Medieval Economy: Women in York and Yorkshire c. 1300–1520* (Oxford: Clarendon Press, 1992), provides a thoughtful analysis of the opportunities for women in the trades and crafts of late medieval York, but his grounding of women's labor in a demographic framework places his explanation perhaps too strongly in a family nexus.

fools" for calling him before them on grounds of employing females. The court, though, was enforcing the weavers' 1596 charter which stated: "no woman or mayd shall use or exercise the Arts of weaving ... except she be the widow of one of the same Guilde."[37]

Paul Ward, in his treatment of the weavers during the late sixteenth and early seventeenth centuries, looks at foreigners as threats to the livelihood and domination of native weavers. Differing with traditional analyses that stress a more negative reaction of rank-and-file weavers to foreign competition, he notes that one of the criticisms of such foreigners was that they went against company regulations as regards their general employment of women. Such regulations from 1578 state that: "No manner of person or persons exercising [weaving] shall keep, teach, instruct, or bring up in the use, exercise, or knowledge of [weaving] any maid, damsel, or other woman whatsoever." Two of the most interesting aspects of this passage are that it contrasts "manner of person or persons" with any "woman whatsovever" and that the justification for such exclusion was given for the protection not of male weavers, but of women and children, "leaving their wives and children in most lamentable misery" (128–29). One of the main reasons for women's work lacking attention from guild historians is the continual juxtaposition in the documents of words such as "person" with others referring only to women, and when women are mentioned, it is as men's economic dependents, even though the specific reference is to their employment in weaving.[38]

Late Medieval Religious and Craft Guilds

Although my primary focus is the early modern economic guild, I must mention the medieval religious guild, its relationship to contemporary craft and merchant guilds, and its relevance to the operation of gender in Tudor and Stuart associations. As has been generally accepted, women were members of late medieval parish guilds. These guilds provided spiritual and social assistance to members and needy persons in the community, including funds for special masses, masses for dead members or candles for the guild's saint day, a priest for members' private altar and burial funds, aid to members down on their luck, and assistance to grammar school and university students, widows

37. Alfred Plummer, *The London Weavers' Company, 1600–1970* (London: Routledge & Kegan Paul, 1972), 60–61.

38. Ward, *Metropolitan Communities*, 128–29.

and orphans, and the poor in general. Records of religious guilds speak of both "brothers" and "sisters," and women comprised from 25 to 39 percent of membership in a group of East Anglian parishes.[39]

Merchant and craft guilds were as old as the religious ones, and many carried out similar functions. They also had women as members but not as officers in the guilds, although charters allowed them to hold such offices. Heather Swanson's study of craft guilds in late medieval English towns documents the minimal importance of members' economic interests in determining the structure and values of craft guilds. She points to merchant guilds that formed city councils or the governing bodies of towns, whose interest it was to control the production of various crafts. Rather than establishing a single product monopoly, members of crafts were better served by being able to work in a range of skills as demand shifted. And histories of craft guilds "suggest a degree of order and coherence ... that is in fact quite illusory." Accounts are based on "administrative" records that for the most part ignore women's work and "reflect the order that the authorities wished to see imposed on society, a hierarchical and above all male-oriented order."[40]

In provincial towns, drapers and mercers did not simply dominate the town's trade but its governance as well. Their combined economic and political role was indicative of their dominance of the towns' economies and social hierarchy, and their ability to dictate craft regulations for the guilds. Such reality undermined the broad-based nature of the family economy, which called upon contributions from husband, wife, and children. Family incomes were supplemented by the sale of fish, through brewing, and by offering hospitality. Women were heavily involved in each of these activities and received a significant amount of brewing equipment as bequeathed by artisans in their wills.

39. From a 1388–89 report on their status required by Richard II, in Benjamin R. McRee, "Bonds of Community: Religious Gilds and Urban Society in Late Medieval England" (Ph.D. dissertation, Indiana University, 1987), 53. Although McRee devotes only a brief portion of his study to gender, he does a gender breakdown of the membership of East Anglian guilds in the late fourteenth century (53–58). Further, his emphasis on guilds as communities that performed a range of activities and offered a sense of unity and status to their members supports my position that one aspect of a guild's functions has been overemphasized to the detriment of its broader purposes and structure. As McRee notes, "The men and women who enrolled in urban religious gilds were seeking more than piety, pageantry and protection from penury. They were looking, more fundamentally, for a sense of community" (4). And ceremony played a "symbolic role as a barrier separating members of the gild from other residents of the city. It compelled those entering the gild to recognize that they were ... a unique social entity, a special community within the larger community of townsmen" (75). Other than McRee's thesis, Westlake, *Parish Gilds*, remains the standard account of medieval religious guilds.

40. Heather Swanson, "The Illusion of Economic Structure: Craft Guilds in Late Medieval English Towns," *Past and Present*, no. 121 (November 1988): 29. Hereafter cited in the text by page number.

They, of course, had traditionally been involved in the textile and cloth trade, and a list of workers who dealt in wool cloth in York for 1394–95 includes the names of 180 women (36).

Swanson's work emphasizes two points: that women's work as artisans, traders, and business people was widespread, and that contemporary records and later accounts have both overlooked this contribution and used institutional documents that obscure such a reality. This has led economic and labor historians to focus on the work of individual artisans rather than the work of the family and to overstress the economic and comprehensive nature of records that were hierarchical attempts at control. "Individuals and family units," she contends, "did not therefore restrict themselves to one occupation. With this flexibility of occupational structure a guild system could not hope to establish craft monopolies" (37).

Craft charters specified clear religious duties, at least through Henry VIII, and to a lesser extent through Elizabeth and the early Stuarts. Such provisions reveal that craft guilds shared social and religious duties along with parish guilds at least into the sixteenth century.[41] References to sisters in charter language, or in by-laws and documents recording the enforcement of guild regulations, declined during the seventeenth century. Yet this does not appear to be a permanent trend because during the early eighteenth century an increased number of women were listed as apprentices and among those admitted to the freedom in a range of London craft guilds.

Linguistic Confusion and Conflation in Contemporary and Historical Accounts

While there is strong evidence of women's role in guilds, and among crafts more broadly, guild directives and advice to apprentices are grounded in issues

41. Stella Kramer, *English Craft Guilds,* continues to offer the most comprehensive coverage of the origin of craft guilds in England; she emphasizes both their religious and political origins, and notes how their charters combined these areas along with economic activity. Examples include the Shrewsbury mercantile guild, which included mercers, goldsmiths, and ironmongers, who in their bylaws of 1480 warned members against missing the celebration of the Corpus Christi festival to attend the Coventry fair or elsewhere "to buy or sell." It oversaw consumer protection by guaranteeing that none pursuing trade would possess "any false Balaunce Weight or measures, wherebie the Kynges People" might be harmed. This guild also maintained membership among a wide range of crafts—pewteres, founders, cardmakers, and cappers—guaranteeing that those crafts also upheld public religious ceremonies and fair business practices (21–23). Those in handicrafts, such as the carpenters and joiners or the armourers and braziers, came together, she argued, not so much to control their trade, but because the divisions between them and similarly skilled workers were blurring and union seemed preferable to competition (52–59). Thus, craft guilds came together at the request of municipalities, for religious and political reasons, to ease

of men maturing to adulthood and economic independence. The false universal of guild-based terms such as "freemen," "members" or "artisans," and the prescriptions that accompanied these terms, have caused historians to take issues of male social mobility and a process of male maturation as both central and universal to the operation of early modern guilds. Such a framework has not only ignored women's role, but overemphasizes that minority of successful men who became either masters or aldermen. One of the reasons for such an emphasis, in addition to the greater accessibility of aldermanic records, is the conflation (especially in the seventeenth century) of the political qualities and efforts of freemen engaged in politics and their standing as artisans based on economic skill and independence.

Difficulties arise when one uses modern studies of individual guilds to extract materials about women in order to understand their economic place within the crafts and trade more generally. For some studies, it is simply that women are not mentioned, but more often individual women are included in the account. Even so, they are treated as exceptions in materials usually offered as an aside, or referred to (but not discussed) in a footnote. The narrative is focused on male family members, and discussion of a woman's life is seldom central to the narrative. A good example of this pattern appears in Elspeth Veale's *The English Fur Trade in the Later Middle Ages*. While Veale's focus is the later Middle Ages, the latter portions of her work go into some detail concerning sixteenth-century guilds. In the author's discussion of livery companies during that century, she includes the following description of relevance to the family of William Gregory: "Some interesting sidelights are shed on them and their life from the letters and papers of the Stonor family, landed gentry of Oxfordshire, into which his grandaughter Elizabeth married. William's daughter Margaret, a capable business woman herself, married John Croke, citizen and skinner whose impressive stone tomb ... is still to be seen in the Church of All Hallows, Barking."[42]

Such an account, along with uninformative references, has been replicated time and again. Women's crafts and trades never seem central to the subjects

boundaries with competing trades, and not primarily to protect a monopoly over their trade. Again, Kramer stresses the complexity and community-based nature of guilds.

42. Elspeth M. Veale, *The English Fur Trade in the Later Middle Ages* (Oxford: Clarendon Press, 1966), 183–84. The note on Margaret Croke's business dealings refers the reader to her will without further explanation of the range or nature of her trade. As for Elizabeth Stoner, who was the daughter of the Crokes, the text offers only the following description: "Dame Elizabeth, masterful, extravagant, shrewd and affectionate, comes vividly to life in her letters." Unfortunately, we lack a discussion of any of these qualities. Hereafter cited in the text by page number.

of a range of guild studies, especially from 1950 on. Another example of the ways in which women are simply dropped into narratives organized in ways to exclude them comes from Steve Rappaport's *Worlds Within Worlds*. In discussing the gifts made by men and women to prospective artisans, he assumes the recipients are all male: "for men 'keeping retailing shops' in London, for 'occupiers into Flanders,' for men 'trading over the seas.'" While Rappaport inserts male identifiers into his narrative, it is interesting to wonder what sex Agnes Suckley, whose beneficence is used as an example in his narrative, had in mind. He states: "In her will Agnes Suckley instructed the Merchant Taylors to grant 2-year loans without interest of £50 apiece to eight 'of the youngest occupiers ... dwelling either in Watling Street or Candelwick Street or elsewhere in London, occupying the trade of retailing of woolen cloth.'" Furthermore, preference was to be given to "apprentices and servants" either of herself or of her late husband, Henry, and also to the husbands of any of her "maidservants," provided they were free of the Merchant Taylors' Company.[43] Given that the individuals could be apprenticed to herself as well as her husband, and that they could be servants as well as apprentices, it is clear only in the specific reference to husbands that she intended only men as beneficiaries. Such accounts make it unclear as to whether men were the sole subjects of guild directives or makers or recipients of wills, as most historians have assumed.

Women are included in detail only in studies that treat them specifically, and then women's work is seldom compared with men's, or discussed as significant in the evolution of crafts and guilds more broadly. Unlike many other scholars, Veale holds a genuine interest in women's work, but that interest only leads to tantalizing comments such as the following on "The Office of the King's Skinner": "It is interesting to note that Thomas Jenyn's (a royal furrier) widow, Katherine, married Thomas Addington, who had been one of Jynge's apprentices. She was herself a silk-woman and had received a royal appointment in 1524" (207). In addition, interconnected analyses that focus on office holding (whether guild or political) and the accepted importance of merchants over individual craftspersons make it difficult to know to what degree women were excluded from the craft, or to what extent they were simply less apt to own substantial businesses or to hold public office. Especially with the case of the skinners, knowledge of the trade seems less important than having a significant role in foreign trade. As Veale notes, "Thus in 1563 only one of the

---

43. Rappaport, *Worlds Within Worlds*, 372–73.

five who held office in the Company was a skinner by trade. In 1606, among the forty who formed the Court, the merchants themselves could only trace fourteen who were either working skinners, sons or apprentices of skinners, or skilful in skins and furs; the artisan skinners, as the craftsmen were then describing themselves, claimed that there were only five" (187).

The question then arises as to whether the great attention paid to aldermen and other governing bodies among guilds undercuts a full understanding of women's role in the trades and overplays the importance of merchants at the same time. It highlights whether concentrating on rules and their enforcement is the best way to understand the operations of crafts during the early modern era, and whether such concentration especially obscures women's place within a particular craft.

Guild Connections and Seventeenth-Century Politics

The limited reference to women in guild records during the seventeenth century corresponds to broader political debates. In those periods when urban freemen strongly defended their political status, especially during the 1640s and 1650s and from 1679 to 1685, it was problematic for them to include women in justifications for men's political standing. Acknowledging women's status as free citizens did not strengthen the argument for the political standing of the freeman or "commonalty," against the claims of mayor and aldermen or Charles II's appointments to local councils. Here, as elsewhere, a group of men cast their political origins in a tradition of the ancient rights of freeborn Englishmen, thereby conflating people with men, in establishing men's fundamental political rights.

In *London's Liberties; or, A Learned Argument of Law & Reason, upon Saturday, December 14, 1650,* John Wildman and John Price argued for the freemen of London against the more limited suffrage of livery men and the dominant authority of the mayor and aldermen in order that "our right in Electing, as we are Freemen, may be restored to us." Such standing was based upon "those very foundations of Common Right which the parliament have declared to us" and thus the ultimate principle (rather than from a charter from James I put forth by mayorial and aldermanic opponents) was that no one had a "Power under God to invest a trust of Government in any but the people." A practical base for such standing came from the fact that the freemen of companies have "hazarded their persons, exhausted their meanes, and freely undergone all services, taxations, and charges imposed on them."[44] While women clearly paid parish charges and taxes and appointed deputies for designated offices, they were not mentioned.

The only question raised concerning the falsely universal term "people" came from their aldermanic opposition, who raised two points. First, that the people did not really elect Parliament, even though "we say the Parliament doth it; as in election of Parliamentmen in the Country, the Writs, run, that the people shal choose; and yet we all know that none choose but such as are Freeholders, although there may be many as good men as Freeholders, yet they have no vote." And, second, that Wildman, Price, and their crowd could face problems in their own guild elections if broadly inclusive terms were taken at face value; if "al power is in the People first: If that shall be a ground to let in all the generality of Citizens into an actual choice of Officers, and will there not be the same reason for Apprentices, and Forreigners, to plead for Votes in your Election?" (14–15).

Wildman, however, did not buy this counterargument and claimed a changed reality since Charles I's death: "wherein the Parliament hath pleased to declare, That the original of all just Power (under God) is from the People, And how Governours shall derive a just power from the People, but by an Assent of the People, I understand not; neither do I know how we can otherwise be a Free People, as the Parliament declared we are" (23). His cohort, John Price, supported these arguments but also tied the need for citizen suffrage to the misuse by mayor and aldermen of funds reserved for the needy, and warned in strong language that as decisions were being made about who should elect the governors of London, the city's officers should "take some speedy course that the blood of the Fatherless and the Widow may not stick to these walls" (14). Here, he questions women's and children's roles in the economic and political claim of the working class, not as contributors but as symbols of need and objects of charity, or as family members requiring support. Women were most valuable in democratic or radical political rhetoric not as equal workers or as members of guilds, but as dependents who legitimized both the independent standing and political prowess of their husbands and fathers. Thus, as democratic arguments incorporated the status of urban citizens during the civil war and among Restoration dissenters, women were rhetorically more valuable not as other members of the freedom, but as dependents.

44. *London's Liberties; or, A Learned Argument of Law & Reason, upon Saturday, December 14, 1650* (London: Printed by Ja. Cottrel for Gyles Calvert, 1651), 4–5. Hereafter cited in the text by page number.

In *The Oath of every Free-man, of the Citie of London,* fees owed, and public duties required, were intermingled although women clearly paid the former while having a substitute perform the latter: "Ye shall be Contributory to all manner of charges within this Citty, as Summons, Watches, Contributions, Taskes, Talleges, Lot and Scot, and to all other charges, bearing your part as a free-man ought to do." Here falsely universal language ignored the existence of the freewoman and conflated duties, some of which were performed only by men and others by both male and female members of the guild.[45] As commercial rather than political distinctions came to dominate guild debates during the early eighteenth century, women's clear economic roles could be acknowledged once more, and significant numbers of female apprentices and freewomen appear.

During the early eighteenth century, and building upon a process begun at the end of the seventeenth century, a small number of women were apprenticed and a smaller number made free. Although it is difficult to determine any clear shift in the desire among certain elements of English society to view women's labor in a more positive and practical light near the end of the seventeenth century, there are some indications that such a trend was in the offing. A number of practical schemes to train and use the labor of those not sufficiently productive were published; one of the most complete and articulate is *Proposals for Raising A Colledge of Industry of all Useful Trades and Husbandry, with Profit for the Rich, a Plentiful Living for the Poor, and a Good Education for Youth* (1696). This work, along with many others, including a plan for Sion College on equally utilitarian grounds, includes the need to train women along with men and stresses the economic value of the female population. These proposals sought contributors for a subscription to establish such a school.

Unlike charity schools, this college of industry was more clearly grounded upon a good return to investors. It did include, as well, strong arguments for the gains to be had by the young people receiving this practical instruction and the general advantage to society to educate its youth and thus avoid the need for workhouses. The program was designed to train eighty-two women and girls in various household, textile, and sewing trades, along with men for various crafts. As was also typical of charity schools, the men were more apt to be apprenticed than the women, but the author does state that "the Men to be Prentices till Twenty Four Years old, and Women till Twenty One Years, or

---

45. *The Oath of every Free-man, of the Citty of London* (London?: Printed by William Jaggard, n.d.).

Marry," then each shall have the liberty to pursue his or her own interest.[46] A similar plan for younger children is discussed in *An Account of the General Nursery; or, Colledge of Infants, set up by the Justices of the Peace for the County of Middlesex* (1686). Here girls were taught reading and practical skills, and parishes were encouraged to save funds by sending their orphans and paupers to the Middlesex institution.[47]

These efforts, along with the attempts to have women spend on a variety of goods and investments, perhaps reveals an increasingly tolerant attitude concerning their relationship to the economy. Much of the earlier guild literature—and for that matter, Puritan and Anglican domestic literature during the 1600s—stresses women's household duties and does not portray them as lower- or middle-class workers or upper-class investors. These disparate phenomena suggest, then, a shifting attitude in women's relationship to the economy near the end of the seventeenth century.[48]

Conclusion

Yet it is still doubtful whether one can trace any clear trend in women's role in guilds or broader involvement in the economy and society of early modern England. To move closer to understanding what trends might define shifts in their guild presence, we need to expand our study of women and guilds into a more integrated picture of economic, religious, and political factors. We need to read guild documents with a more critical eye. For example, the weaver discussed earlier called the court of wardens "a company of fools." His words

---

46. [John Bellers], *Proposals for Raising A Colledge of Industry of all Useful Trades and Husbandry, with Profit for the Rich, a Plentiful Living for the Poor, and a Good Education for Youth* (London: Printed and sold by T. Sowle, 1696), 5–15. This proposal is only one of a large number of practical schemes to enhance the wealth of the country that appeared in the late seventeenth and early eighteenth centuries. See also *The Estate of the Poor in Sion College* (London: Printed by George Dagget, 1688).

47. *An Account of the General Nursery or Colledge of Infants, set up by the Justices of the Peace for the County of Middlesex . . .* (London: Printed by R. Roberts, 1686), 2–5.

48. Other scholars treating the nature of women's labor and economic activities at the end of the seventeenth century are Peter Earle, "The Female Labour Market in London in the Late Seventeenth and Early Eighteenth Centuries," *Economic History Review*, 2nd ser. 42 (1989): 328–53, and L. Wetherhill, "A Possession of One's Own: Women and Consumer Behaviour in England, 1660–1740," *Journal of British Studies* 25 (1986): 131–56. Some attention is paid to women as investors, and some discussion appears in Peter G. M. Dickson, *The Financial Revolution in England: A Study in the Development of the Public Credit, 1688–1756* (London: Macmillan, 1967), 281–82, and in B. A. Holderness, "Widows in Pre-industrial Society: An Essay upon their Economic Functions," in *Land, Kinship, and Life Cycle*, ed. Richard M. Smith (Cambridge: Cambridge University Press, 1984).

could hold a number of meanings: first, they could simply provide evidence for the strict controls on masters who employed women not of their immediate family, or they could be an indication of a master's opposition to guild charter and bylaws, or, and I am inclined to think this is the best reading, they can indicate the foolhardy efforts of the court in their attempt to restrict a practice quite general and widespread. Second, it is essential to cast the net more widely when seeking to understand the forces behind changes in women's economic status. Women's historians have always had problems with the interaction between prescriptive literature and those documents that seemingly contain simply the facts of women's existence. The reader can never be sure whether a lack of references to women in records means they weren't actually there, whether the language of charters or other official rules had any measurable impact on the lives of real women, or, most fundamentally, whether threats or restraints against women for doing a proscribed act document a reality of women's doing just that.

In treating the history of women in guilds, historians need to apply more surely these cautionary concerns, and to realize that the nature of the individual guild, the political values and needs of its members, officers, or even the monarch granting its charter may all have relevance to guild decisions and procedures. The mix of religious, political, and economic elements within the guild and its society may influence women's inclusion or exclusion. It is necessary to think more broadly about how economic, political, and religious values impinge on each other and how they hold both negative and positive impact on the recognition of women's labor and economic contribution to a society. Women obviously worked whether or not someone recorded their names on apprentice rolls, and the reasons their names were or were not included likely had to do with a range of influences well outside traditional economic forces.

3

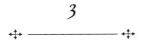

"Acting His Own Part"

Gender, the Freeborn Englishman, and the Execution of Charles I

The trial and execution of Charles I holds a special place in the British imagination. These events have come to symbolize England's lead among European countries in overturning arbitrary rule, and the nation's basic conservatism in carrying out a surgical removal of the monarch's authority while avoiding a social revolution. Charles was executed, in unprecedented fashion as a reigning monarch, or in the words of C. V. Wedgwood, "In the charge against him he is described as 'King of England,' in the warrant for his execution he is still 'King of England.' The last words of the executioner, uttered without irony, as the King laid his head on the block were 'an' it please your majesty.'" Thus the hurried efforts of January 1649 culminating in the king's death have been treated as a momentous event embedded in the nature of the English people, religion, and the state.[1]

1. C. V. Wedgwood, *A Coffin for King Charles: The Trial and Execution of Charles I* (New York: Macmillan, 1964), treats the events leading up to and through the trial and execution; discussion of the trial and its significance can be found as well in Pauline Gregg, *King Charles I* (London: J. M. Dent, [1981]), 432–49), and in Charles Carlton, *Charles I: The Personal Monarch* (London: Routledge & Kegan Paul), 1983), 348–60, who employs psychoanalytical analyses more heavily, and, of course, in Whiggish treatments of the civil war by historians such as Samuel R. Gardiner and G. P. Gooch. For an overview of historians' general treatment of the civil war and their particular understanding of the trial and execution,

Accounts of the king's trial, his execution, and the events immediately following were reproduced for successive generations well into the nineteenth century. There was a strong need to explain what had happened, why it had happened, and what it meant for the nation in 1649 and for the future. Of the 129 tracts I reviewed that questioned the king's authority, or explained his removal (both pro and con), they reveal fundamental political and constitutional assumptions, as well as an ongoing fascination with the execution itself.[2] The king's execution was visualized in physical language with references to the removal of his head from his body as symbolizing both the long-term debate over the king's two bodies and his simultaneous existence as an ordinary man and a monarch. Such debate lent itself to a gendered understanding of both the executed king and those who favored or opposed his death. What exactly was the king's relationship to the body politic? Was he indeed its head, and could it continue to function following his death? On this issue, royalists and parliamentarians strenuously differed. The royalist John Bramhall stated that if the king were not supreme, there would emerge "a serpent with two heads; who make two supremes without subordination one to another, the king and the Parliament." But conflicting claims that sovereignty must rest either in the people or in the monarch more centrally dominated this debate. That conflict was grounded around two definitional concerns: who constituted the people and what was their relationship to the crown?

The latter questions hold significant gender implications that, as yet, have

---

see Michael G. Finlayson, *Historians, Puritanism, and the English Revolution: The Religious Factor in English Politics Before and After the Interegnum* (Toronto: University of Toronto Press, 1983). For a more recent analysis of the English revolution, downplaying the central importance of the king's trial and execution as part of a critique of the revolutionary nature of the English civil war, see Conrad Russell, *The Causes of the English Civil War: The Ford Lectures Delivered in the University of Oxford 1987–1988* (Oxford: Clarendon Press, 1990). For a specific discussion of the image of the king's head in later political rhetoric, see chapter 5 in J. P. Kenyon, *Revolution Principles: The Politics of Party, 1689–1720* (Cambridge: Cambridge University Press, 1977). In this regard, see Patricia Crawford, "Charles Stuart: Man of Blood," in *The Journal of British Studies* 16 (1977): 41–61. Finally, the most useful recent survey of the tract literature is John Sanderson, *"But the people's creatures": The Philosophical Basis of the English Civil War* (Manchester: Manchester University Press, 1989).

2. Tracts used as sources for this chapter were drawn from rare book collections at the British Library; Bodleian Library, Oxford University; Houghton Library, Harvard University; the Seligman Collection, Columbia University; the Folger Shakespeare Library; and the Huntington Library. They were located through chronological listings of works treating broad-based definitions of political, economic, and adult status, and, in addition at the Huntington Library, through reading all titles indexed under Charles I. Further, related materials were used from secondary treatments of the political and constitutional significance of the trial and execution.

received little consideration by historians of the civil war.[3] Most historians treat the constitutional and political significance of the king's trial and execution as untouched by questions of gender. However, contemporaries did not so easily dismiss its importance concerning who constituted the "people" possessing sufficient authority to question and ultimately to overturn the king's prerogative. The king's execution led mid-seventeenth-century tractarians to grapple with the particular qualities the king lost as a "tyrant" when reduced to the status of a "private man," while the men who became the "people" of England recast their standing to empower them to take his life. Thus this mid-century reconstruction of the body politic was done in a manner to define women outside the body and irrelevant to any discourse over whether the king as God's anointed on Earth, or the people with their prior sovereignty, was head of, or coterminus with, the body politic. As John Sanderson notes, those in charge of the king's trial wrapped themselves in the people's mantle or, in the words of prosecutor John Cook, "we are but the people's creatures." Yet here and elsewhere one finds a shifting meaning of "people" influenced, not in small part, by the rhetoric employed by those questioning the king's rule.[4]

The more abstract arguments surrounding the qualities inherent in a "citizen" (in today's meaning) over the traditional qualities of the "subject" were emerging most clearly in the debate over Charles I's personal rule and later in those works justifying his removal as monarch and supporting his execution. One of the more important themes of the 1640s, especially in the antiroyalist pamphlets of 1647–50, was the transformation of Charles (because of his tyrannical actions) into a "private man." Large numbers of works arguing for the unique political standing of the independent Englishman based on supposed pre-Norman liberties appeared simultaneously. As these arguments shifted further from office-conferred political standing (whether in gaining the freedom or in political obligations tied to land ownership), women who had held standing based on such offices lost out to the more abstract qualities

---

3. Some work has been done on women's political role in the seventeenth century, but less attention has been paid to the gender-based implications of the language in tracts exploring the nature of the king's trial and execution. For an early account, see Charlotte Carmichael Stopes, *British Freewomen*. For a general discussion of issues relating to women and politics, see the introduction to *Women Writers and the Early Modern British Political Tradition* (Cambridge: Cambridge University Press, 1998), 1–14, and for a discussion of the possibilities of women's citizenship in early modern England, see "Women as Sextons and Electors: King's Bench and Precedents for Women's Citizenship" in the same volume (324–42). In addition, the volume includes an essay by Lois Schwoerer on women's political writings (56–74).

4. Sanderson, *"But the people's creatures,"* 1. "People," in most of its uses seemed to exclude women, but it varies greatly just which men were included in the term according to the political loyalties of an author, and the intended purpose of a work.

emerging from the origins of individualism. However, in many ways, they retained advantages over their sisters a century later, who not merely had lost any office-based status but had to confront the disabilities equated with the "fair sex."[5]

Those studying mid-seventeenth-century England have considered it a period of intellectual and social ferment, although one that ended ultimately in few changes to the social hierarchy. While emphases on the radical edge of the civil war have recently come under close scrutiny, the language of the Levellers, Diggers, and sectarians still resonates from the 1640s to the present. These radical groups raised serious questions about the individual's relationship to the state and the nature of political and social standing, but ignored issues of gender even though they might have seemed a logical component. Such an omission has been viewed as primarily unproblematic and little related to the nature of civil war debates. This chapter, in contrast, insists on the central importance of gender to those debates and explores the ways in which a focus on gender, as both subject and analytical tool, encourages us to rethink assumptions found on both sides of the constitutional and religious divide.

When it comes to questions of gender, traditional labels of democratic, Puritan, royalist, parliamentarian, and so on are not clear indicators of an author's assumptions concerning women's legitimate role in politics or society.

---

5. The distinction between the arguments excluding women from politics during the seventeenth and eighteenth centuries will be discussed in chapter 5. Discussions of women's role during the civil war can be found in chapter 9 of Antonia Fraser's *The Weaker Vessel: Woman's Lot in Seventeenth-Century England* (London: Weidenfeld and Nicolson, 1984), and in Charles Carlton, *Going to the Wars: The Experience of the British Civil Wars, 1638–1651* (London: Routledge, 1992), 164–67, 295–309 passim, but these are primarily accounts of the exploits of individual women not linked to political language or theory defining the body politic for the mid-seventeenth century. For the revolutionary period, Patricia Higgins, "The Reactions of Women, with Special Reference to Women Petitioners," in *Politics, Religion, and the English Revolution, 1640–1649*, ed. Brian Manning (London: Edward Arnold, 1973), discusses the efforts of Leveller women primarily on their brothers' behalf. See also Mary Lyndon Shanley, "Marriage Contract and Social Contract in Seventeenth Century English Political Thought," *Western Political Quarterly* (Spring 1979): 79–91. A broader treatment for a later revolution can be found in Lois Schwoerer, "Women and the Glorious Revolution," *Albion* 18, no. 2 (summer 1986): 195–218; for a discussion of the role of working-class women in the public arena which concentrates on specific tasks they were assigned, normally society's least desired, see Diane Willen, "Women in the Public Sphere in Early Modern England," *Sixteenth Century Journal* 19 (1988): 559–76. Richelle Munkhoff, "Searchers of the Dead: Authority, Marginality, and the Interpretation of Plague in England, 1574–1665," *Gender and History* 11, no. 1 (April 1999): 1–29, analyzes women as searchers for the dead during periods of plague, and she argues that despite the undesirable nature of the work, it offered some official standing to poor women: "Hired to view their neighbours, searchers policed the plague in an official capacity. Required to examine and codify diseased bodies, they embodied the authority that sought to quantify the effect of plague on the community" (1).

Thus, in grappling with the complex ways in which questions of gender infiltrated actions and writings from 1640 to 1660, it is important to review the language employed during the king's trial and in related works explaining its significance. Although expressed in a multitude of ways, and directed at differing audiences, there is a commonality among these revolutionary-era documents. Whether they contain elaborate and closely considered arguments or are superficial works produced for immediate consumption, all focus on defining those who represented the nation and made independent political and economic decisions. In identifying the politically active, these tracts reveal their gender qualifications.

Historians have either taken for granted, or noted without comment, the equation of political status with manhood in the seventeenth century. Some have argued further that women did not constitute a part of England, but have done so without explanation. For instance, Peter Laslett in *The World We Have Lost,* when describing England for the year 1640, notes that "England was an association between the heads of . . . families." Not simply a class-based nation, England also embodied restrictions based on gender. For Laslett, "Almost no woman ever belonged to England as an individual except it be a queen regnant—scarcely a woman in the ordinary sense—or a noble widow and heiress or two, a scattering of widows of successful merchants and yeomen."[6]

Yet women were discussed, and much was written on the differing nature of the sexes, and their prescribed roles.[7] During the 1640s and 1650s (with the

6. Peter Laslett, *The World We Have Lost,* 2nd ed. (New York: Charles Scribner's Sons, 1965), 20. Unfortunately, recent historians such as Christopher Durston, *The Family in the English Revolution* (Oxford: Basil Blackwell, 1989), have not dealt broadly with issues of gender except to record when wives and husbands agreed on civil war divisions and note parliamentary petitions by women, mostly on behalf of male prisoners. They have not analyzed gender implications of the revolutionary principles and parties themselves.

7. Rachel Weil, *Political Passions: Gender, the Family, and Political Argument in England, 1680–1714* (Manchester: Manchester University Press, 1999), 162–237, and Anne K. Mellor, *Mothers of the Nation: Women's Political Writing in England, 1780–1830* (Bloomington: Indiana University Press, 2000), emphasize cultural and sexual analyses, but do not analyze the gendered nature of male citizenship or focus significantly on women's actual political activities. See also Ann Hughes, "Gender and Politics in Leveller Literature," *Political Culture and Cultural Politics in Early Modern England: Essays Presented to David Underdown,* ed. Susan D. Ammusen and Mark A. Kishlansky (Manchester: Manchester University Press, 1995); Ann Marie Mcentee, "'The [Un]civil Sisterhood of Oranges and Lemons': Female Petitioners and Demonstrators, 1642–1653," in *Pamphlet Wars,* ed. James Holstun (London: Frank Cass, 1992), 92–111; Patricia Crawford, "The Challenges to Patriarchalism: How Did the Revolution Affect Women?" in *Revolution and Restoration: England in the 1650s,* ed. John Morrill (London: Collins & Brown, 1994), 112–28; Crawford and Mendelson, *Women in Early-Modern England,* 394–417. Among these works, their text presents the strongest case for women's political aims, quoting from a number of petitions from 1643 and

possible exception of Margaret Cavendish), no one focused directly on gender as a category determining status. Women did indeed claim (or others claimed for them) standing as members of religious denominations, but this did not lead to inclusion in these groups' enhanced political influence. Only later in the century, and within a royalist and Anglican context (not a Puritan or revolutionary one), works were written that speak directly about the general status of women in English society.[8] Concentrating on the absence of such earlier arguments offers important insights as to how assumptions about social and political hierarchy were implicitly gendered in the mid 1600s.

Official documents, works by political theorists, and the massive tract literature emerging from the English civil war help to uncover what happened linguistically to men and women during the mid–seventeenth century. In what ways did the political shifts of the period, and the need to explain the execution of a sitting monarch, lead to a greater association of terms such as "people," "person," "the nation," or "the commonwealth" with independent men? And to what extent did this enhanced identification require a greater clarity establishing women's absence? When both women and men were the king's subjects, one could afford a less precise gendering of political status. But when more and more subjects sought to compare themselves to the standing of their monarch and to enhance the status of independent men at his expense, it became crucial to separate themselves from the dependent and inferior nature of women.

---

the Leveller petitions from 1647 to 1649, demonstrating women's claim to act publicly in the interest of religion and the commonwealth. Patricia Crawford in both works mentioned presents a more restrained assessment, seeing some gains for women, especially through the efforts of radical religious women, but few real changes by 1660. Crawford sums up the political aspects of women's involvement from 1640 to 1660: "there was no demand for any extension of the franchise to women, even though women were voting in some separatist churches. Nor were there any demands for increased female participation in local government. But, by taking common public action about some of the major issues of the day, some women had claimed the right to participate in politics, a claim of long-term significance" (*Revolution and Restoration*, 127); Hughes is most skeptical about the women's claims, arguing they fit within a broader Leveller rhetoric which debated abstract political categories: "The wives were supporting their husbands and defending their families, and it was made clear that theirs was not an independent voice" (170). Yet, no matter the assessment of these authors respecting the extent of women's aims and efforts during the 1640s and 1650s, none claims women's involvement focused directly on their own status.

8. For a discussion of the development of feminist thought during the second half of the seventeenth century, see my *Reason's Disciples: Seventeenth-Century English Feminists* (Urbana-Champaign: University of Illinois Press, 1982); for the best biographical account of the most important of these feminists, see Ruth Perry, *The Celebrated Mary Astell: An Early English Feminist* (Chicago: University of Chicago Press, 1986); and for selections from their works, consult Moira Ferguson, *First Feminists: British Women Writers, 1578–1799* (Bloomington: Indiana University Press, 1985).

This greater distinction is found in a range of works arguing for a more important political and economic role for independent men during the 1640s and 1650s, and especially in works that appeared in 1649 and 1650 redefining the nature of sovereignty, the basis for loyalty and obedience, or justifying the execution of Charles I. While these works differ as to language and topics, they consistently build up the standing of men at the expense of their sisters. Some authors wrote from religious perspectives, some from political, and fewer from economic, but each offer arguments about men representing independent judgment, on the one hand, and the English nation on the other.

Among these works, women were treated in three distinct, but related, ways: they were omitted from categories or terms to which they clearly belonged, they were thrust into arguments only as asides, and they were the subjects of satire and ridicule, which enhanced the political standing of a particular faction. They were either defined explicitly as inferior, and thus not qualified for political status, or as subjects of harsh satire by both critics and supporters of Stuart rule.

Seventeenth-century political rhetoric and reality grew from the challenge to traditional medieval theories that had viewed office holding as a God-ordained conferring of status. The turmoil of the mid-seventeenth century raised questions and required justifications about legitimate status from all shades of political belief. At one end of the political spectrum, Robert Filmer's *Patriarcha* defended monarchical power and stressed the divine right of kings, but he felt obliged to press this argument by insisting on the analogy between husbandly familial power and that of kingly civil authority. Divine right concepts have correctly been interpreted as limiting women's political role, but it will be argued here that they posited less gender-distinct relationships to the crown than did those at the other end of the spectrum who questioned the monarch's authority.[9]

9. For Robert Filmer's discussion of women's absence, see Gordon Schochet, "The Significant Sounds of Silence: The Absence of Women from the Political Thought of Sir Robert Filmer and John Locke (or, "Why can't a woman be more like a man?")," in *Women Writers and the Early Modern British Political Tradition*, 220–42. Women gained place during the medieval period by taking over the prerogatives of particular offices held originally by male relatives. In these cases, the power of the office was sufficient to overcome the deficiency of sex. For examples of women wielding political power and local judicial authority, see Eileen Power, *Medieval Women*, ed. M. M. Postan (Cambridge: Cambridge University Press, 1976), and Ruth Kelso, *The Doctrine for the Lady of the Renaissance* (Urbana-Champaign: University of Illinois Press, 1956). For the links between royalist and Anglican systems of power and legitimacy and that of the household, see Gordon J. Schochet, *Patriarchialism in Political Thought: The Authoritarian Family and Political Speculation and Attitudes Especially in Seventeenth-Century England* (New York: Basic Books, 1975), esp. 72–84. While I would not question Judith Bennett's argument in "Medieval Women, Modern

The False Universal and Independent Standing

The writings of Henry Parker discuss the importance of independence and its relationship to the false universal in revolutionary discourse. Parker, an anti-monarchist of the early 1640s whose work was highly influential on Leveller leader John Lilburne, suggests the gender limitations of those who insisted on the consent of at least a portion of the governed. "Power," he contends, "is originally inherent in the People," but in defining such power he notes, "it is nothing else but that might and vigor which such or such a societie of men containes in itself."[10] The verbal movement from "people" to "a societie of men" with no conscious sense of difference was typical of such political arguments. Next Parker gives an explanation that helps to explain the verbal disappearance of women. People might consent to pass their power into the hands of a caretaker, but such consent did not limit the right of later dissent. In political society, the strength of independent men, voluntarily bound together, meant that "the whole kingdom is not so properly the Author as the essence itself of Parliaments" (4). However, women's consent to husbandly authority could not be withdrawn. Parker's acceptance of an unlimited patriarchy in the family led to his sharp distinction between the state and the household. While the king derived his authority from the people, the patriarch ruled over those incapable of being his equal, and thus the king lacked the unrestricted power of the latter. "Princes," Parker admits, "are *called* Gods, Fathers, Husbands, Lords, Heads, etc. and this implies them to be of more worth, and more insubordinate in end, then their Subjects are, who by the same relation must stand as creatures, Children, Wives, Servants, Members,

---

Women: Across the Great Divide," in *Culture and History, 1350–1600: Essays on English Communities, Identities and Writing*, ed. David Aers (Detroit: Wayne State University Press, 1993), 147–75, that women lacked a medieval golden age, I do believe that the expanding democratic claims of the seventeenth century offered a new framework to exclude women, and to hide such exclusion in the falsely universal language of the "freeborn Englishman."

10. [Henry Parker], *Observations upon some of his Majesties late Answers and Expresses* [London, 1642], 1. Hereafter cited in the text by page number. Parker presents his objections to the king's claim of constituting the highest authority in the land in some of the most extreme arguments for popular and parliamentary supremacy presented during the early 1640s. Anthony Ascham's analysis in *Of the Confusions and Revolutions of Governments . . .* (London: Printed by W. Wilson, 1649) was one of a number of works that carry forward the connections presented by Parker. He notes that "it is evident that most Contracts . . . made betwixt Politicall or publique persons, are made in this Politicall sence, viz. with a tacit condition of holding their possessions" (37–38), and that "the state of the People, is a state of Privilege, Guardianship, and filiation, not of servitude" (140–41). Finally, he contends that political justice "consists in the reciprocalness of mutuall humane rights paternall and filial duties as we are congregated into common-wealths, and publique Societies" (142–43).

etc." (18; emphasis mine). But in families, power was based on unalterable differences between ruler and ruled that did not exist among men within the civil order. He explains: "The same reason is also in relation of Husband, Lord, etc. for the wife is inferior in nature, and was created for the assistance of man, and servants are hired for their Lords mere attendance; but it is otherwise in the State between man and man, for *that* civill difference which is for civill ends, and those ends are, that wrong and violence be repressed by one, for the good of all, not that servility and drudgery may be imposed upon all for the pompe of one" (19; emphasis mine). Thus Parker laid the ground-work for those questioning the monarch's elevation above his subjects while accepting such an elevation of the husband and father within the house-hold. The monarch was not inherently different from or naturally superior to other citizens within the state, but this fundamental equality required sharper insistence on the natural inferiority of women to avoid troubling domestic ramifications.

In Parker's 1642 work, one can find many themes that reemerged from 1647 through 1650 and which appear in a large body of writings surrounding the king's trial and execution. They included works in support of, and opposition to, the actions taken against Charles, educational reform tracts, economic doc-uments, and Leveller and other political tracts. Most indicative of the general principles underlying these works are those establishing the appropriate path of maturation to independent adulthood. They postulate general principles and then limit their application to the lives of men.

For example, among those works surrounding Charles's reign, such gender-specific views appear in biblical explanations justifying the king's execution and the people's prerogative. Here a number of authors place their arguments within the context of ancient Hebrew kingship. They avoid sexually neutral terms for a ruler and consistently speak only of "king," rather than monarch or sovereign. This exclusive use of the title "king" was most prevalent in 1649 and 1650 when the need to justify Charles's punishment was most pressing. Since his ascension in 1625, many of his subjects had written objecting to his arbitrary rule, but only in 1649 did critics use gender-specific language for the crown and thus avoided the troublesome issue of female rule.[11] It was

11. Examples are numerous, but such gender-specific usage is not found in the constitutionally signi-ficant *Petition of Right* adopted by Parliament in 1628, nor in the Triennial Act passed in 1641 questioning royal authority to dismiss, arbitrarily, sitting parliaments. For these documents and limited background information, see *Sources of English Constitutional History: A Selection of Documents from A.D. 600 to the Present*, ed. and trans. Carl Stephenson and Frederick George Marcham (New York: Harper and

important to show that subjects had the right to take action against even an uncontested male ruler who acted against the legitimate interests of the people and sworn constitutional principles. Among these, and so many comparable works, authors employed language that at once obfuscated and clarified its gender limitations.

Certainly not all of these works agree on the propriety or need for the king's trial and execution, and some argue against it, but their disputes were carried out against a background of what constituted legitimate prerogative, whether situated in the political realm or a related public arena. Among such, the clearest and most consistent linguistic disappearance of women was associated with the conflation of people and men. Such conflation appears in the November 1648 diluted version of the 1647 Leveller document, *An Agreement Prepared for the People of England,* as it clarifies who constitutes the House of Commons and its electorate. Its authors, the army council of officers, note that the members represent the people, in language that appears inclusive: "That the People of England . . . be indefinitely proportioned . . . That the Representative of the whole Nation shall consist of four hundred persons." This was followed by a sentence that stated, "the people do of course choose themselves a Representative." Then the document, as did so many of this era, tries to be precise about who was meant by "the people" in an age of political uncertainly and transition: "That the Electors in every Division, shall be Natives, or Denizens of England, not persons receiving Almes but such as are assessed ordinarily, towards the reliefe of the poore; not servants to, and receiving wages from any particular person. And in all Elections . . . they shall be men of one and

---

Brothers, 1937), 450, 476. Other examples of gender-specific usage for the monarch following 1649 can be found in John Dury, *Considerations Concerning the Present Engagement, whether it may be lawfully entered into* . . . (London: Printed by John Clowes for Richard Wodenoth, 1649), which focuses on the king's trial; and John Dury, *A Seasonable Discourse . . . What the Grounds and Method of Our Reformation Ought to Be in Religion and Learning* . . . (London: Printed for R. Wodnothe, 1649), where he sounds similar to John Canne, arguing that loyalty to the king hinges on his oath to uphold fundamental law, and if he fails to do so, his subjects no longer owed him loyalty. Dury states that "the Parliament did actually lay him aside, . . . from which time forward he was no more an object of your Oath of Allegiance, but to be lookt upon as a private man" (5). Similar language was in John Cook, *King Charls his Case or An Appeal to all rational men Concerning his Tryall at the High Court of Justice* (London: Printed by Peter Cole, for Giles Calvert, 1649), where he notes "That the Kings of England are trusted with a limited power to govern by Law" (6), while one might have thought such was the case for her queens as well. William Ball, *The Power of Kings Discussed; or, An Examen of the Fundamental Constitution of the Free-borne People of England* (London: Printed for John Harris, 1649), contrasts the particular misdeeds of the king with the fundamental rights of the English people. Certainly one of the reasons for the more restricted language was that the king was contrasted as either occupying the place of a monarch or that of a private man.

twenty-yeares old, or upwards, and housekeepers."[12] It is simply not clear here that terms such as "people" or "the whole nation" omitted women, but the authors in some detail explain who is excluded but never concern themselves with women.

A representative example of such works was John Canne's *The Golden Rule; or, Justice Advanced.* As is clear from its subtitle, the *Commons ... have a lawfull power to arraign, and adjudge to death the King, for Tyranny, Treason, Murder.* John Canne was an uncompromising regicide who tried to allay any doubts Parliament or the army might have felt at taking the king's life. Other than accusing the king of treason and murder himself, thus making him a proper subject for trial and execution, the author argues "for the supream and Sovereign power of the People." This work is one of the clearest examples of those numerous works that try to reverse the normal relationship between subject and sovereign, making the former the "Supream Power of the Kingdom," and the king who has become a tyrant "in such a case, no more than private men."[13]

This work also avoids sex-neutral language in identifying the monarch, using only "king" and drawing heavily on the Old Testament to rebut the king's presumed immunity from punishment. In addition, terming Parliament "the supremest Judicatory," the king before it was "another subject ... to be questioned, censured, punished as the Crime and Cause shall be." Finally, when confronting Hebrew precedents that one was not to overthrow a king even though a tyrant, Canne emphasizes the ability of freeborn Englishmen to act in ways not authorized for others: "The Jews were not only subjects of a private condition, but likewise most of them servants and bond-men under the power and Empire of the Caldeans, and therefore for private men to rise up against the Magistrates, or to resist them with force of arms had been unlawfull" (5). Canne comes close to Winstanley's arguments, while differing drastically on issues of economic democracy: "The English are natives, not beholding to their Kings for their possessions, nor ever held the same as *gratis* from them: The Supreme and Soveraign Power of the Kingdom is in their hand; the which Israel in Egypt never had, nor could lawfully challange" (17–18). Again, the English were defined as free persons worthy of confronting

12. Great Britain. Army, *An Agreement Prepared for the People of England, for a Secure and Present Peace* ... (London: Printed for John Partridge, R. Harford, G. Calvert, and G. Whittington, [1649]), 8, 16.

13. John Canne, *The Golden Rule; or, Justice Advanced. Wherein is shewed, that the Representative Kingdom; or, Commons, ... Have a Lawfull Power to ... Adjudge to Death the King* ... (London: Printed for Peter Coke, 1649), 1–5. Hereafter cited in the text by page number.

their sovereign. Thus the need to distribute power more widely led to expansive language that appeared to include all, but surrounding exemplary materials clarifies that that "all" never meant women.

Authors such as Parker and John Canne felt especially obligated to empower the individuals who criticized Charles and later took the king's life; one of their stronger arguments was to distinguish between the more unlimited power men held over their households and that the king held over independent men in the state. They argued as well the unique standing of Englishmen compared to inhabitants of other nations. This led them to employ gender distinctions that diminished women to men's general benefit.[14]

Also representative of the push for inclusion of greater numbers of men, while ignoring women, were a number of works by Gerrard Winstanley. Winstanley is often credited with being one of the most democratic, and in many ways radical, authors to write in the period following Charles's execution. His plan for common lands to revert to the common people has been characterized as an early argument for a communal sharing of wealth. But in both his religious and political works, he frames such a right to the land through Adam and his male descendants. Winstanley's omission of women is linked to a common justification of their public disability, namely women's perceived inability ever to be "free" persons who could represent their own interests. Those wanting to expand the numbers of deliberative adults, both politically and economically, above all valued independence for themselves and those like themselves, and conversely used such independence as a measure to assess who could properly make decisions for the nation. As MacPherson notes in *The Political Theory of Possessive Individualism,* independence was a necessary precondition for citizenship.[15]

Gerrard Winstanley combined a demand for common lands with biblical justifications for men alone. His exegesis on the Creation myth and its link

---

14. Parker, *Observations,* 8; Canne, *The Golden Rule* emphasizes qualities of independence granted clearly only to men.

15. Gerrard Winstanley, *The Mysterie of God, Concerning the whole Creation, Mankinde. To be Made Known to every man and woman* ... (London, 1648); C. B. MacPherson, *The Political Theory of Possessive Individualism: Hobbes to Locke* (Oxford: Clarendon Press, 1962). Although much legitimate criticism has been brought against MacPherson for overstressing the marketplace economy as initiating a competitive individualism in the seventeenth century, still the continued refrain of a person needing to be "free," that is, not a servant or tenant or a wage earner, to qualify for public participation, or to speak one's own mind, supports MacPherson's understanding of the central importance of economic and legal independence in constructing the public person during the 1600s. Such a set of characteristics is surely at the heart of what is meant by a "freeborn Englishman."

to his well-known proposal to allow the Society of Diggers to claim common lands in the period following the execution of Charles I clarifies how he was able to divide women from people in his scheme. Winstanley's *The Mysterie of God, Concerning the whole Creation, Mankinde. To be Made known to every man and woman* (1648), which focused on God's message to be gleaned from the story of the Garden of Eden, told that story as a metaphor for "my Beloved Country men, of the Countie of Lancaster." The message for them to learn was that God did not always turn to the wealthiest or the most learned, "but he chuses the despised, the unlearned, the poor, the nothings of the world, and fills them with the good things of himself."[16]

Astonishingly, Eve does not appear in Winstanley's discussion of the Garden. She was neither a part of Creation, nor was she tempted by the serpent. Winstanley begins: "When God had made Adam, there was then two beeings distinct, the one from the other, that is, God himself, that was an uncreated beeing, and the Humane Nature, that was a created beeing." Winstanley then points to the creation of animals, and of Adam's power over them: "I have made thee the Lord of all my creatures." Adam was then tempted because he "had a secret tickling delight arising in him to be a more knowing man then God made him." He thus ate of the forbidden fruit of the Tree of Life: "And when Adam put forth his hand to take, and eat of the fruit of the tree, in the Hystorie, his hand was guided thereupon by this serpent ... & truly this delight in self, was the eating, and it was the chief forbidden fruit that grew up in the middle of the living Garden." Eve appears nowhere in his sixty-seven-page tract, and women appear only as a part of the comprehensive term "humane nature" in the following passage: "Now the mysterie of God is this, he will destroy and subdue this power of darkness, under the feet of the whole Creation, Mankinde, and every particular branch, man and woman, deliver them from this bondage and prison, and dwell in his own house, or Garden, himself."[17] No woman appears as an individual in this account of man's Fall

---

16. Winstanley, "Dedication," in *The Mysterie of God*. Crawford, "Challenges to Patriarchalism," offers two positive comments on Winstanley's views relating to women, namely that he thought the housework of one hundred women could be done by twenty-five and that he recognized that sexual freedom was available for men as it could not be for women who bore children (113, 115). She does not discuss, however, how justifications for his general platform were clearly engendered. T. Wilson Hayes, *Winstanley the Digger: A Literary Analysis of Radical Ideas in the English Revolution* (Cambridge: Harvard University Press, 1979), 128–73, discusses the rhetorical use Winstanley makes of Adam and his male descendants in his claim for the commons; he does not note any gender implications in those arguments, however.

17. *The Mysterie of God*, 8

and redemption, making clear Winstanley's willingness to offer an account in opposition to Scripture and general knowledge that would showcase the universal male which underpins his subsequent political arguments.

Such a retelling of the Creation myth contributed to Winstanley's justification for his group's right to plow the commons. His writings favored expanding the basic economic access of English citizens in ways that omitted women; it was economic access for those who were free and independent in ways impossible for women. In two works from 1649, he links men's right to till the earth to Adam's experience in Eden. In *An Appeal To the House of Commons.... Whether the Common People Shall have the quiet enjoyment of the Commons and Waste Lands,* Winstanley contends that this: "land of England is The land of our Nativity ... by the righteous Law of our Creation, [we] ought to have food and rayment freely by our righteous labouring ... without working for hire, or paying rent one to another."[18] Insisting that God's creation allowed communal tilling of the soil, Winstanley makes clear gender limitations while at the same time claiming inclusiveness. The "earth was first made and given to the sons of men," according to Scripture, before the Fall "in which there is no respect of persons." Fitting this evolution within the Norman Yoke thesis, he argues that the gentry no longer had rights to common areas because those rights were given to them under the law of the Norman Conquest, which ended with the death of Charles I. Women were omitted from such right to the land here and in another 1649 work, *Letter to the Lord Halifax,* where Winstanley describes the gentry who owned their estates and had enclosed their property as "elder brothers." He then justifies the right of himself and his followers to the commons: "Then in the request of brethren, we desire we may injoy our freedom, according to the Law of contract between you, and us, That we that are younger brothers, may live comfortably in the Land of our Nativity, with you the elder brothers, enjoying the benefit of our Creation."[19]

While it is not clear that Winstanley means women should lack access to the commons, or even that they do not constitute the "people," he presents his evidence for the people's right to common lands in a thoroughly gendered construct, offering no foundation here or elsewhere for contemporary women, or later ones, to argue in support of their political standing. In contrast, men

18. Gerrard Winstanley, *An Appeal to the House of Commons ... Whether the Common People Shall have the quiet enjoyment of the Commons and Waste Lands ...* ([London], 1649), 58.

19. Winstanley, *A Letter to the Lord Fairfax, and His Councell of War ... That the Common People ought to dig ...* (London: Printed for Giles Calvert, 1649), 6.

possessed biblical, political, and legal justifications within Winstanley's arguments for their economic rights.

Just as *An Agreement of the People* had omitted servants and those receiving assistance from eligibility for the franchise, so Winstanley's *An Appeal to the House of Commons* restricted women's independent claim to the commons. Further, when his works were signed by members of his movement, they were signed only by male members. Thus those works that spoke most uncompromisingly in favor of the people's right to unlimited sovereignty and free access to land failed to clarify that women were included in their goals (and rather suggested the contrary). Building upon Henry Parker, the primary aim of these works was to pull down the king while building up his subjects so that they might meet somewhere in the middle as equal citizens of England, and in Winstanley's case, assuring landless men a common standing with their landowning brethren.

Gender and Problematic Social Categories

Because of the universalizing of male experience, it was difficult for authors to treat women as individuals responsible for their behavior, even when they badly wanted to do so. While a woman could certainly do evil, or even just behave badly, seldom were explanations for such behaviors directed simply to her as an individual inhabitant of England. Rather, she was chastised in the context of Eve's temptation, subordination to her husband, or customs demanding her silence abroad and restriction to the home. An obscure tract by David Brown is emblematic of the problems encountered by mid-seventeenth-century authors who wanted to criticize women as individuals for their actions but found it impossible to place them within social and political categories normally reserved for men. Even when women pursued the same goals, or took similar actions, they were not described in the same terms nor placed in comparable categories. Brown, in *The Naked Woman*, criticizes the minister, Peter Sterry, for his failure to demonstrate his authority or to uphold religious orthodoxy; but he had difficulty in directly pursuing his target because of women's problematic place in English society and the nature of the event in question.

In this instance, Brown, an elderly crank accused of being a Ranter, criticized Sterry, who, while preaching a sermon at Whitehall on July 17, 1652, failed to prevent a sacrilegious act. Allegedly a woman about thirty years old entered the church undressed (or partially dressed) and attempted to approach the minister. Brown angrily denounced the minister as the man "most clearly in charge" for not having her held and interrogated.[20] Brown's animus was directed at two points: that the woman was able to enter without being apprehended and questioned as to who was answerable for her, and that the minister did not exercise his authority as the male official in charge of the gathering. In this instance, she upset gender, class, and status hierarchies. The minister "was not only interrupted on his stage, but from acting his own part."[21] As for the woman, Brown fumed, there was no way she could function as an independent individual. While members of the congregation had intercepted her and kept her away from the minister, this was not enough to satisfy Brown. Not merely was her effrontery and lewd behavior a threat, but the minister's status was at risk as well. She must thus be brought before the magistrates and asked the following: "What were the reasons and intentions of that her so presumptuous, impudent, and barbarous attempt? With what Company she Walketh? How long? Whether or not she was sent by them? If not, then by whom? If none at all, then did she not run Unsent? What her name was? If she hath a husband? If yea, what his name was? Where he dweleth?" In addition, Brown states that she could never have a legitimate place in a church setting. Such a woman "is destitute and void of all those gifts and graces, yea, and cannot by any kind of human endeavours reach to the true understanding" of God's grace.[22]

Such a work as Brown's, which made it impossible for him to treat this woman as either a subject he could address directly as an individual or as a person with a legitimate public and religious standing, characterizes so many works from the 1600s. They ignored women as individuals, or as a group with any degree of agency, and thus placed them within various contexts of

---

20. [David Brown], *The Naked Woman; or, A Rare Epistle sent to Mr. Peter Sterry Minister at White-hall* ... (London: Printed for E. Blackmore, 1652). Brown was termed a Ranter in an anonymous, unrestrained attack on his work entitled *Cloathing for the Naked Woman; or, The second part of the Dissembling Scot ... Being a Correction of Mr. David Brown* ... (London: Printed and are to be sold by Giles Calvert, 1652). In this attack, the author claims that Brown has wasted everyone's time with his ridiculous tracts, that Brown and the rest of the Ranters cannot call upon God because "God hath neither decreed, commanded, determined, or drawn them forth to do such devilish actions, God is only good," and, rather mysteriously, that Brown never procured him a place in government (47).

21. [David Brown], "Prologue to Reader," n.p. It would certainly seem that Brown, and likely his critic, would fall within the recent debate as to whether the ranters were an actual group, or whether the word was simply a term of opprobrium directed to one's enemies. See "Fear, Myth and Furore: Reappraising the Ranters," *Past & Present*, no. 140 (August 1993): 155–210.

22. Brown, 8.

authority. Thus women's political nonexistence was symptomatic of a much broader absence tied to the overt and covert conflation of individual and male development as analyzed most thoroughly in Chapter 2. To understand these writings and their underlying values, one should remember that it was not simply women's political status that excluded them from public life but more fundamental considerations of who constituted adults, England, or even humanity broadly defined. As more men defined themselves and their brothers as closer in nature and status to their monarch, as worthy of an education, as competent adults, and as useful members of society, they left their sisters behind as dependent subjects to their husbands, male family members, and the crown.

Satire and Women's Political Standing

Gender was also used in creating imagery to demean the persons or platform of one's political or religious opponents. In John Birkenhead's *The Assembly-man*, the author ridicules the Assembly of Divines by associating it with the "other," including women. In concluding his comments, Birkenhead makes clear that if women were to venture in public, it would be related to sexual function so that women only came to hear Presbyterian clergy as they did "at Paris on Saint Margaret's day, when all come to Church that are or hope to be with child that year."[23]

Clearly such satirical name calling was widespread on each side of the religious divide during the 1640s, and those involved used gender association to discredit the learning, moral standing, and respectability of their opponents. This presented little incentive for them to treat seriously the public standing of the women in their midst. Birkenhead's work thus fits within a substantial literature, some of which had political elements joining women's sexual nature to issues of family, economics, morality, and a range of social issues.[24] In the

---

23. [Birkenhead], *The Assemblyman*, 15. When analyzing this political and religious context, P. W. Thomas, *John Berkenhead*, 146–50, does not discuss the passages concerning women.

24. The most extensive study of semi-pornographic pamphlets, broadsides, and ballads leveled against women is Roger Thompson's, *Unfit for Modest Ears: A Study of Pornographic, Obscene, and Bawdy Works written or published in England in the second half of the Seventeenth Century* (Totowa, N.J.: Rowman and Littlefield, 1979). Susan Wiseman, "'Adam, the Father of all Flesh': PornoPolitical Rhetoric and Political Theory in and After the English Civil War," in Holstun, ed., *Pamphlet Wars*, 134–57, has focused attention more directly on the political aspects of these publications. Her essay is based upon the assumption that there was a broad reading public for political topics from 1640 to 1660 and that the connection

area of politics, most telling were the satirical writings of Henry Neville, an important republican, translator of Machiavelli, and member of Cromwell's Council. He published various editions of works about a mythical parliament of women. These tracts, written from 1641 to 1656, were *A Parliament of Ladies with their Lawes newly Enacted; The Ladies. A second Time Assembled; Assembled in the Parliament of Ladyes;* and *Newes from the New Exchange; or The Commonwealth of Ladies, Drawn to Life.* They were satires devoted to women calling a parliament to indulge in gossip and pass laws demanding sexually competent husbands or lusty young men as substitutes. The women in attendance especially lamented male absence due to the civil wars. But they wanted to subvert marital hierarchies as well. In *A Parliament of Ladies,* their desires were evident: "Further let it be enacted," said Anne EverCrosse, "that whosoever shal hereafter take a Wife, shall doe it with the intent to please her, serve her, and obey her: ... place her at the upper end of the Table ... wait on her till she hath halfe [or three quarters] ... dined; and then (if he have leave) to sit downe, which must be done by her licence." Other than complaining that she would always be "short of what I long for" because it "is beyond your reach," and similar sexual allusions, the work ended with "The chiefe Heads of the Ladies Lawes." Interspersed in the sexual humor were demands for women to displace men's legal and political superiority, but normally with sexual ends in mind, such as: "It is concluded and fully agreed upon, that all women shall have their husbands Tenants at will; and that they shall doe them Knights service, and have their homage paid before every Sunrising."[25]

---

between political theory and popular political tracts is evident. She focuses most specifically on the writings of Henry Marten and Henry Neville, and also analyzes royalist satires against Levellers and republicans. Neville ridiculed women as political agents: "The satire is directed against the inability of women to think politically or discern the differences between one political system and another, because their judgment is made only by the standards of the sexual conduct of the men in question" (147).

25. [Henry Neville], *A Parliament of Ladies: With their Lawes Newly Enacted* ([London]: Printed in the yeer 1647), n.p. *The Dictionary of National Biography* describes Neville as "a strong doctrinaire republican," who joined the Council of State in 1651, printed a series of "rather coarse lampoons," published *Plato Redivivus; or, A Dialogue concerning Government* in 1681, "which was much admired by Hobbes," and "also published an excellent translation of Machiavelli's works" in 1675 (*DNB*, Henry Neville, 259–60). Recent scholarship on Neville includes James Cotton, "'The Harrington Party' (1659–1660) and Harrington's Political Thought," *History of Political Thought* 1 (1980): 51–68, which emphasizes Neville's republicanism, along with that of John Wildman and Henry Marten among others, and these authors' reliance on argument over history as justification for government change in contrast to James Harrington; and Nicholas van Maltzan, *Seventeenth Century* 7, no. 1 (1992): 44–52, focuses on his "political pragmatism" as well as his later importance during the Restoration as a thinker offering a "neo-Harringtonian" position. Neither article mentions Neville's satirical writings. Neville was copying earlier satirical works on women's political gatherings (the *Parliament of Ladies* is a reprint of a 1640 tract on a women's parliament), but his later satires were his own, perhaps after the financial success of the 1647 reprint.

Neville's satirical works fit within a large body of pamphlets characterizing women's political actions and aspirations as a joke. Yet is it appropriate to dismiss them as a sleazy genre, often written by men who were serious authors, scholars, and political figures in other areas? A royalist pamphlet pillories "mistris parliament" when she was betrothed to "Mr. King" and argues against a possible union, in the words of a supposed captain of the army, "for Mrs. Parliament, she being a woman of a light carriage, inconstant, and likely to be fruitlesse, by reason she is troubled with the consumption in her Members, the bloody Issue, and falling sickness, about the time of our approach; yet considering the good service shee hath formerly done us, and now having no more need of her, we commit her to the care of Dr. Period, to be speedily cured of her infirmities."[26] Such works have been discussed, or dismissed, as simply an example of the army's anger against Parliament's unwillingness to pursue sufficiently radical aims, without any mention of their sexual nature. But, by ignoring the easy and continual use of women in political satire, especially their sexuality, have we not missed the far-reaching significance of such demeaning imagery and why women in a political setting have always been thought of as an anomaly, if not a joke. A Puritan tract castigates the papist tendencies of the established church and its royal protector by telling a tale of nuns who operated a brothel within a public market. In *The seven women confessors . . . which lived . . . in Coven Garden,* a group of nuns provided pleasure to passersby, "not only for absolution, but for distraction."[27]

Such works are multifaceted in approach and target, but they all carry the same message: women were effective vehicles for maligning one's opponents, and women as serious and public figures could have no purpose but distraction for kindred readers seeking humorous attacks on mutual enemies. Have these sorts of works been dismissed too quickly as having no political import and no serious negative impact on women's standing in seventeenth-century England? In the mid-seventeenth century, when large numbers were writing angry words denouncing the king's dismissal of the people's prerogative, they did not think of their female counterparts. It is not too far a reach to argue that women were on a more equal footing when both they and their brothers were subjects of the crown, than when some of their brothers in Parliament, and as its electors, were deemed their monarch's equal, or even his superior.[28]

26. *A New Marriage, Between Mr. King, and Mrs. Parliament* ([London]: Printed in the yeere 1648), 4

27. John Stockden, *The seven women confessors . . . which lived . . . in Coven Garden* (London: Printed for John Smith, [1642]), n.p.

28. No group clearly included women in their political or democratic rhetoric, although one could expect them to from introductory remarks to their works. For example, John Lilburne, *The Freemans*

Aristocratic Women and Politics

While there have been studies relating to women's political efforts during both the Tudor and Stuart periods, those studies have focused mostly on the efforts of women on the part of others in assisting husbands and sons to seek office or to use family connections to assist male members of the landowning classes.[29] Less work has been done on women pursuing their own interests. Yet some women worked to ensure that posterity would remember what they had done as individuals. Anne Clifford's diary is a well-known source regarding the management of her lands and the overseeing of courts attached to her office as Countess of Pembroke, Dorset, and Montgomery, but the following sentences from the steps entering Skipton Castle makes clear that Clifford was concerned that her status and memory would not outlive her:

> This Skipton Castle was repayred by the Lady Anne Clifford, Covntesse Dowager of Pembrooke, Dorsett, and Montgomery, Baronesse Clifford, West Merland, and Veseie, Lady of the Honor of Skipton in Craven, and High Sheriffesse by inheritance of the Covntie of Westmorland, in the Yeares 1657 and 1658, after this maine part of itt had layne rvinovs ever since December 1648, and the Janvary followinge, when itt was then pvlld downe and demolisht, allmost to the fovndacon, by the command of the Parliament, then sitting att Westminster,

---

Freedome Vindicated (June 1646) penned one of the age's most far-reaching statements of women's equality. "All and every particular individual men and women," were, he claimed, "by nature all equal and alike in power, dignity, authority, and majesty, none of them having by nature any authority, dominion or magisterial power one over or above another" but "by mutual agreement or consent." Yet this did not lead him or other Levellers to favor women's political rights. For a fuller discussion of this point, see Macpherson, *Possessive Individualism*, 296. The reason for such omission was Leveller insistence on independent status in both person and judgment (negated by women's marrying) as noted in Richard Overton, *An Arrow Against All Tyrants*, quoted in Richard A. Gleissner, "The Levellers and Natural Law: The Putney Debates of 1647," *Journal of British Studies* 20, no. 1 (fall 1980), where he argued that each person "is given an individual property ... so he hath a self property, else could he not be himself." He continues, "By nature we are sons of Adam, and from him have legitimately derived a natural propriety, right and freedom.... It is but the just rights and prerogatives of mankind (whereunto the people of England are heirs apparent, as well as other nations) which we desire ... that we may be men, and live like men" (78).

29. For work on the Tudor period, see Barbara Harris, "Property, Power, and Personal Relations: Elite Mothers and Sons in Yorkist and Early Tudor England," *Signs: Journal of Women in Culture and Society* 15, no. 3 (1990): 606–32, and for Stuart England, see Lois Schwoerer, "Women and the Glorious Revolution," and *Lady Rachel Russell: The Best of Women* (Baltimore: Johns Hopkins University Press, 1988).

becavse itt had bin a garrison in the then civill warres in England. Isa. Chap. 58, Ver. 12. Gods name be praised.[30]

She not merely included her title with its illustrious antecedents, but she had engraved "High Sheriffesse by Inheritance" in case those in the future would forget that she had held that office from her natal family. Clifford had rebuilt Skipton Castle following its destruction by parliamentary forces during the civil war, and she wanted no one to forget who and what she had been.

Bess of Hardwick also used her architectural control to inscribe her identity on Hardwick Hall. She married four husbands, all of whom died before her, and only her marriage to George Cavendish, secretary to Thomas Cromwell, resulted in any children. Hardwick Hall, which was her ancestral home, rather than the seat of her last husband, the earl of Shrewsbury, was designed to emphasize her standing. In the parapet on each side of the house, she had engraved her initials, ES, over and over again; on the inside a plaster frieze was devoted to the life of the goddess Diana, and she included Sappho (even though none of the other figures were poets or literary figures) in a carved listing of prominent Greek political and philosophical figures, including Democritus and Pericles, outside the throne room where she, and earlier the earl, met tenants. She continually displayed her importance in the statuary and design of the home: "Her presence was established throughout the house and still is after four hundred years for those prepared to read the heraldry of the plasterwork." Her biographer also notes that the Diana frieze in the high great chamber was intended to honor the queen as well: "The great plaster frieze which runs continuously round the room shows Diana, the goddess, queen and huntress, with her court of nymphs in a forest setting; it is the first thing to be seen on entering the chamber, it dominates all and is a compliment to Elizabeth."[31] In

---

30. Extract from a guide to Skipton Castle (Norwich: Jarrold Publishing, 1995), n.p. For quotes in this paragraph, see Katherine O. Acheson, *The Diary of Anne Clifford, 1616–1619* (New York: Garland, 1995); while this edition of Clifford's diary is limited to earlier years, its editor notes the advantages that came to her after her uncle's death in 1641 and his son's in 1643 when she inherited northern estates upon "failure of the male line." After pointing to her holding court and riding the boundaries of her property, Clifford complained about its "extream disorder by reason it had been so long kept from me." Quoted in Acheson from the 1916 edition of portions of her diary, *Lives of Lady Anne Clifford, Countess of Dorset, Pembroke and Montgomery (1590–1676) and of Her Parents, Summarized by Herself,* 9. Katharine Hodgkin, "The Diary of Lady Anne Clifford: A Study of Class and Gender in the Seventeenth Century," *History Workshop Journal* 19 (1985): 148–61, emphasizes Clifford's harshness as a landlady, and her insistence on the offices which came with her estates (159). See also Stopes, *British Freewomen*, 60–76.

31. David N. Durant, *Bess of Hardwick: Portrait of an Elizabethan Dynast* (London: Weidenfeld and Nicolson, 1977), 198–99.

each of these instances, the efforts made by such politically astute women to guarantee that their name and accomplishments would be etched in stone may be the most significant symbol of their desire to be remembered by a world that dismissed women's political accomplishments, no matter what their rank.

A related matter was men inheriting political office through the female line or based on their wives' titles. If they had held a post at the instigation of a powerful man, or as the designated family member to serve in Parliament, then historians have consistently discussed the power of the title holder and normally considered that individual even more significant than the office holder himself. Such has not been the case for those analyzing male office holding attached to female inheritance. In a 1832 work on *The Prerogative of Creating Peers*, there were twenty-eight men "whose Titles of Honour are either the Names of such *Heirs Female* from whom they be descended; or the Names of such *Places,* which those *Heirs Female* assumed their Titles of Dignity" and who thereby held their seats in the House of Lords. In addition, nineteen men "had Summons to Parliament in right of their Wives." Again, while the origins of offices have been stressed in both political and legal studies of early modern England, the influence of women has not been assumed when such an office flowed from their titles. This is so even though much work has been done on the family influences of women in early modern politics. Scholars seem more comfortable treating women as members of families and supporters of men, rather than as individuals who attempted to control others because of their social standing.[32]

Certainly political women were continually confronted with confusion and contradictions. Catherine de Medici sought past female figures that she could use for the iconography of her palace. Elizabeth's phrase in her speech at Tilbury, "I know I have the body of a weak and feeble woman, but I have the heart and stomach of a king, and of a king of England too," has been analyzed as her distancing herself from her sex, or attaching herself to the greatness of earlier English monarchs. But it may have as strongly symbolized the inherent schizophrenia faced by any woman who both recognized her sex and claimed political standing.[33]

32. *The Prerogative of Creating Peers* (London: James Ridgway, 1832), 100–103, based on Dugdale's *Summonses* from 1685. The point of this work was more to question the legitimacy and authority of these MPs than any power relationship between them and the female from whom they inherited.

33. Shelia Ffolliot, "A Queen's Garden of Power: Catherine de Medici and the Locus of Female Rule," in *Reconsidering the Renaissance: Papers from the Twenty-first Annual Conference* (Binghamton, N.Y.: Center for Medieval and Renaissance Studies, 1987), 245–56; Christopher Hibbert, *The Virgin Queen: Elizabeth I, Genius of the Golden Age* (Reading, Mass.: Addison Wesley, 1991), 222–25.

Unfortunately, we have mostly anecdotal evidence concerning women's attempts to gain recognition for their political activities. One of the few examples of a man working hard to ensure that the women in his family would attain such recognition was William Cavendish, first duke of Newcastle, the grandson of one of the most important Tudor women and the husband of the most prolific woman writer of the mid 1600s. And, it was not simply his connections to Bess of Hardwick and Margaret Cavendish, but the elaborate epitaphs he wrote for each and the tomb he had designed for Margaret that demonstrated his extraordinary efforts. It is hard to find another man who gave such attention to guaranteeing remembrance of the women in his family. And his efforts were no accident, given his views about the place of women in society. In his advice to Charles II, offered in a lengthy letter, he offers a rare description of Queen Elizabeth's attraction for her female subjects, as a model for Charles II to follow in forging a close tie to his subjects: "And the Queen would say God bless you my good people,—& though this Saying was no great matter, in it selfe, yet I assure your Majestie, Itt went very farr with the people,—nay of a Sunday when shee opend the window, the people would Cry, oh Lord I saw her hand, I saw her hand, & a woman, cryed out oh Lord Sayd shee, the Queens a woman." William Cavendish was unusual in his desire to preserve women's accomplishments and to tie his identity to them. His official portrait has the names of his two wives and the dates of his marriages painted in white letters, very likely to preserve Margaret's memory as his son Henry, who would become the second duke of Newcastle, would have seen to the perpetuation of his mother's memory. In his advice to Charles, he took a number of opportunities to acknowledge women's equal, if not superior, worth. Ever the horseman, in praising women during advice to Charles about hunting with his peerage and gentry, William concluded: "For the most parte in England, the Gray mare is the better horse,—which I profess & acknowledg, for my perticular, for truly I am Not pleased Excepte itt bee so."[34]

The most permanent monuments were the elaborate tribute to his grandmother, which his biographer claims people saw as horribly extravagant, and the tomb designed for his second wife in Westminster Abby, which is

34. William Cavendish, *Ideology and Politics on the Eve of Restoration,* ed. Thomas Slaughter (Philadelphia: The American Philosophical Society, 1984), 45, 60–63. I have written on his views toward women in "'A General War Amongst the Men [but] None amongst the Women': Political Differences Between Margaret and William Cavendish," *Politics and the Political Imagination in Later Stuart Britain,* ed. Howard Nenner (Rochester: Rochester University Press), 143–60.

remarkable even today, as symbolizing scholarship and a career of writing. There are large numbers of books displayed behind the duchess's body and others cascading at her feet. His well-known epitaph that termed her "a wise, witty and learned lady" was intended for both (as was the tomb), and its lengthy paragraph has only the first few words for him, namely "here lies the loyal duke of Newcastle."[35]

C. C. Stopes, who has written more about women's political standing in English history than any scholar before or after her *British Freewomen* (1894), identified the mid-seventeenth century as the moment from which one can date a decline in women's political standing. The focus on men's political rights had devastating effects on the actual political efforts of aristocratic women. A similar argument has been made by Elizabeth Colwill, who discusses how myths surrounding Marie Antoinette's Austrian loyalties, hatred of France, and disdain for the French people were used to vilify the political role of aristocratic women. The misogynist satire by Hébert and other revolutionary radicals formed a "link between aristocratic womanhood and political corruption, and the need for a reassertion of masculine political authority." Colwill states that the queen's execution "signalled the triumph of Rousseau's passive Sophie over the more worldly models of aristocratic womanhood."[36]

Historians agree that no fundamental change occurred in the class makeup of the English electorate based on the revolutions of the seventeenth century, and that the political system of the eighteenth century was controlled by a relatively small elite. Little attention has been directed to women's interests in these discussions. Yet it is quite plausible to argue that the identification of independent men with the standing of the king, the radical rhetoric that reached out to a wider range of men than had traditionally been involved in politics, and false universal language tied to the sovereignty of the people and the place of the freeborn Englishman, may have had their most significant effect in denying political standing to women.

Even though such values did not ultimately increase the power of the men to whom they were addressed, they established language and imagery that

---

35. Geoffrey Trease, *Portrait of a Cavalier: William Cavendish, First Duke of Newcastle* (New York: Taplinger, 1979); Arthur Stanley Turberville, *A History of Welbeck Abbey and Its Owners*, 2 vols. (London: Faber and Faber, 1938).

36. Stopes, *British Freewomen*; Elizabeth Colwill, "Just Another *Citoyenne?* Marie Antoinette on Trial, 1790–1793," *History Workshop Journal* (1990): 66, 74. Jacques-Renee Hébert, in his radical newspaper, *Le Père Duchesne*, posed the question that drove his characterization of Marie: "Isn't the Queen a *citoyenne* like other women?" (68). Colwill argues that to employ *citoyenne* "was simultaneously to elevate her to the ranks of virtuous womanhood and to lower her to the same status as all other women" (68).

formed the foundation for expanding the English electorate throughout the eighteenth and nineteenth centuries. The assumption that women had held no such political standing is refuted by those who held both office and returned members to Parliament. A case from the 1730s over whether a woman could hold the office of sexton saw the chief justice in Kings Bench defend women's past office holding: "I am clearly of opinion that a woman may be sexton of a parish. Women have held much higher offices, and, indeed, almost all the offices of the kingdom; as Queen, Marshal, Great Chamberlain, Great Constable, Champion of England, Commissioner of Sewers, Keeper of a Prison, and Returning Officer for members of parliament."[37] The shift from an office-based status, which large numbers of women from the landholding and mercantile classes held, to a broader citizenship based on qualities restricted to men undercut women's traditional political claims. One would have to wait until the end of the century to hear words such as Elizabeth Johnson's: "We complain, and we think with reason that our Fundamental Constitutions are destroyed; that here's a plain and an open design to render us meer Slaves, perfect Turkish Wives, without Properties, or Sense or Souls; and are forc'd to Protest against it, and appeal to all the World, whether these are not, notorious Violations on the Liberties of Freeborn English Women?"[38] Yet, while such sentiments could be found in isolated feminist works at the end of the seventeenth century, they seldom survived the political atmosphere of the eighteenth century.

37. The case is *Olive v. Ingram* and the chief justice of Kings Bench was William Lee; quoted material from Lord Campbell, *Lives of the Chief Justices* (Boston: Estes & Lauriat, 1873–74); the case itself is discussed in my "Women as Sextons and Electors," in *Women Writers and the Early Modern British Political Tradition*, 324–42.

38. Elizabeth Johnson, "Preface to the Reader," [Elizabeth Singer Rowe], *Poems on Several Occasions* (London: Printed for John Dunton, 1696), n.p.

4

"Interests of the Softer Sex"

Commercialism, Politics, and Gender in the Eighteenth Century

There has been a great deal of research on the nature of gender relationships and the influence of gender on eighteenth-century politics and society in Britain. The scholarship, as it relates to women, highlights two aspects of economic change and popular culture—the growth of commercialism and the dominance of sensibility—as values pervading all aspects of English society during the 1700s. Those who have analyzed the growing link between English nationhood and the values of commerce have not closely tied these analyses to other works on the nature of sensibility. The former are more apt to be written by political and economic historians, while the latter are more apt to come from literary critics and cultural historians.[1]

1. There has been an explosion of works dealing with the eighteenth century over the last three decades, with those works dominating that focus either on the financial revolution and significant economic expansion or those that discuss the interlocking nature of nationalism and imperialism. They include P. G. M. Dickson, *The Financial Revolution in England, 1688–1756* (London: Macmillan, 1967); *The Birth of a Consumer Society,* ed. Neil McKendrick et al. (Bloomington: Indiana University Press, 1982); *Consumption and the World of Goods,* ed. John Brewer and Roy Porter (London: Routledge, 1993); John Brewer, *The Sinews of Power: War Money and the English State, 1688–1783;* Linda Colley, *Britons: Forging the Nation, 1707–1837* (1988; reprint, New York: Vintage Books, 1996); and Kathleen Wilson, *The Sense of the People: Politics, Culture, and Imperialism in England, 1715–1785* (Cambridge: Cambridge University Press, 1995).

Scholars analyzing eighteenth-century Britain tend to pay attention to questions of gender more so than those analyzing the events of the mid-seventeenth century. There is no immediate answer as to why gender did not contribute to arguments for expansion of the politically active in the 1640s, but perhaps most telling is the lack of a discourse of difference acknowledging women's fundamental nature in a way that would proscribe their involvement in politics. In *The Lawes Resolutions,* and other works prior to or during the civil war decades, there is little discussion of women's special nature. Women were either ignored or explicitly excluded based on issues of status such as subordination of the wife, dictates for women's silence in public and obedience at home, or common law precepts that underlay women's legal and political disabilities. Few contended that such exclusion existed because women were incapable of understanding politics, or had natures inappropriate for (and uncomfortable with) political gatherings. Such distinctions did not come up until the eighteenth century, with arguments concerning sensibility.

The works of the eighteenth century concerning the nature of citizenship, educational institutions, and the appropriate training for members of both sexes from all classes are more complex. A number of striking features stand out in an analysis of materials listed for the period 1700–1800 from the *English Short Title Catalogue.* First, when dissecting general terms such as "young man/men" and "young woman/women," or "apprentice," an overwhelming number of works dealing either with crime or biological freaks turn up. Second, in works related to education, there were more class-specific accounts, especially with the growth of charity schools from the late seventeenth century on. As one would expect, works on citizenship and the state differ over time: in the first three-quarters of the century the political standing of gentlemen (and to a lesser extent, merchants) constituted the subject matter, and in its final

---

In addition, there are a range of works that speak of the changing nature of politics and political theory in the eighteenth century, including J. G. A. Pocock, *Virtue, Commerce, and History: Essays on Political Thought and History, Chiefly in the Eighteenth Century* (Cambridge: Cambridge University Press, 1985); H. T. Dickinson, *Liberty and Property: Political Ideology in Eighteenth-Century Britain* (New York: Holmes and Meier, 1977); J. A. W. Gunn, *Beyond Liberty and Property: The Process of Self-Recognition in Eighteenth-Century Political Thought* (Kingston, Ontario: McGill-Queen's University Press, 1983); and Douglas Hay and Nicholas Rogers, *Eighteenth-Century English Society: Shuttles and Swords* (Oxford: Oxford University Press, 1997).

For works focusing on the growth of radicalism later in the century, see Issac Kramnick, *Republicanism and Bourgeois Radicalism: Political Ideology in Late Eighteenth-Century England and America* (Ithaca: Cornell University Press, 1990); Jack Fruchtman, *The Apocalyptic Politics of Richard Price and Joseph Priestley: A Study in Late Eighteenth-Century English Republican Millennialism* (Philadelphia: American Philosophical Society, 1983); and Virginia Sapiro, *A Vindication of Political Virtue: The Political Theory of Mary Wollstonecraft* (Chicago: University of Chicago Press, 1992).

twenty-five years the appearance of more radical publications extended the political population.[2]

While the false universal continued to dominate the broad discussion of aging, education, and citizenship, works on women became more stereotyped, with the "fair sex" replacing the threatening specter of public women during the mid-seventeenth century. While historians of women have written a great deal about the continual castigation of Eve for tempting Adam to eat of the Tree of Knowledge, ultimately placing them outside the Garden of Eden, it is still questionable whether Eve was the most damaging symbol for women's nature and presumed competence in society. Eve has certainly stood for evil, and her ill-informed and sinful choice has stained the reputations of women who followed her. Yet one could argue that Eve was also the most powerful person, one with the capability of reducing mankind to a state of mortality and removing them from the possibility of a comfortable eternity with God. To overcome such an act required Christ's sacrifice and a hard and constant path of faith and effort geared to salvation. In the eighteenth century, women became more attached to qualities of helplessness, of needing protection, of requiring separation from public venues, of a greater focus on dress and cosmetics. Such views heightened society's love affair with the young; older women lacked the innocence and beauty to be worthy of men's attention. Under these circumstances, the evil but powerful Eve, from the endless Puritan and Anglican tracts of the seventeenth century, could easily have been a more positive model, even for what was wrong with the sex.[3]

2. Colley, *Britons,* stresses women's unique relationship to citizenship and patriotism, while undercutting broader class divisions. She notes that Britain developed a cult of royal women especially appropriate for female subjects: "Princess Charlotte, like Queen Charlotte, like Queen Caroline, and like the future Queen Victoria, supplied British women with a focus for their patriotism that was peculiarly their own" (272). And on women's exclusion, she contends, "One answer was by placing renewed emphasis on the physical, intellectual, emotional, and functional differences between men and women." She later discusses women's active role in such things as processions (238–50). Wilson, *Sense of the People,* includes an explicitly gendered analysis of the growth of imperialism and its connection to "the effeminate body politic" in which the aristocracy is seen as especially suspect because of its weak, effeminate nature. (185–205).

3. The most comprehensive recent study of the nature of sensibility and its spreading influence during the eighteenth century, along with a thorough analysis of its gender implications, can be found in G. J. Barker-Benfield, *The Culture of Sensibility: Sex and Society in Eighteenth-Century Britain* (Chicago: University of Chicago Press, 1992). Barker-Benfield outlines the evolution of sensibility that built upon Lockean psychology and emphasized the senses, but ultimately was harmful to women. He states: "Sensibility signified revolution, promised freedom, threatened subversion, and became convention." As for women, "the promise soon began to be short-circuited by the restoration of a model of innate difference" (1). I disagree with Barker-Benfield over this being a reversion to an earlier sense of inherent difference and argue rather that it was an enhanced view of difference based more on "feminine" qualities than that found in the literature of the previous century.

In comparing the language of the 1632 *The Lawes Resolutions* with *The Laws Respecting Women* (1777), and a compendium on women's nature entitled *Woman. Sketches of the History, Genius, Disposition, Accomplishments ... of the Fair Sex* (1790), one can begin to pinpoint the significant shift in definitions of women's nature from the mid-seventeenth through the eighteenth century. *The Lawes Resolutions* uses either biblical admonitions or common law realities along with discussions of women's proclivity for marriage and their adopting husbands' names. These prescriptive norms and commonplace realities were all that divided women from men. By the late eighteenth century, there was much more. In *The Laws Respecting Women,* women were portrayed as lesser beings beyond the state whose rights required protection, but not as political beings or as a threat to the state or groups within it. After discussing the "bravery, generosity, and a love superior to mean suspicions" among English men (which prevented much violence against women), the author notes how women were to be seen: "England has been stiled the Paradise of women; nor can it be supposed that in a country where the natural rights of mankind are enjoyed in as full an extent as is consistent with the existence and wellbeing of a great and extensive empire, that the interests of the softer sex should be over looked."[4]

The nature of such views was introduced in an early eighteenth-century satire. While the earlier satires of the mid 1600s, such as the series focusing on a women's parliament, ridiculed women's political ambitions and presented the ridiculous outcomes that might emerge from such ambitions, still there was an edge of fear in women's potential power. But in eighteenth-century satire, the focus was more apt to be on young women than threatening matrons, and these young women were most apt to be interested in marriage and romance and to be less serious and potentially threatening creatures. One of the more interesting examples of such satire, *The Levellers: A Dialogue between two young ladies ... proposing an Act for Enforcing Marriage,* reveals a continued use of the categories and language from the civil war period, while trivializing both the topic and the young women involved.[5]

The work focuses on the need to support marriage since the young women who were its subjects, Politica and Sophia, believed their urging of human

---

4. *The Lawes Respecting Women, as They regard their Natural Rights, or their Connections and Conduction,* 4 vols. (London: Printed for J. Johnson, 1777), v–vi.

5. *The Levellers: A Dialogue between two young ladies ... proposing an Act for Enforcing Marriage* (London: Printed and sold by J. How, 1703), reprinted in vol. 5, *The Harleian Miscellany* (1765). Hereafter cited in the text by page number.

procreation was more important than proposed legislation, namely an act prohibiting importation of foreign cattle to encourage "the Breed of English cattle." Rather, the young ladies supposedly argued that "Increasing the Breed of Englishmen" would be "far more advantageous to the Realm." The anonymous author, putting words in their mouths, termed them "two young Ladies of great Beauty and wit" who saw themselves as "useless Creatures, not answering the End of our Creation in the Propagation of our Species, for which, next the Service of our Creator, we came into the world." While named "Politica" and "Sophia," their political wisdom was restricted to issues of getting a husband and producing an heir (416–17). Later, Politica, in responding to Sophia's demand that all young men should be householders who have come into their inheritance, asked "whether the Law you mention be not destructive of Magna Charta, since, without Cause or Offence, it deprives a Man of his Property," but Sophia answers, "A Person who has broken, and forfeited his Right to the Magna Charta of Nature, ought to have no Protection by the Magna Charta of Englishmen," thus clarifying both their biological aims and the political standing of men (422). Here, women were evolving into the passive creatures of the late eighteenth century and Victorian era, where they had "interests," and arguments concerning their "rights" were left mostly to those concerned with their specific political status (such as Mary Wollstonecraft) and later emerged from those engaged in the women's suffrage movement.

Woman. Sketches of the History, Genius, Disposition, Accomplishments ... of [the] Faire Sex (1790), written by "a Friend to the Sex," made even clearer that the softer, sensitive female of the eighteenth century did not fit the requirements of the British state. After terming patriotism "the noblest sentiment of the human mind," he ties it to "ideas of interest, and property," clearly a set of values and loyalties most applicable to men: "These sentiments, it will readily be perceived, do not correspond with the condition of women. In almost all governments excluded from honours and from offices, possessed of little property ... they cannot in general be supposed to be eminent for patriotism." Women existed "more in themselves, and in the objects of their sensibility ... [and were thus] less susceptible of that enthusiasm which makes a man prefer the state to his family, and the collective body of his fellow citizens to himself." Women lacked that universal love "which extends to all nations and to all ages" because "they must have an image of what they love." Finally, women's incapacity for patriotism was linked to their intellectual and imaginative limitations, again part of their essential difference as seen by the late eighteenth century: "It is only by the power of arranging his ideas, that the philosopher is able to overleap so many barriers; to pass from a man to a people; from a people, to human kind; from the time in which he lives, to ages yet unborn; and from what he sees, to what he does not."[6]

The more grounded female, stuck in the family circle of the here and now, lacked the imaginative capacity of such connections, and that is why it was important for the state to protect her interests, as noted in *Lawes Respecting Women*. Men, who could become "domestic despots" in this enlightened age even though "the politeness of such times" might restrain them from open violence, still had unlimited power over a weaker creature, and "the torture of a susceptible mind is superior to any bodily suffering."[7] Thus the emphasis on female difference, weakness, and sensitivity was used by the end of the eighteenth century, ostensibly on women's behalf but in reality to bar them from equality.

Had women been admitted into the political community during the seventeenth century, there was no discourse of sensitivity to transform their inclusion into characteristics of difference that did not threaten men's primary tie to the state. They would have had to be admitted on the same grounds, and utilizing the same arguments, as that "freeborn Englishman" who was seeking to join his more privileged brothers. After 1750, and in the future debates over women's suffrage, women could be brought under the political rubric without necessarily having to claim equal or identical natures and standing to their male counterparts.

Perhaps the seventeenth-century language and imagery of equality were at the heart of the general omission of women, or their direct ridicule, among those debating the political nature of England during the 1640s and 1650s. And, while later arguments based on essential differences might ultimately have softened the opposition to women's political involvement, they allowed a continued confusion and conflation of qualities associated with the independent male and a supposedly nongendered citizenship.

Recent scholarship has given scant attention to issues of gender as they relate to broad conceptions of citizenship, nationalism, and the state during the 1700s. Kathleen Wilson's study is the most concentrated effort to insert gender into the political alterations of the eighteenth century, but it is encased in a class analysis that is more centered on the conflict between a rising

---

6. *Woman. Sketches of the History, Genius, Disposition, Accomplishments, . . . of [the] Fair Sex*, by a Friend to the Sex (London: Printed for G. Kearleys, 1790), 136, 138.

7. *The Lawes Respecting Women*, v–vi.

middle class (and to a lesser extent to the independent but economically less well off) and the landed aristocracy. The negative stereotypes of the aristocrat were more gendered in her account, and the positive qualities ascribed to the freeholder, citizen of the city, or those trying to displace an unrepresentative government were less gendered. Other studies focus on the enhanced standing of commerce without going into much detail concerning its gender aspects. These studies treat women almost wholly as consumers, although they were shopkeepers, craftpersons, investors, and stockholders of chartered companies in significant numbers. In designating women as consumers, these economic and political histories integrate the values and stereotypes of sensibility into their economic and political analyses. It is because women were concerned with dress and appearance that purchasing a wide range of goods was central to their lives. This has led to women being left out of the productive activities of commerce, but important as representing demand in shops and among merchants. It is a one-sided and incomplete view of women's role in the eighteenth-century economy.

Neil McKendrick, John Brewer, and J. H. Plumb, in *The Birth of a Consumer Society*, introduced women's importance as consumers. While the authors discuss the growth of consumerism generally, noting that during this consumer revolution "more men and women than ever before in human history enjoyed the experience of acquiring material possessions," women's buying habits are stressed, although men both practically and legally controlled the greatest amount of money during the 1700s. Domestic and fashion purchases are highlighted, and the authors mention that the "fashion doll" meant that women did not have to rely on their memory after seeing fashionable attire on the aristocracy, as the method to direct and purchase a copy. While women might have been consumers disproportionately, in terms of taking the initiative for such a movement, the authors engender the advance as male: "It needs to be pursued into the political world of 18th-century England, into the commercialization of leisure, and of childhood, and into the world of invention and creation, where unabashed by any sense of the plenitude of Nature men deliberately sought to create new and improved species and exciting novelties with which to delight the eye, to exhibit one's taste and to assert one's wealth."[8]

8. Neil McKendrick, "Introduction," in *The Birth of a Consumer Society: The Commercialization of Eighteenth-Century England*, ed. Neil McKendrick, John Brewer, and J. H. Plumb (London: Europa Publications, 1982), 1–3, 9–10. While McKendrick identifies men's initiative as consumers, he employs female imagery in his dispute with historians who have been too quick to find consumer revolutions in the

Consumer spending reached a "revolution" by the third quarter of the century, and while men purchased more, the expansion in women's shopping was crucial. More women were working because whole families were employed and women's tastes were more apt to dictate spending choices, such as "clothes, curtains, linens, pottery, cutlery, furniture, brass and copper for the home; buckles, buttons and fashion accessories for the person" (9, 20–22). The authors sum up their general perspective with a birth analogy:

> By 1700 the embryonic development of a consumer society had certainly begun, but the pregnancy had still had some way to go. By 1700 the barriers to retail trade were certainly coming down, but there were still too many in place to prevent the protracted birth pangs of a nation giving birth to a consumer society from being seen to be over. By 1800, however, those barriers had given way and the consumer society had been announced by so many observers … that its arrival should no longer be doubted. (31–33)

One of the difficulties in pinpointing the gendered nature of consumerism is that historians differ according to whether they are treating consumerism in a political or national context, or are describing the habits of a small group of consumers.[9] As happens so often in historical scholarship, women are included as individuals (when they are included) or as people who spread a set of current values or behavior, but seldom as either the initiators of such values or behavior or as essential to their symbolic or actual nature.

Eighteenth-Century Conceptions of the Citizen

While there were vast changes in the writings regarding citizenship over the course of the eighteenth century, still the language of the 1600s continued to

sixteenth and seventeenth centuries: "One has to admit that there have been many false pregnancies, and some births so premature that the infant so fondly announced by one historian has been allowed to die without regret by the consensus of his historical colleagues" (3). Hereafter cited in the text by page number.

9. Amanda Vickery, "Women and the World of Goods: A Lancashire Consumer and Her Possessions 1751–81," in *Consumption and the World of Goods,* ed. John Brewer and Roy Porter (London: Routledge, 1993), offers a detailed treatment of Elizabeth Shackleton (274–304), while John Styles, "Manufacturing, Consumption and Design in Eighteenth-Century England," in ibid, 527–54, and John Brewer, "Commercialization and Politics," seldom mention women or gender.

be employed in much of the radical focus on a male individual that emerged following 1775. Numerous works that appeared early in the century treated the nature of English citizenship in a satirical manner. Some were written by two of England's more prominent authors, Daniel Defoe and Joseph Addison. Addison's the *Freeholder* was a periodical defending the Whigs against a threat from the Stuart pretender to the throne during 1715 and 1716. While it had much in common with his joint adventures with Richard Steele in the *Spectator* and the *Tatler*, the *Freeholder* was most like his early newspaper, the *Whig-Examiner*, which was full of political propaganda. He described it as a written defense allied with the troops on the field fighting for George I against his Tory enemies. It is a common blend of Protestant and Whiggish sentiments, guaranteeing Englishmen that George would uphold their liberties and their religion against the tyrannous and Catholic threat of the Stuarts. In doing so, Addison harkened back to revolutionary arguments of the seventeenth century and claimed that his paper was directed to a range of English citizens who best fell under the rubric "freeholder." In this work, which combines political satire and support for Hanoverian rule, Addison maintains the familiar connection among England, political access, economic independence, and men standing for all inhabitants. He says that all freeholders possessed their rights as English citizens, which they "enjoy in common with myself." To make clear that women fell outside this circle, whether or not they were freeholders, he addresses numbers four and eight directly to the "fair sex." In urging their support, he claims that "it lies in the power of every fine woman, to secure at least half a dozen able-bodied men to his Majesty's service" because "arguments out of a pretty mouth are unanswerable." In number eight he proposes a "Female Association" where women could use their beauty and feminine wiles to aid the government's cause, and here he urges virgins to withhold sexual favors and married women to nag their husbands in order to bring them to a state of active loyalty.[10]

Such comments were tied to his satirical treatment of Tories, especially boorish country gentlemen who most loved fox hunting, and hated foreigners, dissenters, and trade of any variety. In his Tory satires, Addison continually had his Tory gentlemen blanche at the dress and behavior of independent women in London; they could not tell women dressed for a costume ball as a Quaker and a nun from the real thing. It was an interesting mixture of ridicule

---

10. For a discussion of the *Freeholder*, see Robert M. Otten, *Joseph Addison* (Boston: Twayne Publishers, 1982), 128–33.

of the unsophisticated country gentleman and Addison's supposed greater sophistication. While reflecting his urban knowledge of the more complex eighteenth-century woman, in his newspapers directed to women he still urged that they should be demure and dependent and seek only to influence individual men, not society or politics.[11] He made similar distinctions in a series of essays in which men stood for the nation and various professions while women appeared normally as "ladies." While he edited numbers entitled "the citizen's journal," "the vanity of fame," "the coldness of English oratory," "the fine taste of writing," and so on (all of which could encompass women), women appeared only in the "lady's journal," "women's tongues," "the female passion for China," and the like. Each of these works built upon stereotypes of women's flighty, superficial, delicate, and self-indulgent natures. Addison, however, while presenting typical comments on women's loquaciousness, such as "there are many among them who can talk whole hours upon nothing," in comparison to men who only talked too fulsomely about something, he still notes women's past learning: "We are told by some ancient authors, that Socrates was instructed in Eloquence by a woman, whose name, if I am not mistaken, was Aspasia. I have indeed very often looked upon that Art as the most proper for the female sex, and I think the universities would do well to consider, whether they should not fill the rhetoric chairs with she-professors." In the other essays, Addison continues his satirical treatment of women as "gossips" or "coquettes," and of their hats, which exhibited "a kind of molting season," their dull journals, which recorded such events as "drank two dishes of chocolate in bed, and fell asleep after them," or their love for fancy table settings: "China vessels are playthings for women of all ages." In an essay on "patriotic ladies," which places women in the political satire directing most of the *Freeholder,* he criticizes not only Tory women such as the "little lively rustic, who ... will prattle treason a whole winter's evening," but also loyal Whigs who joined a female association. These Whig comrades identified qualities to aid the cause as "teeth," "a good neck," and "hands," of which each had a handsome example.[12]

While Addison and Steele, as well as Swift and Defoe, wrote a range of satires directed against male as well as female subjects, for men to be attacked

11. *Selections from the Writings of Joseph Addison,* ed. Barrett Wendell and Chester Noyes Greenough (Boston: Ginn & Co., 1905), 244–54.

12. *Essays of Joseph Addison,* ed. Sir James George Frazer (London: Macmillan and Co., 1915), 2:41–45, 69–73, 109–14, 406–9, 410–15. These essays are drawn from *The Spectator, The Guardian,* and *The Freeholder* and appeared from December 1711, through January 1716.

they required an opposing political attachment, backward or unsophisticated origins, or lack of knowledge of cultural or current events. For women it was sufficient simply to be a member of their sex. Again, as noted in Chapter 4, such satire and ridicule have been either overlooked or dismissed as insignificant, certainly not thought to hold significant social or political import. If treated at all, such works were most often analyzed for their sexual content or as emblematic of a period's popular culture, but not to be considered substantive social and political commentary. But if such judgments about women were repeated constantly, even in satire, and one's sex alone proved damning, it could easily have had an important impact on why women, no matter the reality, were not seen as political or economic actors.

Daniel Defoe wrote a number of works defending the freeborn Englishman at the heart of Whig ideology. The most relevant for this study were the epic poem, *The True-born Englishman,* and the works, "The Free-holder's Plea against stock-jobbing elections of Parliament Men," and "The Complete English Tradesman." While Defoe lacked some of Addison's satirical edge, defended married women against sexual misuse by their husbands in *Conjugal Lewdness; or, Matrimonial Whoredom,* and offered a plan for a school for young women based on Mary Astell's proposal for a Protestant academy, he still employed the false universal when speaking of England's essential nature, both economic and political.[13]

In *The True-born Englishman,* he offers both a dissenting and Whiggish interpretation of those who supported arbitrary religion and government in England. After castigating Spain, Italy, and Germany for their pride, sexual excess, and drunkenness, he turned to England. England is described as a female, the victim of a number of invaders coming to her shores while she was yet unable to defend herself: "Who conquer her as oft as they invade her; / So beauty's guarded but by innocence / That ruins her, which should be her defence" (189). Out of all those invaders there emerged: "That vain ill-natured thing, an Englishman" (190). He then continues a history of England, based on a Norman Yoke model, in which Norman rule undercut the rights of freeborn Englishmen. Because of others imposing their offspring and their systems of government on England, "A true-born Englishman's a contradiction, / In speech an irony, in fact a fiction" (195). The satire continues with England

---

13. Daniel Defoe, *Conjugal Lewdness; or, Matrimonial Whoredom. A Treatise Concerning the Use and Abuse of the Marriage Bed,* facsimile, 1727 (Gainesville, Fla.: Scolars' Facsimiles and Reprints, 1967), and "An Academy for Women," in *An Essay Upon Projects,* facsimile, 1697 (Menston, England: Scolar Press, 1969).

breeding up rascally poor who take to liquor and irresponsible monarchs and gentry and who set the model.[14]

After portraying Englishmen as greedy and not able to recognize true liberty, he moves on to praise William and Mary. William could take the country toward the perfect blend of order and liberty which would bring the freeborn Englishman to his true heritage and allow him to emerge from being a mere member of a mob. But such would not be easy, given the problems inherent in current English citizens:

> All men are bound by conscience to submit;
> But then that king must by his oath assent
> To *postulatas* of the government,
>
> . . . .
>
> This doctrine has the sanction of assent
> From Nature's universal Parliament.
> The voice of Nature and the course of things
> Allow that laws superior are to kings.
>
> . . . .
>
> Nor can this right be less than national;
> Reason, which governs one, should govern all.
> Whate'er the dialects of courts may tell,
> He that his right demands can ne'er rebel,
>
> . . . .
>
> Thus England groaned—Britannia's voice was heard,
> And great Nassau [William] to rescue her appeared,
> Called by the universal voice of Fate—
> God and the people's legal magistrate. (193–95)

In the early days, invading nations formed the Britons for "still the ladies loved the conquerors" (195); this, and a reference to Queen Mary as the pull to

---

14. *The Earlier Life and Chief Earlier Works of Daniel Defoe.* (London: George Routledge & Sons, 1889), 186–218. This lengthy poem is a satire about English citizens not recognizing their own interests as they relate to the religious establishment as well as the monarchy, and the political domination of the landed oligarchy. While continuing at some length, sometimes positively, other times negatively, about the contrariness and independence of English character, he tells the story without women. His reference to Queen Mary is as follows: "He dwelt in bright Maria's circling arms, / Defended by the magic of her charms / From foreign fears and from domestic harms." His only other reference to particular women was to Charles II's mistresses, who left the kingdom "six bastard Dukes" (208, 193, 195).

draw William to the English throne, were the only mention of women in this religious and political history of the English people. This poem again incorporates God's intention, universal human qualities, and the particular place of the English in the larger scheme, all without reference to women.

At about the same time Defoe's poem was gaining such attention, there was an anonymous satire, *The True-born English-woman. In a letter to the publick ... By a true-born English-man* (1703), in which the author began with an apology addressed to women with the heading "Madams" and reminded them that he came from a woman and had no interest "to wrong your Sex, or vilifie your Nature." As Anne was on the throne, he felt obligated to treat her with respect terming her "Solomon's Vertuous Woman."[15] He argues that she was "a Mirror for all her Sex to dress themselves by." Her attributes include a "Humble, Meek, and Lowly" character, "no Extravagant Apparel," a "Lover of Decency," "truly Pious and Devout," and one who did not employ paint to improve upon nature. The "Best of Queens, the Best of Wives" had much to teach her female subjects, but if this work was any guide, her instruction had little to do with the status or actions of "trueborn Englishwomen." In contrast to the queen, court ladies were prideful creatures who dressed lavishly and spent their time at the playhouse rather than the chapel. "City-Ladys" were just as bad and could be characterized as "High-Spirited, Self-conceited, Talkative," persons who stole from their husbands and displayed false interest in religion or morality.

The qualities of these women had little to do with politics: "Most *True-Born English-Women* are Extraordinary nice in their *Dresses* and *Houses,* and that's one of their Best Faculties; but thanks be to their Servants; For my Lady her self is not us'd to't" (6). He continues with the indulgences demanded by these women during their lying-in. In contrast, a good woman was a farmer's wife who "picks not her Husband's pocket," but added to his wealth "by good Housewifery and Marketing." Gentry wives, though, were almost as extravagant as their City sisters and would be "Mistresses in their own provinces," namely, *"Dairy Kitchin, Buttery, &tc."* He then concludes by saying there were a few good women whom he should mention, "lest a Female Civil War is Proclaim'd against me." Yet, lest the positive might outweigh the thrust of this brief tract, he concludes: "'Tho in the best of their Sex, the Crooked Rib may be discovered, and A Tincture of Grandame *Eve* wil remain in that

---

15. *The True-born English-woman. In a letter to the publick ... By a true-born English-man* ([London]: Printed in the year 1703), 3. Hereafter cited in the text by page number.

perverse Generation to the World's end" (8).[16] This satire even plays with Queen Anne's relationship with her female subjects, involving her in a familiar attack against her sex, and displaying scant respect or deference.

Defoe's *The Complete English Tradesman* went through a number of revisions after it was written, and Defoe scholars have listed its publication date from 1725 to 1727 because of the large changes in the various versions that appeared during these years. It was originally intended for those who were only beginning a trade, but he later extended his audience to experienced tradesmen. He distinguishes between artisans and tradesmen, and the latter incorporates a range of "warehouse keepers, shopkeepers, whether wholesale dealers, or retailers of goods." Those who made goods but did not own shops where they were sold were termed "handicrafts, such as smiths, shoemakers, founders, joiners, carpenters, carvers, turners, and the like." And, if they made goods for others to sell, then they were "manufacturers" and "artists." In establishing this economic hierarchy, Defoe left no place for women. He is quite elaborate about the interaction between craftsmen and tradesmen, and notes that there were those both below and above these groups, namely merchants above (those who trade with foreign countries) and those below, "such as workmen, labourers, and servants." The introduction to the work is wholly given to definition and categorizes a hierarchy of trade and crafts. The last sentence of the introduction includes language that is emblematic of the false universal, using inclusive terms to enhance one's subject and to link it to the broadest of human qualities, while at the same time excluding women: "These are the degrees by which the *complete tradesman* is brought up, and by which he is instructed in the principles and methods of his commerce, by which he is made acquainted with business, and is capable of carrying it on with success, after which there is not a man in the universe deserves the title of a *complete tradesman,* like the English shopkeeper."[17]

---

16. While this poem picks up the political terminology made popular by Defoe's work, it is similar to other satirical works considering women's nature and had little or nothing to do with women and politics. Good examples of such satire appeared in the late seventeenth- and early eighteenth-century editions of Robert Gould's *Love Given Over; or, A Satyr against the Pride, Lust, and Inconstancy, &c of Woman* (1682; reprint, London: H. Hills, 1710). It was answered in [Sarah Fige (Fyge) Egerton], *The Female Advocate; or, An Answer to a late Satyr against the Pride, Lust, and Inconstancy of Woman, written by a Lady in Vindication of her Sex* (London: Printed by H. C. for J. Taylor, 1687). Egerton's *Female Advocate* was written while she was young and angry, "I think, when a man is so extravagant as to Damn all Womankind for the Crimes of a few, he ought to be corrected" ("To the Reader," n.p.) The correction includes a defense of Eve's behavior, given that Adam received the admonition not to eat of the Tree of Knowledge, and a range of examples of women exhibiting purity and good judgment from the ancients to the present.

17. Defoe, *The Complete English Tradesman*, in *The Versatile Defoe: An Anthology of Uncollected Writings*

"The Freeholder's Plea against Stock-Jobbing Elections of Parliament Men" was a brief tract written by Defoe during the parliamentary election of 1701. It reflects his views from the *True-born Englishman* and is directed against the growing influence of stock companies over the outcome of elections. He criticizes the policy of companies in sending in a candidate to a region where he is unknown, "he is no inhabitant there, nor ever was, has no freehold, or copyhold, or leasehold estate there." There was collusion between local gentlemen (those most likely to be elected to Parliament) who sold such office for one thousand guineas, and financial interests from the City who hoped to gain from controlling the House of Commons. Competition between companies led to this corruption because they "suppose which company so ever gets most friends in the House" would gain over the other.

His criticism of such efforts was twofold: one, that rich and corrupt men would buy elections just to see the price of their stock rise, and two, that it would lead to incompetent persons sitting in the House of Commons. The work thus reached out to the freeholder in democratic language, but disparaged—in contrast to his treatment of tradesmen—the commercial types who might end up in Parliament. His first statement emphasizes the nature of Parliament as representing the general interests of the nation while the latter castigates the types of persons brought into Parliament through the influence of stock jobbers: "The Parliament of England is the governing council; their breath is our law, and on their breath under the direction of God's Providence we all depend, the greatest nicety that is possible should be used in chusing men of untainted principles, and unquestioned wisdom, to compose a body so eminent in their power and influence." Yet this influx of city money would lead to "Fill[ing] the House with mechanicks, tradesmen, stock-jobbers, and men neither of sense nor honesty ... and [will lead to] undermining the nation's felicity at once."[18] Such a reality would undercut the king's "confidence in his people" and subvert the English Constitution. While women were equally affected by such events, they were not included either as freeholders or as

by Daniel Defoe, ed. Laura Ann Curtis (Totowa, N.J.: Rowman and Littlefield, 1979), 381–84. He also moved without notice from the use of "person" to "tradesman" to "complete man" (my emphasis) in one sentence and without acknowledging the wide range of shops operated by women during the early eighteenth century (383).

18. Daniel Defoe, "The Freeholder's Plea against Stock-Jobbing Elections of Parliament Men," in Curtis, ed., *The Versatile Defoe,* 251–58. Defoe obviously created a complex, self-reliant, and interesting character in *Moll Flanders,* and he was concerned both about women's education and their treatment by husbands, but we have only a partial understanding of his views regarding women if we ignore those works addressed to men but which encompass the interests of the nation.

individuals with something to gain from the financial success of the chartered national companies. Such narratives recognized that not only did men alone serve in Parliament, but gave a false impression that Parliament's actions affected only the male half of the population.

Popular Periodicals

Because of the prominence of Addison, Steele, and Swift, their works have come to be treated as works of literature. There were, however, innumerable newspapers that appeared during the eighteenth century, often produced anonymously or by editors whose reputations have not survived the century. One was a paper which continued throughout 1755, *Man;* its subtitle was "A Paper for Enobling the Species." The opening issue noted that the authors hoped to be instructive and entertaining and that they had chosen the topic "man" after "survey[ing] all the regions of nature ... either in the heavens or the earth" and could find nothing that more "deserves our attention." And thus they decided "to make him the subject of our paper."[19]

They turned to this subject because it satisfied their personal wishes: "Men, in general, have a love for themselves; and this so justly, that no part of the visible creation has been found, in the course of almost six thousand years, more amiable than man" (1–2). Thus, they "properly make ourselves the centre of all things," and "we seek ourselves in all things." The other major reason for choosing man as their subject matter was that other "Men carry their researches through all nature; attempt to know whatever exists, or is capable of existing; and yet remain ignorant of themselves" (2).

Under the general rubric of "man," the authors explore three principal heads. The first was religion, "which must exactly suit our nature" and presented man's relationship to "the Supreme Being." The second head "regards the dignity of our nature; and instructs us how we should act up to it." In this area they would discuss issues of morality and virtue. The final head discusses "the lower powers, or faculties, of the soul, depending upon the use of our senses." In this section, they explore the "little known doctrine of the sensible and the beautiful" (2–3).

---

19. *Man. A Paper For Enobling the SPECIES: Designed to be continued weekly* (London: Printed by J. Haberkorn and sold by J. Robinson and A. Linde), no. 1 (Wednesday, January 1, 1755): 1. The price is listed as two pence. Hereafter cited in the text by page number and/or issue number and date.

They eschew any systematic analysis as being "unfit for a weekly paper": "As we propose examining into human nature, we shall promiscuously treat of whatever occurs, provided it be human." They then define the word "man" in laying out the appropriate subject for their "periodical essays": "MAN was created majestic: he has dignity stamped in his nature. Revelation informs us he has the prerogative of being made after the Image of the Supreme. Reverence therefore is due ... We shall never Sport with man, ... A contrary procedure is due to those who unman Themselves, by debasing their nature" (4).

The authors state that they will avoid both dry and foreign materials. They will write in an animated fashion and work for the "improvement of men." They mention women in this introduction, but their description veers from the qualities stressed earlier: "The fair sex, the most pleasing half of our species, we shall always consider as the mothers of men; and accordingly pay them the utmost attention. Men have by their nature a most particular regard for the ladies; as our subsequent papers will abundantly shew" (5).

Subsequent issues directed general topics to male readers, while specialized discussions on romance, beauty, dress, and the like were addressed to women, or on some occasions to both men and women. But broad philosophical topics were not thought to be of interest to women. A letter signed only "Woman" written on January 29 in the fifth number was concerned over the title of the paper and the implications it held for her sex. While it was not uncommon for editors to enlarge sales by penning their own controversial missives, still the bulk of the letter reflects the values of Mary Astell and other feminists writing early in the eighteenth century, except perhaps for its conclusion, which sought "every female virtue":

> But whilst the cause of man is likely to be thus nobly defended, I tremble for my own. If you would know from whence my apprehensions arise, you must give me leave to repeat your own words [seeing women as mothers].
>
> The compliment at the beginning I thank you not for; [those who speak such] flatter me to my ruin; they lead me in golden bands to gaudy slaughter; and make perdition pleasing. I hoped you would have treated this subject in a more manly manner; that you would have considered me in a more enlarged light, than merely as the mother of men, or, in other words, than as an object of desire, and, as such only, think me worthy your attention. Much too long have

I been considered in this light alone; as such I prostitute my charms at every place of public appearance that is open to receive me.[20]

The authors' response to the letter was a typical argument for male superiority; they claimed that they had no plans for comparing particular men and women in their publication, but taking the two sexes as a whole, "we find that the females, in general, are both in their bodies and minds, weaker than the males." In supporting such views they argue from distinct offices held, so at the heart of the false universal, to uphold their perspective, "It is justly expected from men, to provide for their families; defend their country; perform the laborious exercises; and engage in all the robust employments of life; for which they are fitted by their superior mental and corporeal strength" (2). Such a judgment, as with their endless counterparts past and future, ignores class differences, never contrasting the physical labor of the vast majority of women as against the leisure of the classes writing, and likely reading, this newspaper. The authors continue their arguments with the various virtues tied to men: "conquering the passions ... requires a strength of mind, and a firmness of resolution, more to be expected from the male" (3), they "defend and protect the women," and are thus "formed to stand firmer, and behave braver, in dangers," and "history indeed is incomparably more ornamented by the names of illustrious men, than of illustrious women." Women did have more limited, but positive qualities; they were mistresses of their toilet and good at assessing cloth. "Expertness, and readiness, in judging of lace and needlework, is doubtless an accomplishment in women, that would ill become a man" (4). Finally, the innate differences tied to the growth of sensibility and the qualities of the "fair sex" are clear in their final statement: "Superstition, credulity, prejudice, and hasty judgments, better suit the softer female, than the rough, masculine sex. Such foibles are unbecoming a strong understanding; and should be avoided by men, merely on account of their sex; even though they had no other reason" (5).

While such comments are common throughout history, they took on a new edge of sexual difference during the eighteenth century. Most significantly, they do not jibe with the grand discussion of human nature offered by the authors the previous month in the opening issue of the newspaper. How can

---

20. *Man*, no. 5 (Wednesday, January 29, 1755): 2. The authors do anticipate a claim that the letter is not genuine and they include the following in introducing it: "The public will do us the justice to believe it genuine. We have too sincere a regard for our readers to attempt any thing like imposition upon them," and hope to bring such letters before them in the future (1).

the falsely universal "human" incorporate both the qualities of the rough and nonsuperstitious male with the soft female given to prejudice and hasty judgment? Can they logically belong to the same species? And if human qualities point only to male characteristics, where do women fit into the general discussions of this publication, and so many like it. While many have commented on the self-interested prejudice exhibited in such judgments, more problematic are the previous qualities of human nature which ignore supposed feminine attributes existing at once both within and outside their boundaries.

In following issues, the authors claimed their interest to "defend and enoble the character of women" and further both "natural and acquired excellencies that properly belong to their sex." And while women might not do well with sciences that require "long abstract meditation, and an uninterrupted series of reasoning" they often best men "in the politer sciences" (April 16, pp. 1, 3). In advising a young woman who wondered whether she should marry, they urged her to soften men's rough edges: men, because of their "laborious employments" were "obliged to arm themselves with resolution and intrepidity." And if these rough virtues were not moderated, and softened, by the tenderness of women, men would become too rigid, and intractable, for civil society (4). Marriage was also good because men's "labour and fatigue . . . require refreshment and comfort at home" (April 23, p. 5). This issue, supposedly addressed to encourage a young woman to marry, ends by entwining man and humanity: "Marriage, therefore, being human in the highest degree; and man in his height of dignity when he becomes a virtuous husband, and a good father; we shall always esteem it a noble sign, whenever single persons, like our accomplished correspondent, declare they are not unwilling to marry" (6).

The next issue (April 30) urged "representing human nature as it really is, so as to form the moral history of man" (1). In reality, it was a tale of a man being cuckolded and his wife bringing up their daughter to such ill behavior as well. The following issues were mostly similar stories of young women who failed at love, were not attractive enough to engage the social scene successfully, or sought advice from the authors for problems in dealing with men. The males in their stories usually could not succeed at university or profession, had some serious character flaw, or had committed an act with immoral or unwise consequences. These stories were interspersed with moral platitudes and information from those presumably wise in the ways of the world. They spoke of husbands who had been absent for fifteen years and loyal women who sought better treatment from their spouses. In addressing a response to the husband of a complaining wife, they stated, "Neither does she require you to stay perpetually at home, keep no company abroad … but would delight in your taking the pleasures of friendship [and] to have some little share of your conversation" (July 2, p. 5).

- Women's complaints were normally treated as reasonable, but women were portrayed as weak supplicants. While women were offered specific responses to romantic or marital problems, the work was filled with general moral aphorisms for men, such as "Whosoever would behave as a man, must conduct himself by a knowledge suitable to his nature. He who acts without knowing his own nature, acts like a machine" (August 20, p. 1). In the September 24 issue the authors assured their female readers they were as interested in their ennobling as in that of their brothers and that they should not be "startled" by the word "philosophy" (September 24, p. 3).

The November 5 issue focuses on education and reaffirms the earlier confusion of "man" and "human," "children" and "boys." It pushes parents to seek "the rational education of children" (1). And the authors continue at great length associating such education with the central qualities of humanity: "Those who have not this regard for their children, highly dishonour their own nature, by suppressing and stifling the noble sentiments of humanity" (1). There is a lack of evidence to support the claim that men are superior to beasts, which intensely nurtured their young. The shift from inclusive language to gender-specific terms begins: "Parents are apt to flatter themselves that they really perform this duty; but he must have little knowledge of human nature, who is not thoroughly convinced they grossly deceive themselves. What is the reason that so few real men are to be found? Is it not owing to inhuman education, as the poisonous fountain of numerous vices; and the almost universal cause of our transgressing the laws of our nature?" (2). "Parents" was used in a sex-restricted way for those who aided their offspring to find suitable matches and positions but ignored "the best ways of improving their rational faculties." The subject of this attention narrowed even more severely when the authors complained that "young gentlemen of birth, family, and fortune, are usually, from their infancy, brought up in a soft, effeminate manner." But shortsightedness was not limited to gentlemen, "wealthy citizens, in general, have no better notions of education than gentlemen of birth and fortune; whence their sons," whether educated for advancement or to remain at their rank, seldom learned "a right knowledge of the sciences" (3). On page 4, when they turn to daughters, concern is reduced to the "false idea of their own beauty" in those who focus too greatly on dress. What they need, in contrast with either the fashionable or isolated and dull regimen afforded most females of "rich or of middling families," is to have instilled in them "the habitual practice of the essential virtues."

Their discussion concludes with a general comment on children and confirms its identification with boys: "A very little knowledge of human nature shews us, that the general methods of education are extremely wrong calculated for promoting the real perfection and happiness, either of individuals or of the community. A new scientifical method, a new set of rules should be introduced, as the foundation of a suitable practice for the forming of men" (5).

Two other November issues expand the focus on education to analyses of the nature of the species and the requirements of the state. They even more dramatically deny a place to women within the human species, if they hold the feminine qualities designated for them in earlier issues of *Man*. The authors note that "there are many duties to which men may be compelled" (November 19, p. 1). Governments have the right to force debtors to pay, parents to compel children to behave, and "every man has a natural right, forcibly to oppose and resist another" who would deprive him of his rights and property (5). These obligations were linked to the nature of the species: "If the whole species were humanly affected towards one another, there would be no occasion for compelling these duties. Every man would still have a power to compell them; but there would be no call for its exertion." And, finally, in characterizing the human species in contrast with those beneath it, the authors state that men are distinct "from brutes and plants," but above all "the advantages of humanity, and the excellence of one man above another, depend not upon the climate we are born, or the country we live in: for though the complexion and stature of men may differ in different countries, yet, with regard to the soul, we find it human in all countries; [any difference] entirely depends upon education and custom" (November 26, p. 1). The work continues with a tolerant attitude to "Laplanders and Hottentots" whose ignorance proceeds from "the want of education, and proper instruction" (2). Such status was linked only to males; "every real man should shew himself in his full strength and glory; without attempting to set up for a dogmatical teacher of others." And this would happen if children were rightly instructed; "it is of the utmost consequence in the education of youth, to let them converse with proper persons, capable of giving them manly notions," thus providing them with a true understanding of themselves. They should at all costs be kept from ignorant and superstitious persons (3).

Such a discussion of race fits within a much wider set of concepts tied to European hegemony and the meaning of "whiteness." Scholars have recently devoted a considerable amount of attention to Europeans' assuming their identity and experience is universal. Certainly in their language usage and visual imagery Europeans discussed their experience as not simply superior but as the essential experience of human beings. I contend, though, that these views are closer to the ideas surrounding the "other" as discussed in my analysis of *The Assemblyman* in the introduction. While early modern English writers, as well as more current ones, used words such as "we" or "us" or "English" without acknowledging the existence or legitimacy of other cultures, there is no word comparable to "man" that allowed authors to write in ways that were simultaneously inclusive and exclusive. When using terms such as "white," "English," "European," or "American" authors do not believe that those terms include "black" "African," "Asian," or the like. But many authors in the past, and continuing today, do claim that when they use "man" they mean all people. And this is the case even when their examples and explanations are drawn wholly from men, or they employ only the male pronoun to stand for all humans. This is not to claim that the false universal is more overtly discriminatory, or carries a greater belief in women's difference or inferiority, than works concerning race and region, but it does argue that linguistic constructs make it easier to hide omission or stereotyping of women than those dealing explicitly with race.[21]

While *Man* was perhaps unique because of its explicit tie between men, their qualities, their pattern of maturation, and the human species, still other eighteenth-century periodicals addressed themselves to male interests as comprising the interest of England as a whole. The most well-known among eighteenth-century newspapers are likely the *Gentlemans Magazine* and the *North Briton.* For the most part, these and other popular periodicals from the 1700s have been analyzed for their political viewpoints and as reflective of popular values. But they have not been discussed as perpetuating a false universal that equated male experience with the central needs and values of English society, using language that only at times seemed certainly to include women; at other times it clearly did not. While there were some periodicals directed specifically to women such as the *Ladies Diary,* the *Ladies Library,*

---

21. The literature on issues of race and imperialism is massive, but some of the more important works include Edward Said, *Orientalism* (New York: Vintage Books, 1979); Rein Lewis, *Gendering Orientalism: Race, Femininity, and Representation* (London: Routledge, 1996); *Displacing Whiteness: Essays in Social and Cultural Criticism,* ed. Ruth Frankenberg (Durham: Duke University Press, 1997), and *Tensions of Empire: Colonial Cultures in a Bourgeois World,* ed. Frederick Cooper and Ann Laura Stoler (Berkeley and Los Angeles: University of California Press, 1997).

and the *Old Maid,* the vast majority had a male audience and conflated their interests with everyone else's.[22]

The *Adventurer,* an example of one of the many newspapers addressed specifically to men, established broad principles in its various numbers, such as the nature of courage and "intellectual and corporal labour compared," and the authors placed women in retellings of individual tales that reaffirmed the weakness and vulnerability of the sex, such as "Distress encouraged to hope: the history of Melisssa," or directions for their relationships such as "The Ladies directed in the choice of a Husband," and "Directions to the Ladies for their conduct to a Husband." Stories and lessons directed to men dwelt on broader, human dilemmas: "Happiness and misery how far the necessary effects of virtue and vice," "Happiness properly estimated by its degree in whatever subject," "Religion the only foundation of Content," "Parallel between ancient and modern learning," and "On Lying."[23] The broad directions to men began with number 1: "As every man in the exercise of his duty to himself and the community, struggles with difficulties which no man has always surmounted, it was soon found, that without the exercise of courage . . . life itself [is] set at hazard, [and] much cannot be contributed to the public good nor such happiness procured to ourselves as is consistent with that of others" (1). But one (a man), while needing courage to further the common good, did not include women among "others," from whose behavior he sought consistency. So much of the significance of the false universal was, therefore, in the effects of writers and readers characterizing such comments as if they were generally relevant, while in reality they were both framed and read with only male experience in mind.[24]

The first sentence of the *Briton* continues the pattern: "The Briton thinks it unnecessary to produce himself amidst the parade of pompous professions, which serve only to excite idle curiosity, and raise expectations which may be attended with disappointment." The *Country Journal; or, The Craftsman* was

---

22. *The Ladies Diary; or, The Womens Almanack for the Year of Our Lord, . . . Containing many Delightful and Entertaining Particulars for the Use and Diversion of the Fair Sex* (London: Printed by J. Wilde, 1707, 1710, 1712); *The Ladies Library,* 3 vols. (London: Published by Mr. Steele, printed for Jacob Tonson, 1714); "Mary Singleton, Spinster," *The Old Maid* (London: Printed for A. Millar, and sold by S. Bladon, 1755). The last newspaper continued from November 15, 1755, through July 24, 1756. The vast majority of newspapers, however, were addressed to men, including the *Adventurer,* the *Briton,* the *Country Journal; or, The Craftsman,* the *Englishman,* the *Gentleman's Magazine and Historical Chronicle,* the *Monitor; or, British Freeholder,* and the *North Briton.*

23. *The Adventurer* (London: Printed for J. Payne, 1752, n.p.); as listed in "Contents of the First Volume," nos. 7, 30, 32, 10, 37, 49, and 50, respectively.

24. *The Adventurer,* no. 1 (November 7, 1752), 1–2.

written by Caleb D'Anvers, a lawyer from Gray's Inn, and treated issues of trade and taxation. But it employed the same conflation of male experience with the interests of England as those publications dealing more specifically with politics: "All proposals, which seem really calculated for the Good of the People, either by promoting any valuable Branch of Trade or easing them of any bruthensome Tax," will be his subject, and "it is not to be doubted that my Readers will be highly pleased." The editor hopes to "lighten the burthen of the *Subject,* without diminishing the Revenues of the Crown," but while women were obviously subjects who paid taxes, they were omitted from his paper as audience or subjects.[25]

The *Englishman* claimed to be directed to "plain Freeholders as have just sense enough to form an opinion of your own" rather than "Scholars and Gentlemen." Its editors focused on the great harm done by the current ministers from 1772 to 1779, and they were sure that "every-well wisher to the liberties and prosperity of this country" was better informed about misgovernment (even foreigners who had only read English history), than the average freeholder who had kept his head in the sand. Such newspapers have been analyzed for the growing factions against William Pitt's rule, but again not for the conflation of man, freeholder, and "every well-wisher" to England's well-being. While the contemporary impact of such efforts had clear political import, they have had a long-term impact on women's being defined outside politics, no matter the later Herculean efforts of the duchess of Devonshire to unseat Pitt.[26] Further, in volume 54 of the *Gentlemen's Magazine,* the editors often claimed their efforts to improve the periodical was based on the comments of readers, and their original intent, "to give to the World pleasing and profitable communications" still directed their policy. Yet, with complaints that it had sometimes been too greatly directed to antiquarians and others of specialized interests, they claim, "But it is not to the Antiquary alone, however

25. *The Briton,* no. 1 (Saturday, May 29, 1762); *The Country Journal; or, The Craftsman,* no. 45 (Saturday, May 13, 1727), n.p.

26. *The Englishman, Number 1. Addressed to the Freeholders of England, Saturday, March 13, 1779,* 1. Much has been written on Georgiana, duchess of Devonshire, and her contribution to Whig politics, but she generally has been treated as an anomaly or as a female aristocrat interfering in a political scene where she did not belong. For a recent essay that emphasizes her importance in late eighteenth-century politics, see Amanda Foreman, "A Politician's Politician: Georgiana, Duchess of Devonshire and the Whig Party," Barker and Chalus, eds., *Gender in Eighteenth-Century England,* 179–204. Of the election of 1784 when she canvassed for Fox for the last time, "her contribution to the Whig campaign is well known because she was then, and is now, generally held responsible for Fox's victory" (184). The election is also discussed in Colley, *Britons,* 258–63.

Fig. 6   The eighteenth century introduced wide-scale political cartooning. While explicitly
sexual cartoons were common, men were seldom portrayed in sexual situations for
simply carrying out an electoral function, as in this cartoon depicting Georgiana,
Duchess of Devonshire, canvassing for Fox. Reproduced from *The Common
People and Politics, 1750–1790's* by John Brewer (London: Chadwyck-Healey,
1986), 217.

respectable, that the Editors ought to devote their attention. The Philosopher,
the Historian, the Physician, the Critic, the Poet, the Divine, and above all the
PUBLIC, have an undoubted claim to the utmost exertion of their abilities."
In following through with this promise, they built upon a need to diversify
by agreeing to expand their catalogue and accounts of books. Yet these books
would still be based on an assessment of "the general merits of works of
genius." But general merit had little relevance for their female readers,
whose interests they described as follows: "We have been told, that a due
regard has not been shewn to our Fair Readers, a numerous class of literary

judges, who are charmed with fine writing; that there is little or none of that fine sprightly kind of composition calculated to kill time, and furnish fashionable conversation; none of those select novels, love-stories—those brilliant sallies of wit and humour, that captivate the young, and delight the gay."[27]

The *North Briton,* which focused on British liberties and especially the importance of the freedom of the press, did not link its broad principles to any women who might have lived in England. In defending the current monarch against the perfidy of the Stuarts, the editors referred continually to the Briton in italicized terms such as "*His* assertions are every where much more general than the MONITOR'S," and "*He* affirms, *the administration is conducted with such integrity as defies reproach.*"[28]

The rhetoric, stories, platitudes, and teachings of these newspapers have been discussed since their inception, and they have been studied with much more sophistication recently because of the growing scholarly focus on popular culture and cultural history. Yet less attention has been paid to their broadly gendered language. Feminist scholars have noted their satire against women, but not given as much attention to their falsely universal language or their gendered constructions in the portions of works addressed to men. While there has been a growing critique of aristocratic politics, and its effeminate nature, less concern has been shown about the rhetoric of politics and male maturation separate from class, party, or regional differences. Such rhetoric is so endemic that we tend to overlook it or consider it insignificant in its repetition. One of the primary reasons for this lack of attention is the continued use of false universals by contemporary historians.[29]

27. "Preface," in *The Gentleman's Magazine and Historical Chronicle* 54 (1884), Part the First, by Sylvanus Urban, *Gent.* (London: Printed by John Nichols, for D. Henry and sold by E. Newberry, 1784), n.p.

28. *The North Briton,* no. 1 (Saturday, June 5, 1762) 1–2. The paper to which *The North Briton* was in opposition was *The Monitor; or, British Freeholder,* from August 9, 1755, to July 31, 1756. The *Monitor* was in opposition to the Hanoverian rule of the 1750s, identified with the traditional English freeholder and criticized those men who threatened the nation's liberties "without respect of persons." Its attachment to such values were grounded in the falsely universal language surrounding the freeborn Englishman: "The Liberty, which every Briton has of delivering his sentiments freely on public measures, is essential to the nature of our government; and our history abounds with instances, where the exertion of this right in the collective body has produced great and noble effects." (no. 1, August 9, 1755, 1).

29. For a discussion of the satire against the aristocracy, see Wilson, *Sense of the People,* and for discussions of the nature of popular periodicals, see Jeremy Black, *The English Press in the Eighteenth Century* (Philadelphia: University of Pennsylvania Press, 1987), and *Newsletters to Newspapers: Eighteenth-Century Journalism,* ed. Donovan H. Bond and W. Reynolds McLeod (Morgantown: West Virginia University Press, 1977); for pictorial political satire in newspapers and other eighteenth-century venues, see John Brewer, *The Common People and Politics, 1750–1790* (Cambridge: Chadwyck-Healey, 1986).

Eighteenth-Century Works on Education

As noted earlier, works on education and the proper training of the young were divided among those directed to the curriculum and needs of charity schools and those directed to the education of the middling and upper ranks. While differing along class lines, and between works representing parish and public policy and those offering private advice to the young, they differ little on questions of gender. In each type the general principles for training were directed to males; secondary, additional, and specialized programs were established for girls. The authors of works relating to charity schools were overwhelmingly clergy, and the works themselves were most apt to be appeals for community support for the schools. Charity schools emerged during the last decades of the seventeenth century and grew significantly in number during the 1700s. They had as their goals the spreading of religion among the poor, the teaching of useful skills to poor youth (which could prevent them from becoming adult charges on the parish), and maintenance of social order to prevent crime and insure deference to superiors.[30]

Francis Gastrell, who was canon of Christ-Church and preacher to the Society of Lincolns Inn when he offered his 1707 sermon, spoke before gentlemen meeting to promote charity schools in London and Westminster that had to that point educated three thousand children. In his sermon, he compares the needs of the children of Israel to those of these poor children. His text was drawn from Psalms 97:12, 13, and introduces the false universal, which characterizes the sermon as well. After the Hebrews returned from their lengthy captivity, "the People, the Priests and Levites, and all they that had separated themselves from the Filthiness of the Heathen unto the Law of God, they, their Wives, their Sons and their Daughters," made a covenant with God. Such godliness for the good of a people could also be detected in

---

30. See M. G. Jones, *The Charity School Movement: A Study of Eighteenth-Century Puritanism in Action* (Cambridge: Cambridge University Press, 1938). For examples of works relating to charity schools, see Francis Gastrell (Bishop of Chester), *The Religious Education of Poor Children, Recommended in a Sermon Preach'd in the Parish Church of St. Sepulchres, June 5, 1707 . . . Promoting the Charity-Schools Late Erected in the Cities of London and Westminster* (London: Printed and sold by H. Hills, 1707); John Jackson, *The Blessedness of Communicating to Charity-Schools. A Sermon Preach'd at Dursely, in Glouchester-shire, Feb 19. 1710* (London: Printed for and sold by H. Hills, 1710); Philip Bearcroft, *The Wise and Useful Institution of our Charity Schools: A Sermon Preached in the Parish-Church of Christ-Church, London; on Thursday April the 28ᵗʰ, 1748* (London: Printed by J. Oliver and sold by B. Dod, 1748); and, Frederick Cornwallis, *A Sermon Preached in the Parish-Church of Christ-Church, London, April 29ᵗʰ, 1762: at the yearly meeting of the Children Educated in the Charity-schools [of] London and Westminster* (London: Printed by J. and W. Oliver, 1762).

English victories and economic successes. Gastrell claimed that to ensure that such national purpose pervades all, it was necessary to reach the nation as a whole, and thus the mission of charity schools was "Educating the Children of the Poor." He claimed that the nature of "this charity ... is purely Religious; the whole Aim of it being to give those Persons, to whom it is extended a just Account of the Being and Providence of God, and of the End and Duty of Man."[31] It was wise to focus on childhood, for "this is certainly the best Season for all manner of Learning and Instruction, and the most proper Seedtime of Religion." It was thus important to bring the children "to the Guidance of Reason," and this would lead to their being "nourish[ed] ... in the Words of sound Doctrine and Wisdom." Such a wise early training would prevent their later lamenting "a vicious Education." This religious instruction was tied to occupational training, and these two curricula, together, gave poor children the ability to resist temptation:

> Here therefore, not only the Ignorant are instructed, but the Poor are also relieved: ... put also into a Condition of supporting themselves afterwards; by being taught and exercised in all sorts of honest Labour. By which means they are preserved from the greatest Danger incident to Human Nature, *Idleness*. We know that idleness is tied to human nature, for it "was inflicted upon Man for the Punishment of his first Transgression; *that in the Sweat of his Face he should eat Bread.*

The familiar punishment for Eve, of course, was: "I will greatly multiply your pain in childbearing; in pain you shall bring forth children, yet your desire shall be for your husband, and he shall rule over you" (Gen. 3:16).

Gastrell continues that labor furnished everyone "with all the Necessaries and Advantages of this Life," and he does not doubt that this is what makes it so difficult for the rich man to enter the kingdom of heaven (9). He continues with the life course set out for the "children," and notes that they would contribute to society in the future as "faithful Servants, honest Traders, useful Subjects of the State, and sincere Members of God's Church." Not simply that, but they would grow up to hold their own responsible positions within their communities: "These poor Children will ... be placed at the Head of distinct Families: And then the just Sense they have of the Advantages of their own Education, engage them to breed up their Children and Servants, and

---

31. Gastrell, *Religious Education of Poor Children*, 5. Hereafter cited in the text by page number.

all such to whom their Advice and Direction extends, in the same pious and useful manner" (11).

Not simply were "children" boys, but their education also prepared them specifically to hold the positions they were intended to follow in their path to male maturation. In reality, of course, large numbers of girls attended these schools, even though their curriculum stressed reading over writing and arithmetic and encouraged domestic skills, spinning, and needle trades over a period of apprenticeship. But it is key that the nature and goals of the schools, in Gastrell's conception, could be subsumed under religious, political, and economic categories reserved to men.

John Jackson's sermon from 1710 was directed to the inhabitants of Dursely and began: "Brethren!" pleading with them to support the proposed charity school the town had agreed to. He spoke of the sacrifices Christ asks and the importance of charity. He warns that "bestowing our Charity at Random" may do more harm than good and support "Idleness and Vice." Rather, charity should be directed toward these poor children who, because of their parents' poverty, would "run up and down *like wild Asses Colts as they were born* (Job 11.12)." Under this scheme they would be "taught how to live like Reasonable Creatures"; such a school moved them immediately "to Mens better Parts, their Souls" and aided them for a longer term with "*a quiet and meek spirit,*" and thus the child would gain over the course of his life and eternally.[32] Others who "live near him will be better thereby; whilst he becomes a careful Parent of his Family, a good peaceable Member of the Commonwealth; in a word, one diligent to discharge his Duty in all Respects." While this work, along with the others, camouflages its conflation of child and boy, man and human, it does not lead to a positive result for those in question and has strong elements of social control: "When they, on whom the drudgery, and slavery of a State lies, and by whom all the servile Offices (as necessary as the highest) are to be borne, when these, I say, will willingly yield their shoulders to the Burden, and ease others not so fit for it, it can't but be of unspeakable good to a Commonwealth." Jackson asks the residents of Dursely to contribute toward the costs of the students' clothing, education, and occupational training, for "the benefit of which would be unspeakable to every Man and the whole Community" (11–12). This work does not simply employ a model of male maturation for both justifying and organizing the project, but also mixes high-minded principles of faith with a way for the community to get the most

---

32. John Jackson, *Blessedness of Communicating,* 2–5. Hereafter cited in the text by page number.

work for its investment, epitomizing why numerous historians have found such schemes distasteful.

Philip Bearcroft's and Frederick Cornwallis's appeals appeared later in the century, but continue the pattern. The former links the fear of God to the need to train up young people and suggests the following categories: "a noble and generous Fear, and in opposition to the other, which termed *servile,* this is called *filial* Fear, or that of Children and Sons, as the other is that of Servants and Slaves." After bestowing this better fear on the poor children in the audience, he then states its relevance for others, "to Persons of all Ages and Conditions among us," again representing the distinct categories into which the male half of humanity fell.[33] He again links the purpose of the charity school to male aging:

> *It is good for them* to begin *to bear the Yoke* in their greener Years, To be early accustomed to Work, as well as to Instruction; that the Organs of their Bodies, and the Faculties of their Souls may acquire Strength and Vigour from Action; that as they rise up towards Manhood, They may be no longer chargeable, nor *eat any Man's Bread for nought,* But earn it for themselves; and as faithful Servants, brave Mariners and Soldiers, diligent Workmen, laborious Husbandmen, ingenious Artificers, And honest Tradesmen. (11)

Thus, while including themes relating to infants who had recently come from their mother's womb, and using as a guide to the trustees that Christ said to his disciples, "Suffer little Children to come unto him," he treats charity school students as if they were only boys. Not simply were girls in attendance at charity schools, but they were much more apt to do work early in life and forgo the training afforded their brothers (8).[34]

Frederick Cornwallis, who later became archbishop of Canterbury, continued the same themes, but focused on masters, ministers, teachers, and others who filled in for parents. His summary of the schools' goals fit the mixture of social utility and religious mission that is so typical of these works: "And above all, to impress upon their Minds such a just Sense of practical Religion,

33. Bearcroft, *Wise and Useful Institution of our Charity Schools,* 4–8. Hereafter cited in the text by page number.
34. Jones, *Charity School Movement,* notes that while much of boys' time in charity schools was taken up with vocational training, it "was the predominant element" in girls' schooling (80–84).

as may induce them to lead sober and virtuous Lives, in all Godliness and Honesty; and with all Diligence to do their Duty in that State of Life unto which it shall please God to call them." The security of the nation "depends principally on the Dispositions of the Poor; and where the Poor are virtuous and industrious, there the Rich have a security for the Blessings vouchsafed unto them." "Poor parents [fathers] were unable to give a proper Direction to the Minds of their Children ... how great a Part of their Time is taken up in providing Sustenance for themselves and their Families."[35] Because of this, "nothing can be more agreeable to the Character of a good Man, and to the good Works I have been recommending, than the Design of this Charity we are met to inforce." In concluding his discussion, he incorporates that now familiar combination of a vast improvement for English society avoiding any reference to women:

> Particularly when the Execution of it is vested in proper Hands, and is under the Management of discreet and religious Persons, that it will always claim the Countenance, and be intitled to the Approbation and assistance of all those who are Friends to the Civil and Religious Liberties of their Country; that are desirous of establishing *Peace and Goodwill among Men,* and of promoting the temporal and eternal Happiness of their Fellow-Creatures—or the Poor and Fatherless. (18–21)

There were, of course, a large number of works directed to the training of gentlemen, and certainly one of the most prominent was *Lord Chesterfield's Advice to His Son.*[36] This work notes on the title page that it built upon Lord Burghley's precepts for his son from the late sixteenth century, linking this genre of works over two centuries. While Chesterfield's guide, along with a range of works arguing for the establishment of new directions in learning (especially focusing on science and mathematics), and other works addressed to sons, continued to direct their message to males, they both expanded their subject matter and justification for such education beyond that found in the seventeenth century. Also, as James Bramston's *Man of Taste* makes clear,

---

35. Cornwallis, *A Sermon Preached in the Parish-Church of Christ-Church,* 17–18. Hereafter cited in the text by page number.

36. *Lord Chesterfield's advice to his Son on Men and Manners: ... To which are added, EXTRACTS from VARIOUS BOOKS, Recommended by Lord Chesterfield ...* (London: Printed for W. Richardson, 1788). Hereafter cited in the text by page number.

women were not the only ones caught up in the influence on society of ideas associated with sensibility.[37]

Chesterfield's work was a combination of social manners, knowing when to speak and what to say in polite conversation, how to read people, as well as gaining basic knowledge. It emphasizes the greater sociability of the eighteenth century, noting that only men with great minds were allowed absent-mindedness. "Sir Issac Newton, Mr. Locke, and perhaps five or six more since the Creation, may have had" such a right, "but such liberties cannot be claimed by, nor will be tolerated in, any other persons." Like earlier works, Chesterfield's writing had a universal reach but was limited to the male condition. While "the knowledge of the world, is never to be acquired without great attention," such attention was reserved for men: "What is here said of this inelegant distortion of the face is applicable to every other part of the human body. It is ungenteel to be continually thrusting out your tongue, or stroking up your heart, as many do" (3–7).

In advising his son not to stereotype whole groups he categorized women by their sex and men by occupations, thus repeating that ubiquitous pattern of only identifying women as women, but distinguishing men by occupation and training. One should avoid such stereotyping, for

> you may thereby unnecessarily make yourself a great number of enemies. Among women, as among men, there are good as well as bad, and it may be, full as many, or more good than among men. This rule holds as to lawyers, soldiers, parsons, courtiers, citizens, etc. They are all men, subject to the same passions and sentiments, differing only in the manner, according to their several educations; and it would be as imprudent as unjust to attack any of them by the lump. (29–30)

The work as a whole prepared him above all for polite society and seems to incorporate women as much as men, but while individual women are mentioned, such as the quality of Mme. Sevigne's letters, they are not to be treated

---

37. James Bramston, *The Man of Taste: Occasion'd by an Epistle of Mr. Pope's on that Subject* (London: Printed by J. Wright for L. Gilliver, 1733). See also Lewis Maidwell, *An Essay upon the Necessity and Excellency of Education. With an Account of Erecting the Royal Mathematical Schole* (London: Printed for S. B. and J. B. and sold by J. Nutt, 1705); Phillipe Sylvestre Dufour, *Moral Instructions from a Father to his Son* (London: Printed for the author, and sold by W. Owen, 1760) (a reprint of a seventeenth-century French work); John Ash, *Grammatical Institutes; or, An Easy Introduction to Dr. Lowth's English Grammar, Designed for the Use of Schools,* 4th ed. (London: Printed for E. and C. Dilly, 1762) (this is the only work that mentions "ladies," but outside of schools and likely because of its focus on English grammar).

as men in polite society generally. While Chesterfield advises his son not to stereotype whole groups of people, he does just that in directing him how to judge women: "Women have in general but one object, which is their beauty; upon which scarce any flattery is too gross for them to swallow. Nature has hardly formed a woman ugly enough to be insensible to flattery upon her person. If her face is so shocking, that she must, in some degree, be conscious of it, her figure and her air, she trusts, make ample amends for it. If her figure is deformed, her face, she thinks, counterbalances" (63, 81). Although a work directed to his son, it treats his life course as the norm and advises how to deal with women only through flattery.

Limitations of Women's Education

In contrast, works addressed to girls' education, beyond those written explicitly from a feminist perspective, emphasize their distinct and more limited curriculum, and are not tied to the broad requirements of human advancement. The most important explicitly feminist educational treatise was Mary Wollstonecraft's *Thoughts on the Education of Daughters,* along with Catharine Macaulay's *Letters on Education,* in which she wanted "Amusement and Instruction of Boys and Girls to be the same." Wollstonecraft united arguments for a sound pedagogy such as "Above all, try to teach them to combine their ideas," to more traditional lessons concerning appearance and preparation for marriage; but the latter was framed less in a romantic and ordained path than within a skepticism over the limited choices open to women. After speaking of the resentment and discrimination against governesses and teachers, which left women significantly fewer options than men outside of marriage, she concluded: "the few trades which are left are now gradually falling into the hands of the men, and certainly they are not very respectable." Catharine Macaulay, in the fourth letter from her *Letters on Education,* was particularly upset about the separate education of the sexes, which, she claimed, could only be based on "the absurd notion, that the education of females should be of an opposite kind to that of males." This was especially harmful to girls whose movements were constrained unlike their brothers who "are suffered to enjoy with freedom that time which is not devoted to study, and may follow, unmolested, those strong impulses which Nature has wisely given."[38]

38. Mary Wollstonecraft, *Thoughts on the Education of Daughters,* in *A Mary Wollstonecraft Reader,* ed.

Sarah Fielding, in a letter concerning her work on a female academy addressed to Mrs. Poyntz, states that she wanted to focus on pupils' "entertainment and instruction" to best prepare them "to arrive at true Happiness, in any of the Stations of Life allotted to the Female Character." The work is directed to Lady Poyntz as the ideal model, who, though prominent at court, as soon as she married, "turned her Thoughts to all the Domestic Duties that Situation requires, and made the maternal Care of her Family her first and chief Study." In the preface addressed to young readers, she offers quite general advice, admonishing them to be neither too prideful nor too modest to believe that they could not grasp materials being taught. She encourages them to read a few books thoroughly rather than trying to fill their heads with superficial knowledge from a massive assortment of works. In the remainder of the work, which is supposedly based upon the ideas of a governess who ran a school in northern England, Fielding's curriculum incorporates the mix of domestic and cultural preparation, tied to morality and a superficial survey of a number of academic subjects, which was so common to the education of middle- and upper-class girls.[39]

H. Cartwright states that she was encouraged by Elizabeth Montagu to contact the "married lady," the intended audience for her work, to whom she described her intentions. While Montagu, who gained the title "queen of the blues" because of her standing as a bluestocking and thus a female scholar, might devote herself to serious reading, Cartwright wrote for that great majority "who take up a book merely with the design of passing away, an idle hour," and for whom "it is necessary to blend precept with amusement." The work continues with the broad but superficial curriculum that was intended to introduce girls from the middling and upper ranks to a wide range of subjects, but which expected little understanding from them, even though Cartwright stated she explicitly wanted to avoid such training.[40] John Bennett, who wrote his *Strictures on Female Education* from a more integrated study of religious

---

Barbara H. Solomon and Paula S. Berggren (New York: A Mentor Book, 1983), 29–44; quoted material from 34, 38. Catharine Macaulay, *Letters on Education: With Observations on Religious and Metaphysical Subjects,* ed. Gina Luria (New York: Garland, 1974), 46–50. Other works addressed to girls' education, other than those discussed in this section, include Ann Murry, *Mentoria; or, The Young Ladies Instructor in Familiar Conversations on Moral and Entertaining Subjects* (1791; reprint, New York: Robert Moore, 1812), and John Moir, *Female Tuition; or, An Address to Mothers, on the Education of Daughters* (London: Printed for Messrs. Murray and Highley, [1800?]).

39. [Sarah Fielding], *The Governess; or, The Little Female Academy. Calculated for the Entertainment and Instruction of Young Ladies in their Education,* 4th ed. (London: Printed for A Millar, 1758), iii–x.

40. [Mrs.] H. Cartwright, "To Mrs. Montagu," in *Letters on Female Education, Addressed to a Married Lady* (London: Printed for Edward and Charles Dilly, 1777), n.p.

values and domestic principles, was identified on the title page as "a Clergy-man of the Church of England." After dedicating his four essays to the count-ess of Clarendon, he outlines their purpose in his preface. The work combines a serious attempt to bring greater knowledge to women, while at the same time pointing out "the comparative difference of understanding in the sexes." He found boarding schools unacceptable institutions in which to educate young females, and he wanted to offer appropriate romances, moral lessons, and "the necessary, domestick duties, as well as the proper manners, graces and accomplishments of the sex" that young women could be taught at home. There is little evidence that he perceived any conflict between his discussion of "the treatment of women in the different ages and nations of the world . . . the causes, which have contributed to the obvious and shameful negligence in their education," and his mixing of serious moral lessons with the more restricted regimen of domesticity and social graces.[41]

The most substantial of these works is James Burton's *Lectures on Female Education and Manners.* The printer noted in the work's advertisement that these lectures were intended to be read in "a School for Female Tuition." The goal was to have "a series of plain and familiar discourses" to aid women, "for though there are some Duties of a general Nature, yet there are others, which may be strictly called feminine." It was conceived as an elementary work intended for younger girls. While the advertisement for this work might have acknowledged some general duties relevant for both sexes, the curricu-lum as outlined not merely is directed to such topics as "On the Duties of Wives," "On the Duties of Mothers," and "On Beauty and Dressing," but introduces the feminine creature so cherished by the end of the eighteenth century. Under "childhood," the qualities to be stressed were "Docility," "Cautions against Obstinancy, Sullenness and Self-conceit—a docile Temper acquired by Attention." While the work includes twenty-eight lectures, there is no progression based on enhanced cognition as a girl matures to adult-hood. Only two lectures have anything to do with academic education, and the first discusses whether "the natural Talents of men be superior to those of Women."[42]

41. [John Bennett], *Strictures on Female Education; Chiefly as it Relates to the Culture of the Heart, in Four Essays, by a Clergyman of the Church of England* (London: Printed for the Author, and sold by T. Cadell, J. J. G. and J. Robinsons, J. Murray and Dodfley, [1787?]). It is interesting to note the similar-ity to the title of Hannah More's *Strictures on the Modern System of Female Education, with a view of the Principles and Conduct prevalent among Women of Rank and Fortune,* published in 1799.

42. J[ames] Burton, *Lectures on Female Education and Manners,* 3rd ed. (Dublin: Printed for J. Mil-liken, 1794). Hereafter cited in the text by page number.

Lecture 11 begins with "a definition of mind" before debating the relative merits of the sexes, and speaks of "Instances of Female Erudition" that require that "the Female Sex should acquire a certain Degree of Literary Knowledge." It is followed by chapter 12, which focuses on recommended readings and bemoans that "the Female Sex [is] too fond of Novels." After arguing that men and women have similar intellectual abilities, he contends that girls are more perceptive younger because boys are busy with their books "for the purpose of civil Society" and girls "are more at liberty to read the World." Yet, examples of women's scholarship and writing make clear that some women had become learned; his examples include a number of scholars and novelists from the first half of the eighteenth century. Even so, the example of these exceptional women did not mean that women should be educated as men, or outside domestic demands. They needn't be taught "the learned Languages," although modern ones such as French and Italian were acceptable (139–50).

In Burton's next chapter, women are encouraged to gain knowledge through reading since he has demonstrated that they have the ability to absorb lessons that were taught. "By Books, likewise, your Passion would be agreeably animated; and you would be susceptible to the nicer feelings of pity and benevolence." Books separate us "from savages" and "enable us to compare past ages with the present; and to observe what, in our forefathers, is worthy of imitation" (152) While he urges a range of works upon women including religion, history, morality, and the like, he continually returns to their peculiar needs as women. There seems a strong disconnection between the small portion of this work that presumes women's ability and suggests books they should pursue and the large portion that focuses on socializing, domestic skills, and needlework. It is hard to see how one reinforces the other, and easy to see how the latter would detract and take time from the former. This work, and the ones noted above, slights academic training and inserts sentences such as the following in the academic section, reminding women that they do not pursue scholarship to learn for themselves, to further a career, or to fill a useful post in society. Rather, they learned to enhance their ability to fill a restricted and predetermined role: "Reading will also prepare you for Society. Your sex, it must be confessed, are fond of ornamental accomplishments. And can there be one more ornamental, than the art of pleasing in conversation? An exterior grace ... strikes the Beholder ... yet where externals only have been studied, what you gain at first, you would lose afterwards ... Conversation must be insipid where the mind is void of ideas, and is not capable of thought or reflection" (155–57).

This horribly familiar refrain means that women, even in those limited portions of works that deal with academic subjects, were reminded not only of their sex but of the social roles directing their reasons for such learning. It is an example of being drawn up short, as mentioned in the introduction, as in a female reader believing the general principles are for her, but recognizing that they are not. She might read or hear the lecture and be interested in both the earlier and contemporaneous women who demonstrated female erudition and the substance of what was being discussed, but then is reminded that, no, you should not be reading this in a general, unrestricted way; you must read this as a woman and apply it to relationships that control your life from childhood to the grave. It means that identical materials and lessons to be gleaned could not be applied equally to men who used them to improve themselves as adult humans, while the woman read to aid her in conforming to the needs of a series of other people.

Conclusion

While these common sentiments regarding women's training for future domestic duties, religious piety, and their appropriate place within the nuclear family may seem unremarkable, when contrasted with the educational and social goals for men, they remind us of how men's life courses were equated with human aspirations in ways women's were not. Such a reality was most clear in the proximity within a work, as in the educational works and popular newspapers discussed here, where the work's aims were laid out for humanity, humans, or human nature and a discussion follows immediately on the aims of men's lives. Not simply were they identical, or at the least compatible, but then a discussion of the needs and training of women or the fair sex followed, and that discussion was contrasted with the former, and possessed restrictions and qualities not found earlier. Such construction verified the identification of men's existence with the broad realities of human choices framed by God's plan and earthly realities. But the works concerning, or addressed to, women (while often employing the same broad-based set of values) were more specialized, moving easily from a recognition of female abilities, and the physiological and social characteristics of human beings, to women's more restricted nature and life pattern.

Epilogue

"Masculine Gender ... Taken to Include Females":
Gender, Radical Politics, and the Reform Bill of 1832

As we move closer to the end of the eighteenth century, and through the difficult years of the Napoleonic wars, larger groups of British men were becoming unhappy with the prospect of permanent exclusion from the English constitution. Influences on these efforts emerged from the writings of Thomas Paine and Mary Wollstonecraft, although the latter was the only radical theorist to give significant attention to women's political standing. The arguments for extending the franchise spanned the interests of middle-class men of the industrial classes and working-class men, usually mechanics and other skilled workers, to be included in the suffrage based on their industriousness. Men of increasing wealth from commercial and industrial backgrounds who paid substantial taxes lacked the vote most commonly because they did not live in a borough or region that held traditional voting rights, but sometimes because they lacked title to the appropriate type of property. The more radical elements in the reform movement sought the suffrage for any man who could be considered independent, and not subject to influence from the peerage, landlords, or the moneyed interests who regularly bought the votes of traditional electors.

Yet, whether pursuing a more limited suffrage for those of the middle ranks whose income was more apt to come from industrial production or commercial transactions than from rents, or pushing for votes for all independent men, proponents continued to employ broad, falsely universal language. Especially by the first half of the nineteenth century those pressing for inclusion in the political community, through utilizing more straightforward democratic language, characterized men in even more grandiose and inclusive terminology than had their predecessors. Traditional accounts of the history of the passage of parliamentary reform in 1832, and the ideology and effort that went into that passage from the 1790s to the early 1830s, have focused heavily on the impact of reform efforts on the competition between Tories and Whigs to dominate the national, and to a lesser extent local, political stage. As regards the Reform Bill itself, accounts have stressed the day-to-day political maneuvering by one side or the other, the conflict between Lords and Commons, the role of the king, and the growing importance of public opinion as expressed through newspapers and broadsides and through the large numbers of political unions. There seems a disjuncture between the older accounts that treat political maneuvering and the role of a few important leaders on each side, and the newer ones that give greater attention to events and people outside Westminister.[1]

The language of late eighteenth- and early nineteenth-century radicalism highlighted the strong desire of middle- and working-class men to attain the standing, while questioning the character, of their social betters and political superiors. They did so by arguing that they performed a range of responsible tasks that contributed more to the needs of the nation than the less productive aristocracy and equaled their standing as heads of families and individuals exercising independent decisions. The Reform Bill of 1832 holds a significant place in the evolution of women's protracted efforts to gain the vote. Up to that point, women as members of the privileged classes took active roles in

1. The standard treatment of the struggle to gain passage of the bill is found in J. R. M. Butler, *The Passing of the Great Reform Bill* (1912; reprint, London: Frank Cass & Co., 1964). Another work that continues this emphasis is Michael Brock, *The Great Reform Act* (London: Hutchinson & Co., 1973). A work that uses the same emphasis on applied politics, but expanded from Westminster, is J. A. Philips, *The Great Reform Bill in the Boroughs* (Oxford: Oxford University Press, 1992). Kevin Gilmartin, *Print Politics: The Press and Radical Opposition in Early Nineteenth-Century England* (Cambridge: Cambridge University Press, 1996), focuses on the role of public opinion and the print media in radical politics, while *Re-reading the Constitution: New Narratives in the Political History of England's Long Century,* ed. James Vernon (Cambridge: Cambridge University Press, 1996), includes a range of approaches. See also Anna Clark, "Gender, Class, and the Constitution: Franchise Reform in England, 1832–1928," in *Re-reading the Constitution,* even though the bulk of its attention is directed beyond the disputes of 1832.

politics, and isolated numbers held office. But with the expansion of the franchise to middle-class men, and serious debate over its extension beyond the middle classes, those drafting the reform bill felt it prudent to add the phrase "male person" to clarify that women were not included in the suffrage, no matter their property or tax status.[2]

While the Reform Act was finally passed in May 1832, historical treatment has focused on its nature as a bill, and the threat to political and social order which the House of Lords' opposition to reform constituted. Tories, Whigs, and Radicals have been treated as three protagonists in a great struggle for the nation's soul. On one side the Tories, and to a somewhat lesser extent the Whigs, feared a revolution similar to that which installed Louis Phillipe in France in 1830 (with strong resonance of the English Revolution of the seventeenth century and the French Revolution of 1789). On the other side— those representing radical viewpoints and the demands of working-class men—continually feared betrayal, either in being left out of reform or gaining no alteration to the traditional electoral system at all. That system, of course, reflected a preindustrial Britain with dominant agricultural interests and geographical localities with small populations voting in overwhelming disproportion to the new industrial cities and the classes who resided there. In addition, such small numbers of electors in individual districts led to corruption, either through a local family dominating their social inferiors and often tenants, or through financial interests openly purchasing their votes.[3]

While radical ideas from the late eighteenth century influenced political debates during the 1830s, much of the anger and distance between the working classes and their governors emerged from the economic hard times of the Napoleonic wars and their aftermath. The government's rigidity and unflinching support of property and moneyed interests, reflected in acts such as the use of force in 1819 against a popular protest in Manchester which came to be termed Peterloo, radicalized a wider proportion of the population and led their leaders to write uncompromising and angry attacks against the Tories

2. The Reform Act, or "Representation of the People Act, 1832," other than including detailed listings of the boroughs and counties that were to be included in the franchise and the number of their representatives, included the following phrase that, for the first time, explicitly excluded women from the English constitution: "XIX ... That every male Person of full Age, and not subject to any legal Incapacity, who shall be seised at Law or in Equity of any Lands or Tenements of Copyhold ... of the clear yearly Value of not less than Ten Pounds over and above all Rents and Charges." From *The Nineteenth-Century Constitution, 1815–1914: Documents and Commentary,* ed. H. J. Hanham (Cambridge: Cambridge University Press, 1969), 262–64.

3. Butler, *Passing of the Great Reform Bill,* 1–50.

and those in authority generally. Moderates sought reform, but made little headway in the 1820s. Only with the fall of the Tory government in 1829, and with the revolutionary events in France and Belgium in 1830, did it look as if there was any hope for reform of Britain's electoral system. It was a great struggle, which threatened a constitutional crisis when the king supported a measure of reform adopted by the Commons, and the Lords rejected any reform late in 1831. Yet, in the long term, the Reform Act that went into law in 1832 has not been seen as a definitive moment in the reformation of British politics because it expanded the franchise only to middle-class men and continued to allow the nation's politics to be decided by a limited number of important men, although the identity of those men shifted somewhat in favor of industrial over agricultural wealth. For those whose cry was for democracy and whose loyalties were to working-class men, it was an inadequate victory and one that delayed real change. Such views led to the Chartist movement of the later 1840s and the push for greater expansion of the electorate in 1867 and 1884.[4]

Scholars of modern British politics, especially those who attempt to link political and cultural phenomena, have given limited attention to either gender or the Reform Act of 1832. Dror Wahrmam, Margot C. Finn, and James A. Epstein each embed class in nineteenth-century political debates while offering scant attention to gender as a category providing similarly important qualities both for the men who were and were not included in the political nation, and the women who were not. Wahrman gives most attention to the reform debates of 1832 both because of his focus on middle-class politics and his greater concentration on the earlier nineteenth century. He does not include gender in his discussion of those debates, but links middle-class standing and qualities to men later in his work. His analysis, though, is tied most clearly to the masculine and public sphere in contrast to the private and feminine, and he does not analyze the gendered nature of the male political figure standing for the English people or the competent and responsible individual.[5]

4. For an analysis of the interaction of class and radical politics in the period following the passage of the Reform Act, see Margot C. Finn, *After Chartism: Class and Nation in English Radical Politics, 1848–1874* (Cambridge: Cambridge University Press, 1994).

5. See ibid.; Dror Wahrmam, *Imagining the Middle Class: The Political Representation of Class in Britain, c. 1780–1840* (Cambridge: Cambridge University Press, 1995); and James A. Epstein, *Radical Expression: Political Language, Ritual, and Symbol in England, 1790–1850* (Oxford: Oxford University Press, 1994). Wahrman, as with the other studies noted here, emphasizes class as the key concept for understanding political reform, and his discussion of class is separate from his brief comments on gender. Typical of his analysis is the following summary of what was most significant for reform in 1832: "Key issues in the

The most important gender analysis of nineteenth-century politics is found in the work of Anna Clark in *The Struggle for the Breeches: Gender and the Making of the British Working Class,* and in her essay in James Vernon's collection of new perspectives on the British constitution. In each study she argues the centrality of gender to understanding the nature of the English working class. Her *Struggle for the Breeches* deals with issues beyond politics, especially questions of sexuality, violence, and power in working-class families, but her chapter 8 on "Manhood and Citizenship" treats many of the issues central to this study. While not immediately relevant to the debates of 1832 since the chapter focuses on radical politics in the period 1767–1816, she still offers a range of analyses that substantiate the tie between manliness and working-class values. Clark differs with feminist scholars who see "rational citizenship" as the basis for excluding women from politics and rather argues that its true origin exists in "the fact that radicals were so caught up in the association of masculinity with political power that they could not carry their philosophical principle to its logical conclusion."[6] She provides evidence for the connection discussed in Chapter 5 between effeminacy and aristocracy in

heated debate were the existence of the 'middle class', its identity, its boundaries, its social and moral characteristics, its political nature, its pretensions, its power—in short, the various implications of endorsing a 'middle class'-based conceptualization of society" (301–2). While a useful explication of the language used in 1832, it ignores the identification of the middle-class male with people or humans more broadly. The collection *Gendered Nations: Nationalism and Gender Order in the Long Nineteenth Century,* ed. Ida Blom, Karen Hagermann, and Catherine Hall (Oxford: Berg, 2000), is a recent effort to engender nationalist and imperialist movements of the nineteenth and twentieth centuries. Catherine Hall, in an essay on the Reform Act of 1832, "The Rule of Difference: Gender, Class, and Empire in the Making of the 1832 Reform Act," works to integrate empire, nation, class, and gender in her assessment of the act's limitations. However, her discussion of gender is quite brief and, while discussing the role of masculinity in Irish nationalism, devotes little space to the gendered nature of enfranchised middle-class Englishmen or working-class men seeking to join them (see esp. 124–27).

6. See Anna Clark's *The Struggle for the Breeches: Gender and the Making of the British Working Class* (Berkeley and Los Angeles: University of California Press, 1995), 141–42; and "Gender, Class and the Constitution: Franchise Reform in England, 1832–1928," in Vernon, ed., *Re-reading the Constitution,* 239–53. *Women in British Politics, 1760–1860: The Power of the Petticoat,* ed. Kathryn Gleadle and Sarah Richardson (New York: St. Martin's Press, 2000), includes a range of essays on women's political efforts ranging from Hannah More's politics to British women working to end *sati* in India, but the collection does not address women's exclusion from the efforts for democracy in the 1800s, except for a voter's reaction following 1832 urging men to use this opportunity to overturn "petticoat politics." Yet more attention needs to be paid as to why these reform movements overlooked gender privilege, which often went hand-in-hand with expanding numbers of men voting. Elaine Chalus, "Women, Electoral Privilege, and Practice in the Eighteenth Century," in ibid., 19–38, offers an interesting distinction between women's electioneering in the eighteenth century with their omission from official political structures. Eric J. Evans, *Parliamentary Reform, c. 1770–1918* (London: Longman, 2000), does not mention women as part of his analysis of the struggle for reform, even though he discusses the 1832 Act as part of an unfinished effort at extending British suffrage.

contrast to masculinity and the economically productive citizen. She does not discuss explicitly, however, the easy movement from "human" to "man" and vice versa which also characterize radical works and emphasizes more than I would do secondary characteristics of masculinity as key to men's public roles. While the bulk of her essay on gender and franchise reform is devoted to the post-1832 period, Clark again offers highly valuable insights regarding the ties between gender and citizenship which continue to be ignored by the great majority of political historians. She argues that the connection between masculinity and citizenship not simply kept women from voting, but also limited the number of men who qualified for suffrage: "The manhood of citizenship always had to be earned, rather than claimed as an inherent human right based on reason. From the era of the French Revolution to the First World War, working men were consistently told that they had not yet attained the full masculine status of the citizen." She continues with the conflicts over household and individual suffrage and their gender implications. However, she begins her essay with a quotation from E. A. Leatham, an MP who opposed women's suffrage in both 1867 and 1884 and was the brother-in-law of the great Liberal leader John Bright; his statement clarifies why it is so difficult to identify any particular quality or status of masculinity that underpinned men's claim to suffrage: "It is not because men pay rates or taxes, or own or occupy property, that they have the vote, but because they are men . . . independent and free."[7] In the debates surrounding 1832, as in those political disputes preceding and following it, as the sands of parliamentary qualifications shift, the only ongoing requirement seemed simply that one be a man.

Radical Arguments During Reform Efforts

Although political reform during the 1830s did not encompass as wide a class of men as the radicals hoped for, their language and imagery was more expansive than that used during seventeenth- and eighteenth-century political debates and popular writings. In radical demands for broad inclusion of the "people" during the 1830s, both authors and radical leaders built upon earlier demands for change and altered their usage of falsely universal language to enhance the standing of wider groups of men. The demands and publications of the political unions, which grew up especially in large industrial cities in

7. Clark, "Gender, Class and the Constitution," 230–38, 230.

England and Scotland, emphasized the importance of their members (middle-class and better-off working-class men) and tied their economic contributions and independent standing to the political standing of Englishmen of the past. In an effort to mobilize the country for reform, they called upon their members to reveal their strength in numbers:

> See, see, we come! no swords we draw
> We kindle not war's battle-fires;
> By union, justice, reason, law,
> We'll gain the birthright of our sires,
> And thus we raise from sea to sea,
> Our sacred watchword, Liberty![8]

One of the more interesting linguistic shifts is the addition of "populace" to "people" as inclusive nouns that excluded women. "People" was a term reserved for those men who qualified for the vote, either middle-class or working-class, depending on the political loyalties of the author; "populace" referred to the broad population (often associated with the mob) who were clearly not qualified to vote. Yet both terms took on the familiar, manly characteristics of either the industrious and independent citizen, or the threatening and irresponsible mob, which was a threat to social and political stability.[9]

In the massive debates that took place in the House of Commons over reform, those pressing for reform were not the only ones who tried to show that their principles were tied to the status of the lowest of His Majesty's subjects. Thomas Pemberton, member of Parliament for Rye, in arguing against reform, noted how those who favored it spoke at length about what was wrong with the current system, which he summarized as being "of corruption, of close boroughs, and of the scandal of Peers nominating the Members of that House [the Commons]." But, he claimed, the advocates of reform were short on explaining how these problems could be solved through reform. He then emphasized a common antireform theme, that representation was based on more than simply numbers, as "if property, intelligence, and the common interests of the mass of society were not entitled or intended to be represented in the House of Commons." And, he said, such representation had reached

8. From the *Call of the Unions,* quoted in Butler, *Passing of the Great Reform Bill,* 377.
9. The following comment by Lord Cockburn, emphasizing a distinction that appeared in tracts on all sides of the Reform debate, makes the distinction clear: "The *public* was the word for the middle ranks, and all below this was the *populace* or the mob." Quoted in Clark, *Struggle for the Breeches,* 141.

well beyond the groups seeking the vote. As for the interests currently represented, he enumerated them as "the agricultural, the commercial, the manufacturing, the colonial, the military, the naval, or the professional." But he did not stop there in describing the reach of the British constitution: "He would ask what individual was there, not only in this country, but in the almost boundless empire which she has extended to the remotest parts of the world—what individual was there, to the lowest bondsman, down to the negro slave, who, if he had a complaint to make, real or imaginary, would not find in that House a hundred tongues ready to give it utterance, and make it heard."[10]

To gain victory over a struggle which each side saw as essential to the successful advancement of the nation, and a "way of life" they believed crucial to human improvement, their spokesmen used inclusive language and goals that never mentioned women and which continually employed male identifiers, leading one to assume that women were not included in the political vision of radicals, reformers, or their opponents. While each would have argued that women's interests were represented by husbands or other male friends and relatives, those on the radical and reformist side continually said such virtual representation was no representation at all for those they were urging to be included in the franchise. And radical MPs, in making their case for the needs of those who lacked political standing, spoke only of the male members of their class. On October 11, 1831, Michael Sadler spoke regarding the needs of the laboring poor, outlining the decline of England's independent peasantry and the gains of both the commercial and agricultural interests over them. "The best of the cottages have been demolished," and this has led to wage labor which often resulted in the following scenario: "Thither, then, the unhappy parent, when employed, carries his wages, which, with the exception of a few short weeks in the year, are utterly inadequate to supply the necessities of a craving family." Such is the image of "tens of thousands—of the labouring poor." As with John Wildman's *London's Liberties* in 1650, women who were workers at even lower wages were enveloped in the "family" and used to build sympathy as dependents, not as members of the laboring poor.[11]

In addition, radical gatherings, such as exemplified in the meetings and publications of the political unions, used the language and symbols of respectability while at the same time terming the aristocratic and merchant

10. *Hansard's Parliamentary Debates: Forming a Continuation of The Parliamentary History of England, from the Earliest Period to the Year 1803, Volume III, Fourteenth Day of September to the Fifth Day of October, 1831* (London: Printed by T. C. Hansard for Baldwin and Cradock et al., 1832), 169–70.

11. *Hansard's Parliamentary Debates*, vol. 8, 501–2.

classes vile representatives of these qualities. While gathering in Birmingham in May 1832 to pressure the government for political reform, the author of the *Report of the Proceedings of the Great Meeting of the Inhabitants of the Midland Districts* described the glorious scene and made it both an all-male event and one that spoke continually of the "royal standard" and "prominent gentlemen" and the grand train of all the members throughout England attending the event. It was both a glorification of public resistance to the Tories and the Lords and an attempt by the members of these radical unions to identify their actions with the political dealings in Parliament. It represents a clear example of the inherent conflict between a radical critique of English society and politics and an effort to emulate the efforts of those who dominated it that had significant gender implications which have received less attention than its class and ideological elements.[12] The meeting convened the Council of the Political Union, bringing together reformers from around the region: "150,000–200,00 outsiders were in Birmingham yesterday and virtually all of them came to express support for reform." Attendance was so great that those present "greatly exceeded in numbers the memorable review of the National Guards in Paris by Louis Phillipe in 1830." The royal standard "from Somerset House," along with many "banners showed above the large crowd, were displayed, and were gathered," the author claims, "not to console but to terrify the borough tyrants."[13]

Yet the author's association with the king, and the description of the ritualistic aspects of the meeting enhanced the standing of those in attendance as much as it represented radical political organizing. The crowds were entertained and encouraged by "a thousand musical-instruments." In addition, decorations lent a festive air to the proceedings. Each officer of individual unions was on horseback with a sash that designated his office, "embroidered with the Union Jack." This event exemplified the growing importance of Romanticism as in the following description of a Polish representative who was overcome with the crowd's support for his cause: "His heart was more sensible than his head; he wept, and instinctively, as it were, dried his eyes with that banner on which was inscribed the simple but beautiful sentiment."[14] While including radical phraseology in the work, the author gives much more attention to the meeting and greeting of leaders of unions around Britain and the glorious nature of the event—again emphasizing the need to enhance the

12. *Report of the Proceedings of the Great Meeting of the Inhabitants of the Midland Districts, held at Birmingham, May 7, 1832* (Birmingham: Printed by William Hodgetts, 1832).
13. Ibid., 1, 4.
14. Ibid., 4.

standing and ceremonies of working- and middle-class men as part of the call for reform.

A tract following the passage of the Reform Act is probably most complete in reproducing the range of arguments used in favor of expanding the suffrage. An analysis of it as a model for the massive literature offering such views points out the complicated set of values that formed the falsely universal language, which excluded women from the political nation. Was it necessary so thoroughly to ignore women for working-class men to be considered eligible for the suffrage? It is obviously not the kind of question that has a simple, or perhaps any, answer but it is important to speculate on whether women were simply forgotten or whether there was a calculated strategy of excluding them in order to make a stronger case for men. We have no definite answers to such a question, but certainly the explicit links between men's lives and the central qualities of the nation make it appear an overt, if not calculated, set of arguments. The author of *What the People ought to do, in Choosing their Representatives at the General Election, after the Passing of the Reform Bill,* argues that the "rights" of Englishmen had been pyrrhic for most up to that moment, and it was necessary to organize if the vast majority of the English population was to enjoy the rights they deserved: "It has been a custom with the English people of all classes, for a long period of time, to talk of their "Rights;" yet but a very small proportion of them have, in fact, possessed "Rights. The word has, in reality, possessed different meanings, according to the grade in society held by those using it."[15]

This tract, written under the pseudonym Junius Redivivus, was a letter directed to the electors of Great Britain, which tried to convince them of the wisdom of using their expanded suffrage (following the passage of the Reform Bill) wisely. In urging such an action, the author does not simply tie the voting rights (or lack thereof) of men with the "rights" and interests of all people, but he argues, as did virtually all of those pressing for an extended suffrage between 1790 and 1832, that class was the only determining factor separating those with the suffrage from those without.

This tract, although somewhat more magnanimous than similar radical tracts in the heat of the contest over the bill, possesses qualities found in the great majority. Most prevalent, as noted before, is the conjunction of class and privilege and the sense of oppression under which the "people" have suffered

---

15. Junius Redivivus, *What the People ought to do, in Choosing their Representatives at the General Election, after the Passing of the Reform Bill,* A *Letter directed to the Electors of Great Britain* (London: Effingham Wilson, 1832), 3. Hereafter cited in the text by page number.

by lacking membership in the political community. While large numbers of radical tracts explicitly included the term "rights" and discussed the manner in which the people had been denied them, they give greatest attention to an overview of English history where average citizens lacked political standing. Significantly for this study, virtually all of those debating reform, whether in the anti or pro camp (and whether radical, reformist, or conservative) returned to the seventeenth century as the crucial precedent for defending or criticizing the demands and actions of the late 1700s and the explicit efforts to seek reform from 1830 to 1832.

According to these tracts, it was either a glorious period that saw common Englishmen stand up for their importance in English society, or it was a horrid time in which order and deference disappeared and the people, unlawfully, took the life of a sitting monarch. *What the People Ought to Do* was directed to those who had just come within the body of the electorate and presents a radical, but sometimes more reformist and moderating perspective. The work devotes the greatest attention to the evil influence of wealth on the political system of England, both now and in the past, and the need for constant vigilance not to allow the wealthy to make decisions for all. Its major thesis, which was continually reiterated in reform tracts, was that those with "wealth or political power" used it for "the enactments of law or custom, by which they held their wealth and share of appointment in government," and they looked with disapproval on "just claimants to a share in that appointment." The privileged perpetuated such policies even though "no rational man" would dispute their property claims, "for any insecurity in the possession of property would effectually destroy all production; valuable property being only the accumulation of human labour" (3–4).

The author spoke for "the community at large," which had been ignored in earlier guarantees of British liberty. This was evident in the most famous of these efforts, for while Magna Charta was indeed a claim for rights, they were limited rights: "[The barons] did well in this, but they did well only for THEMSELVES; they recognized no 'Rights' in those beneath them." Here, and throughout the tract's narrative, economic standing is all that divides human beings, and the broad rights of "the community at large" had no place for women (4). Nor did the tract's author ever recognize that the principles he outlined for the wrongs associated with nonrepresentation could just as easily apply to the half of the population hidden in a range of false universals ranging from "people," to the "nation," to the "whole community." Such impassioned pleas for expansion of the franchise, utilizing universal principles and inclusive language, was associated in the minds of readers with the fact that such goals related only to male experience and standing. This made it even more difficult for women to apply such principles to their own status, and forced them to speak not of a "democratic" suffrage, but rather "women's" suffrage when seeking an extension for themselves later in the century.

In continuing his constitutional history leading up to reform in 1832, the author states that kings originally granted charters to towns to create a partnership against the overweening power of the barons, but over the centuries such boroughs came to be bought and sold, especially if they had lost the trade that originally had supported them. This led to the barons regaining control over them through money and creating the pocket borough. The Tories, however, called such a system the "Constitution, and worked to perpetuate it." Only reform will end this system, and "thus, when the whole nation obtains equal 'Rights,' plunder will cease, for it will be of no use to plunder when the subsequent division must again return to every man his own" (5–7). But, again, there seemed little need for women to be empowered to prevent the plunder of their resources.

This ongoing struggle between the Tories and those seeking their legitimate rights was a dispute based on the differing status of the two sides, those with and those without rights: "The former meant their legal 'Rights'; the latter meant the CLAIMS OF JUSTICE." In order to attack those seeking to join their club, Tories called them by outcast names: "Levellers, Jacobins, Republicans, Radicals" and claimed such men were the "thieves" when actually the Tories were the villains, but such disinformation could not last forever because "the schoolmaster is abroad" teaching the people who the real thieves are. While the author supports those who succeeded in obtaining the Reform Bill, he was no friend to Lord Grey and other Whig leaders: "Devices were then got up, of sending forth sham schoolmasters; a species of Tories in disguise, called Whigs.*" While the people were at first fooled, they learned and established their own schoolmasters to teach the truth (7–9). At the bottom of the page, in response to the asterisk above, the tract's author explains his views of Whigs: "I mean nothing personal. I speak of them as a body. The present men who have been the agents of the people in carrying the Reform Bill, although they may be designated Whigs, have acted upon Radical principles in doing what they have done. The Reform, so far as it goes, is a 'root and branch' one" (7–9).

The author of *What the People Ought to Do* continually returns to the interests of the people, and the means that had been used to ensure their understanding and control of their political destiny. For the most part, this has been against the efforts of the Whigs. For some time the people were fooled by the Whigs, but soon designated their own schoolmasters who could alert them to their real interests. Because the "Whigs were sleek and fat" they thought they should retain their "plunder" "peaceably," but "the more ferocious members of the community of thieves" were willing to use force to keep what they had taken. But when the news spread among the people, "each man girded on his weapon to resist." And when the people revealed their arms, "the cowardly bullies melted away." While the barons had won in 1215 through threatening force, the people ultimately won through "moral force," and it was a broad-based victory: "The first gave freedom to a caste—the last gives freedom to a nation. It ensures the welfare of the world. And after ages will appreciate it, even more than the present." While the Magna Charta was based on "selfishness," current reform efforts were built upon "principle." And it was not simply the political gain of those added to the electorate, but a wider victory: "The reign of brute violence is ended, and OPINION, as it should ever do, reigns paramount" (10–11).

While the breadth of the people's gains would seem to include women, the author throughout the remainder of the work shifts from people or populace to the interests and actions of a single man, and vice versa. Scholars have written a great deal about the uncompromising individualism of radical doctrine, and this quality is most determinate in denying women a role in either political reform or its rewards. Radical doctrine both recognized and rewarded the long-suffering Englishman who had contributed to his community and his nation without public recognition. Now he would receive that recognition; and, as many argued, his greater industriousness would be valued over the more parasitic existence of the upper ranks, especially landlords who lived off the labor of their tenants.

In establishing the historical trail that led to current reform, the author did not end with Magna Charta but quickly moved to the glorious triumphs of the mid-seventeenth century: "there is one green spot to which the memory of the patriot will ever recur with unmixed delight; I allude to the short period previous to the Protectorate of Cromwell." But even though Cromwell did not fulfill the hopes of those who had sought a fuller representation of the people, the author still supported him: "Cromwell was bad enough, but when compared with either of the Charles, he shines forth an angel of light.... But the names of Hampden, Marvel, Pym, Elliot, and the rest of the glorious band of patriots, impart a feeling of national pride, in which there is no cause for shame." It is interesting that he selected some of the more moderate leaders during the civil war, and did not note either Lilburne or Winstanley as great models from the past. And the reasons he admired them were tied as much to character as to program: "They were men of pure and noble principle ... worthy to be called patriots" and were not motivated by "petty selfishness, but by a desire to call forth human freedom, and to ennoble human nature, by awakening it to the exercise of all its higher faculties." Again, the qualities of a small number of male revolutionary leaders are equated with the best among human beings, and their actions had positive influence on "human nature," generally enhancing its "higher faculties" without a thought of women either as human beings or ones with higher faculties (11–12).

While one could say that he was speaking of areas where women had little role, and where he envisioned even less, the conflation of male experience with the political realm, with public roles and space, and with the qualities that formed the best human beings, did have a significant impact on women having such a long and arduous path to political rights, and one where they felt they had to argue as women, not as British inhabitants, subjects, or citizens. Women lost a range of court cases where they argued that their past history of voting, office holding, or existence simply as English persons who paid taxes and owned property that qualified men of similar standing to vote. This lack of notice of women created severe barriers for them to overcome. If explicit barriers are specified, then one can work either to overcome them or argue their inappropriateness or unfairness, but if one is simply left out of language standing for all, then it is hard to discover the proper target against which to struggle.[16]

For those arguing reform in the early nineteenth century, the great heroes of the seventeenth century "set the example of resistance to tyranny" and provided models for future action tied to the broad scope of humanity; these models wavered in the eighteenth century and fell back to the rule of its "ancient, imbecile rulers" because "there was no PUBLIC, no enlightened mass." But they hoped reform would change these realities and make a better political situation than that of past victories. In the seventeenth century, leaders set the direction, and when they died the momentum was gone. But by 1832 that was not the case, as "the public are as a mass enlightened, and every man who thinks, has the capacity of a leader for the purposes of resistance

---

16. For a brief discussion of the legal aspects surrounding women's suffrage, see Susan Kingsley Kent, *Sex and Suffrage in Britain, 1860–1914* (Princeton: Princeton University Press, 1987), 186–88.

to injustice" (*What the People Ought to Do,* 12–13). This study has sought to pinpoint the continual and unthinking use and significance of such language.

What the People Ought to Do insisted, as well, that political reform did not simply bestow rights on people; it also required duties from them. Up to this point, they had been "a mass of irresponsible slaves," but now they must also "take up their corresponding DUTIES, with a resolution well and truly to execute them." Reform was important because it acknowledged "that the great body of the people are the real source of power," and if a government is to function well it must "administer justice equally to every citizen alike" (13–14). One of the other points of this, and similar radical tracts, was the role of people with informed knowledge and political standing. The importance of such knowledge emerged from the myth that the king, the House of Commons, and the House of Lords were to watch each other to ensure that no one branch dominated. But in reality, while the Commons possessed the power of the purse, they were still inferior to the Lords, who actually controlled them through "the elder Lords sitting in the upper room, and their offsets, sons, brothers, nephews, and cousins, in the lower" (18–19). Yet it was both the people's greater authority and understanding that was crucial to changing this system: the political rights "which the people are about to possess, they do not owe to the freewill of the majority of the House of Commons, but to the fact, that their growing intelligence and determination operated upon the fears of the majority of that body" (19).

The goal of all government, in strongly utilitarian language, "is the furthering of human progress," and the British government has not fulfilled this goal. But things should change with the advance of public opinion, which brought sufficient pressure on the Lords to allow reform to be enacted. The tract finally stresses the broad representation of the new franchise that was essential to prevent corruption. Falsehood must be avoided because it "has a tendency to debase the national character of a free people.*" Again, in his definition of a "free people," he continues his falsely universal framework and situates it in utilitarian values: "By a free people, must be understood a people free from all restraints not conducing to human happiness" (24). Full representation was essential, "but until nearly the whole of the community shall be politically enlightened, the only security there can be for a tolerably just government is to keep to the democratic form as extensively as possible." While some voters could not be trusted, republican government allowed the state "to maintain peace among human beings of different degrees of intellect" (27). This phrase reiterates the link between class and intelligence employed by so many during the Reform debates; it also reflects the concern of reformers that not all electors were apt to vote intelligently and thus a few "noble-minded self-sacrificing patriots, who would only have looked straight forward, to promote 'the greatest Happiness of the greatest number' should vote" (31). The tract ends with strong support for expanding the franchise to all independent men, with a large dose of morality and essential knowledge thrown in, reflecting again the importance of setting high standards for political involvement, apt to be met only by those men most committed to their nation's benefit.

Nature of the Debate over the Reform Bill

The debates over the Reform Bill of 1832 often seem to be totally different sets of conversations. Those in the House of Lords and the House of Commons (but especially the former) discussed issues as if the topics and individuals were members of those two bodies, or individuals closely tied to them. Attacks are pointed and personal. While those pushing for reform certainly identified their opponents, especially in the Lords, as enemies, they were apt to characterize them in broader terms based on rank and wealth. Further, those from the political establishment who opposed reform spoke often in more anecdotal, and to a degree historical terms, emphasizing the great accomplishments witnessed under England's present system, while those seeking reform were more apt to speak the language of principle and proposal. It is not that the latter did not use the past in their arguments, but more to ferret out those few moments where common men, or efforts on their behalf, held a significant sway. And, there were, of course, great differences between the Whig leaders of reform and their radical allies, who were more apt to be outside of Parliament. Not merely did the radicals seek a wider expansion of the suffrage, they also avoided the compromising language favored by Lord Grey and his allies. In terms of rhetoric, the Whigs and Tories—although on opposite sides of reform—often sound more alike than those pressing more radical solutions. Certainly the level of anger is greater in the latter, but some of the Tory old guard mounted angry attacks on those who would threaten an English Constitution that had worked well for centuries. While the Tories had little faith in the working-class radical outside of Parliament who lacked the interests that would make him a responsible Englishman, still often their harshest attacks were saved for reformers among their midst who were seen as selling out their social peers, as well as king and country.

While these specific realities characterized the debate over reform, both sides spoke of the dire consequences for the nation as a whole if the other side were victorious. In these statements they create a community, a society, a nation, and an empire devoid of women. While all factions felt the urge to enhance their ability to speak for all, the radical political unions and press especially felt most compelled to create both a grandiose sense of themselves, the nation, national purpose, and the essential need that they be represented in the franchise.

In *A Letter to the Farmers of the United Kingdom*, B. Escott exemplifies the pattern of linking the status of only one group of English people (here characterizing all farmers as men) with the broader nature of Englishmen and England generally. The tract is an antireform document that argues that farmers are better off staying with a peers-dominated Commons whose primary loyalties are to British agriculture and who gain their income from the land just like the farmers. But in making this case, which was a common one for those speaking to the particular interests of agriculture, the author expands his reach to topics seemingly well beyond his scope.

Escott begins the work, addressed to "My Friends," with the incredible importance of the moment; it is "such an important subject that in our lifetime, or in that of our forefathers for many generations, has ever occupied the minds of men." Such an important topic should discourage prevarication, but that is just what one has from the Whigs; "we despise vain seekers of temporary popularity. We hate falsehood, and therefore abhor the Whigs."[17] He links the particular interests of farmers, on one page, with the broad, timeless interest of England and Englishmen on the next: "Do not tell me that the Members of Minehead are the nominees of Mr. Luttrell, or those of St. Mawes of the Duke of Buckingham; but tell me this,—Who are most likely to protect the interests of Agriculture in the House of Commons? Gentlemen returned by the influence of great landed proprietors, or the Radical Delegates of manufacturing Towns?" (4–6).

While the tract was above all a defense of the corn laws, Escott links his stance to the British Constitution, the greatness of the nation, and farmers' place within it. After a lengthy discussion on this topic, he apologizes: "but I had almost lost sight of you as Farmers, in considering you in your and our general character as Englishmen" (12). Farmers, in their vested interest to

---

17. B. Escott, *A Letter to the Farmers of the United Kingdom*, 2nd ed. (Taunton, London: J. Poole, Hatchard and Son, 1831), 3. Hereafter cited in the text by page number.

oppose the Reform Bill, are joined to the best of England; those in opposition include England, all the judges except one, bishops and clergy, the learned of the universities, and historians ("those who have made the events of other climes their study and know the signs of Revolutions") (14–15). And, to drive home the point as to the ultimate outcome of such changes to the political establishment, he reminds them: "The last successful Reformers of the House of Commons were *the murderers of their king.*" They should thus continue their allegiance to the gentry and peerage, and, he reminded them, it has been the yeomanry and gentle classes who have been the best defenders of "the Constitution of King, Lords, and Commons" (19).

The tract urged no compromise in the nature of the Reform Bill, which was tabled by the Lords in October 1831 over, among other objections, the fact that it made no distinction between large cities and smaller towns as regards the £10 requirement for householders, where many more could qualify within the large cities both because of higher wages and the number of residences that would require £10 taxes per year. In smaller regions the values of homes were less and salaries lower, which undercut the numbers of those who could purchase qualifying homes. This, it was claimed, would lead to an over-representation of larger population centers and favor the Whigs and commercial interests generally. For this reason, reform as framed in the bill should be reorganized to allow greater representation of the village and small town constituencies.[18]

In making this distinction—guaranteeing that urban inflation did not mean that cities had the greater advantage—the author established property

18. One of the clearest and most convincing arguments for equalizing the franchise based on property values and tax rates was expressed in an anonymous tract: Anglicus [pseud.], *A Letter to the Right Hon. Lord John Russell ... containing suggestions towards the improvement of the English Reform Bill* (London: Printed by Mills, Jowett, and Mills, 1831). The author claims a strong expertise about parish rate books, and is more familiar with how they are calculated and how they differ dramatically by parish than many members of Parliament and Lords. If the bill were to overcome its opposition in the Lords, then it "should exhibit as few anomalies or inconsistencies as possible" (3). He developed a list of the representation of the various boroughs taken from the census of 1821. While the bill's principle, which he characterizes as follows, is sound, it is based on an inaccurate set of facts: "It proceeds upon a simple and avowed principle, but it only carries that principle into operation in a partial degree. It began with the assumption that a large extent of property and population entitles a town to have representatives, in preference to other towns of trifling size and small population" (9–10). The anonymous author wanted to reduce the representation of open boroughs by one half and admitted that some towns with 20,000 will lose from two to one representatives, but they would be able to select that one, unlike at present, "a much more satisfactory representation, in returning a single member chosen by themselves, than they now do, in having two chosen for them by other persons" (14). As in so many other accounts, he highlights the pernicious role of "outdwellers" and argues against the propertyless voting, without placing women in the category either of property holders or the poorer workers he discussed.

and labor categories that in reality included women, but in his discussion of the conflicting interests involved in reform did not. His views most resembled the Whigs, namely that property and responsibility tied to gradual reform were key rather than a faster and more democratic political transformation of the British electorate. His analysis which follows reveals the categories that mattered to him, and their omission of women. In larger areas, he notes that one could raise the property requirement to £50 and still have enough voters able to resist bribery or control. But in such instances a £10 standard would be wrong: "To maintain the *ten-pound* qualification, will necessarily form an elective body of the worst description; that is to say, an immense mass of the working classes, who must inevitably act as a mob; and who will, of course, be acted upon by the usual mob motives,—either the oratory of the demagogue, or the temptations of the public-house" (21).

The bill carried with it the appropriate principle to handle this problem: "For what is that principle? The extension of the elective franchise as far as it can safely be extended;—stopping short, however, of Universal Suffrage, and assuming that there is a class of the community into whose hands the franchise cannot be committed, either with benefit to themselves, or advantage to the community." In defining this proscribed class, he describes them thus: "the labourers of the community;—meaning thereby those persons who have no other property than their labour, and whose talents are either of so low a description, or their economy of their time and money so deficient, as to force them to depend upon each day's toil for each day's bread."[19] Obviously as many, if not more, poor women fit into the latter category as men, and if women were not invisible in falsely universal language and imagery they would have required attention as individuals with adequate property worthy of the suffrage, or as workers whose income disenfranchised them.

Contrasting Treatments of Gender and Race in Reform Debates of 1832

There were few tracts which dealt with women in the debate over the Reform Bill; one which did was supposedly written by a woman, but was clearly a call from a clergyman to recruit women to aid him and his compatriots in their efforts to avoid reform and support the role of bishops within the House of Lords. It is interesting to contrast it with a racist tract that follows; the former

---

19. Anglicus, *A Letter to the Right Hon. Lord John Russell,* 22–23.

did not consider the enfranchisement of women while the latter discussed the enfranchisement of blacks, but in horridly racist and negative stereotypes. *An Address to the Females of Great Britain,* written in 1832, is a good example of those works that pressed gender stereotyping while supposedly being favorable to women. *To De Black Electors ob Emboro,* a broadside from 1832, supposedly was written by a "Caessaa" Thompson who was urging his black brethren to support him for election to the Commons given his contribution to the community. The first is respectable, but it removes women's potential as individuals in ways equally effective, but dissimilar, to its racist companion. Both are anti-reform; *An Address* focuses on the harm reform could bring to the Church of England and by extension the women of England who fell within its protective arms; *To De Black Electors* ridicules the radical political unions by demonstrating their appeal to as unworthy a group of potential voters as free blacks.

An Address to the Females of Great Britain was supposed to have been written by a gentlewoman who is urging her sisters to oppose reform. Early on, the author makes clear "she" accepts women's traditional roles; she is "no advocate for an undue assumption of power over those to whom, by nature and Divine authority, we are subservient; no exciter to a presumptuous interference in matters at once out of our province and beyond our capacity." In continuing the appeal, the author urges women to be careful only "to exert an influence which the Almighty himself bestows, which religion sanctifies, and the highest civilization approves and encourages." It was especially urgent that women act, for a radical journal had called upon them to support reform, and it was most important that women resist such a call "in the inflammatory language of a popular journal."[20]

The author was concerned that women might be tempted to do so because such appeals were addressed to "the best or the worst parts of our character, our vanity or our affection." The pamphlet was an interesting work in that it included cajoling and threat, and an internal contradiction that berated women for considering any political involvement (through responding to the appeal in the popular press) while encouraging them to resist reform, thereby

---

20. *An Address to the Females of Great Britain,* 3rd ed. (London: J. G. and F. Rivington, Whittaker, Treacher and Co., and Roake and Varty, 1832), 3–4. Hereafter cited in the text by page number. While acknowledging the absence of women in the 1832 debates, Anna Clark, in "Gender, Class and Franchise Reform," notes that Macaulay, in criticizing the views of James Mill and Jeremy Bentham in supporting universal suffrage, stated that householders could "kindly protect" the poorer members of society, just as they now were doing for the women of their society (234).

taking a political position but on the opposite side. The work's general principles are outlined in a rigid sex role framework, often combined with what seems a genuine fear that women might be attracted to the cause of reform: "Distrust those who would involve you in political disputes, which are irrelevant to you as females, and, with the clear-sightedness [with which you are credited] withdraw your footsteps from the brink." Women should find it easy to resist the call for involvement because "the general principle of Reform" has no relevance; for them reform was only "carried home to our bosoms, to our families, to our domestic economy, and to our public expenditure." The two pillars of their existence, religion and nature should guide them, and thus they should be prepared "to serve the sacred cause of nature, of the God who made you, and of the land which gave you birth." While the latter seems an unremarkable phrase, most reform tracts did not acknowledge that women were indeed "of the land which gave you birth" (5–6).

The rigidly gendered argument often seems a cold and calculated appeal (although likely not seen as such by its author) in the degree it portrays an uncompromising and negative view of women's lot on Earth while at the same time trying to draw them to antireform efforts. The serious and immediate threat was clear: "A deadly blow is aimed at our constitution, and the impoisoned arrow is thrust first through the side of religion. The holy barriers of our Church, as the acknowledged bulwarks of national liberty and safety, are the chief points of assault." It was essential that women understood the gravity of the threat and acted upon it; in urging such an action the author amends Marc Antony's words: "Friends, sisters, countrywomen! lend not yourselves to so dreadful a purpose, nor bring down on your devoted heads the frightful catastrophe that must inevitably ensue from their success" (5–6). But the call for action was tied to a belief in the passive early nineteenth-century woman, surely a weak reed to save the established church:

> Man goes forth exulting in his strength: great in bodily as in intellectual power, he creates a world around him; and variety, whether in the ardent pursuit of pleasure or of business, makes him, for a time at least, insensible to other wants, and independent of other resources. But woman is a being born for retirement and for suffering—delicate in constitution, and doomed to subjection, the evils entailed on her for original transgression, render her life a scene of much endurance and of much sorrow. (6–7)

After painting this unhappy picture of women's existence, the author claims that such misery has forced them to turn to God for protection, and in one of the tract's more offensive lines of argument, the author says not only would they be harmed if reform were not defeated, but so would those around them. Above all, they must resist this attack on God's clergy or they would be truly miserable: "You may be punished directly in yourselves, but you may be more severely punished in your children." "She" was sure they would protect the clergy because no mother would place her children at such risk. But the threat does not stop here; women might lose their familial connection altogether: "Suffer me to ask you, what are the ties by which the husbands, on whom you repose for all that earth can bestow of felicity, are bound to you? Are they not those of religion? Let no woman delude herself that the powers of her charms, and the strength of affection which she excites, are sufficient to retain in con-jugal fidelity the being on whom her happiness depends" (8–9). Not merely had the church solemnicized matrimonial bonds, but if women did not pro-tect them, such action could lead to "the division of the lawful inheritance of your own offspring with the children of the strange woman" (10).

While the work sounds throughout as if it were written by a clergyman, near the end this assumption is confirmed by the use of "we." The author adds up the many things a minister has done for the female reader, such as the christening of an infant where she took "her new-born babe," again from the hands of that same minister, no longer "the heir of wrath," but "the child of God, and an inheritor of the Kingdom of Heaven." The work concludes with a direct and grandiose appeal from the clergy of England, couched in language both of appeal and threat:

> A new and powerful claim has very recently been made upon your gratitude. We have trembled under the visitation of an appalling malady, "and with humble supplication have approached the Throne of Mercy. . . . By all your expectations, then of present happiness; by all your hopes of future felicity, whether temporal or eternal . . . as you love yourselves, as you love your families, your husbands, your children, your country, and your God. . . . Reverence the God whom you serve, through all the channels of His delegated power, and win. (14–15)

The racist broadside supposedly by Caessa Thompson, *To De Black Electors ob Emboro,* aimed to undercut radical claims for an extension of the franchise by placing the ridiculousness of the demands of common men in the words of an ill-educated and ill-informed freeman. While the tract claims he came from New York, the speech was satirized more as West Indian than African American, although identities were confused throughout. It satirizes the goals and institutions of radical reform during the debate over the passage of the bill. Written throughout in black dialect, it assumes the freeman was from America, and offers ridicule based on both racial and cultural stereotypes, as well as lack of information or intelligence. While supposedly directed to blacks, it omits any reference to women along with the works both for and against reform directed toward English men of all classes.

The work is addressed to "Dearly B'lob'd Broderin," and asks them whether they have not heard: "dat Lor Grey has pass one great law for whitewash de buckra man? Black niggas, hab you heaa dis, and why I no heaa you voice, crying loud, loud, like de wind'mong de suggacane, like de watta rushing down from de rivaa to de sea, dat you may be whitewash too?" In *To De Black Electors,* Caesar Thompson notes that he was from "Back Settlements Indiana, [and] last from New York" and that he was the only black man to ride about Emboro [most likely Edinburgh] on horseback and "is alway on de street." From his prominent position, he continually watched the black community, and noted when some men came and others left. He had devoted himself to making the race greater and stronger: "I hab done all in my powaa to increase de breed and to keep him puaa,—I hab lay in great stoaa of hominy and rice, and to ebbery he and she Niggaa dat marry, I hav gibben,—to ebbery new Niggaa dat cum, I hab gibben,—I hab nebber allow true Niggaa to beg in de street;—der is no Niggaa in Emboro but can read and write him tongue,—*I hab taught dem all.*"[21] This continual degrading imagery, based most often on purported ignorance or enhanced sexuality, dominates the satire. But the author did make clear that politics was its primary subject when characterizing the political unions through the vision and language of his foil, Caesar Thompson.

Not simply had his arrival from New York increased the black population of Edinburgh from 304 to 403, but he was now willing to lead the community into political activism. The following portion of the broadside mixes his

21. *To De Black Electors ob Emboro,* a broadside that lists no place or date of publication, but the British Library has determined that it was printed in 1832. Edinburgh is the most likely identification for "Emboro" both from its mispronunciation of the city and because of the predominance of radical reformers there. Such an association of Thompson and his fellows originally from the United States with Edinburgh would have highlighted the non-English nature of the call for a radical expansion of the franchise.

political ambitions with the "Great Spirit," as later the author links the origins of African Americans and Native Americans, and tied his goals to Peter Cooper, who founded Cooper Union in New York City in the early 1830s to further the education and influence of working-class men:

De Great Spirit appeaa to Caesaa Thompson, as him did to Petaa Coopaa.— *"Caesaa Thompson de houaa is cum, when de bottom will be de top, and when de black will be white,* Go, Caesaa to Emboro, *and collect de black man for dat houaa.'* De houaa has come now,—de bottom is de top.—Black man,—free niggaa,—I ask of you, will de black also be made white? I tink I heaa youaa answer;—de voice of de Great Spirit hisself is no louder dan dat answer; "De houaa is cum,—de black is no yet white, but him *shall be white.*

He assumes that his brothers will ask him how could this be, and he states that it was because something had forced the king "to gib de whitewash to de people." And, when he thought they asked him what could have forced such, he offered an explanation based on the radical politics of 1832: "One stick, man break at once.—tousand stick togedder him no can break—One dirty man cum for whitewash to de King,—for white was widoup de money for pay for him, and de King send him to the debbil wid a kick in him behind;— tousand, ten tousand dirty man cum togedder to de King, de King gib dem de whitewash, cause he no got 'nuff feet for kick dem all.—Dis is de Po-lick-it-all Union." He next calls upon his brothers to meet him at Blackfriars on the upcoming Friday at 8:00 P.M., and he asked them to consider before they come

dat de eye ob Europe will hear ob you dat ebening,—dat all good niggaa praise you, or will send you to de debbil,—dat de Great Spirit hisself will be dere. Tink what has been done,—de tinker, de tailor,— de nightman, de sailor,—de scaffenger, de sweep,—de whisky-man, de plumber, de fish-man, de fleshman, de fowl man, all buckra man, dirty man and clean man, dey hab all got what him call vote to sit in what him call Little House [Commons];—de black man only, him no can sit in dat house;—him no can send one man out ob de foaa hunder hunder thousand hunder niggaa in Britain foa sit dere. What is de use ob whitewash, if him no can make white from blackface?

The broadside concludes, after his appeal for their support, with his ethnic and racial credentials. But before establishing his legitimacy, the author pokes more fun at Thompson's political naivete:

> Dere is de corn law: black man hab corns same as white man. Dere is de civil list: black flunky mush moaa civil dan white. Dere is mush talk of war: black man hab enemy and eat him too … dere is noting for black man in dat house. Where is de law for hominy? Where is de law for rice? Where is de law for maize? Where is de law for banana? Where is de law for Guava? Where is de law for roast monkey,— for stew snake,—for alligator tail? Where is de stinction 'twix woolly nigaa and quadroon?

After stating that there were none of these things, he makes clear the need for black representation if they were to be considered: "Make Po-lick-it-all Union, and send a me to sit dat Little House, and I will go to de King, and I will say to de King, 'dere is foaa hunder and tree niggaa in Emboro dat want dese tings,' and de King will say, Caesaa Thompson, you 'sahll hab dem all.'" Finally, he was particularly well qualified to represent them: "I am true woolly niggaa,—no quadroon, my sistaa was chief ob de flat nose Cherokee, and my dam was tird sister ob de thick lipped Mohauk. Trust a me,—I say ebbery ting dat you bid;—I no care dam to morrow what I say to day. I no care dam for noting."[22]

These two works pose interesting contrasts. The work directed to women appears less offensive because it employs domestic and sexist ideology that continued well beyond the debates over political reform during the early nineteenth century. Certainly such racist sentiments were also common, especially in antebellum United States, but they carry a clear message of racial stereotyping. The integrated vision of protection within the home, tied to impending punishment awaiting women if they either stepped outside the domestic circle or threatened the ideology or institutions that buttressed it, created a more complex and subtle set of values. Such values made it difficult for people to see the negative stereotypes tied to protective language and institutions.

---

22. Not merely does the broadside employ the typical racist stereotypes regarding sexual prowess and ignorance, the author also uses improper word choice and punctuation to emphasize his lack of education. He places quotations marks out of place, and in expressing the numbers of blacks in Edinburgh, he scatters the word "hundred" throughout, both before and after the number "thousand" to signify that Thompson also did not understand proper numbering or amounts.

Only in tracts such as this message to the females of England, which portrayed the inherent ties among women's defined inferiority, their domestic comforts, and the power and threats that underpinned them, can one discern the control that underlay them. This religious plea to women placed them within traditional domestic qualities and demands, but escalated the connotations of such works by using them as threatening agents for women who would consider reform and not place support of the clergy above all.

Other than offering the age-old distinction of their lesser abilities and courage than men, there was nothing of the stereotypes of ignorance and child-like misinformation to be found in the satire on black electors in Edinburgh. Yet, even though they were the butt of jokes and ridicule, black men, and their political aspirations, were the subject of this broadside and their status was thrust into the name calling that was so common in the emotional, and often vicious, attacks each side hurled at each other during the reform debate. Women were simply the audience here, designated as individuals who had the ability either to further or hinder reform, in siding with the latter to protect the interests of the Church of England and its clergy. Women were excluded but avoided the worst of character assassination and name calling; here, at least, black men were included only to be attacked and ridiculed. Each approach led to both groups being viewed as beyond the English Constitution, with the latter being framed in more political terms (but only in a negative and satirical vein.) The final distinction between these two works is that the former was supposedly addressed to real women, whose loyalty to the church would guide their decisions, while "Caesaa Thompson" and his followers were characters created for the purpose of undermining the serious political aspirations of working-class men.

Repercussions of Reform

While the nineteenth century saw continued efforts for the extension of male suffrage, there were also the beginnings of the women's suffrage movement. As noted earlier, larger groups of men gained the vote in both 1867 and 1884, and all remaining men were enfranchised in 1918. Women over thirty gained the right to vote in 1918 and finally all women were enfranchised in 1928.

There were also efforts during the nineteenth century to overcome women's exclusion through linguistic changes in the law that did not ultimately lead to their enfranchisement. The most important instance was Lord Brougham's

efforts at standardizing the meaning of the law codes and those rules designating the procedures for local government. Brougham's legal reforms, which
became effective as of 1851 and 1852, tried to overcome the conflict between
explicit exclusion of women such as in the language of the 1832 Reform Act,
which included "male person" and a range of other statutes which used "man,"
"person," "people," and the like. The act read as follows: "That in all Acts
words importing the masculine gender shall be deemed taken to include
females, and the Singular to include the Plural, and the Plural the Singular,
unless the contrary as to gender or number is expressly provided."[23]

Although this clause had both significant legal and political import,
Brougham's proposal received almost no discussion in Parliament at the time
the law was enacted, and later historians have shown little interest in it as well.
While it did not prove definitive as to whether women would be included in
the franchise, the parliamentary franchise was extended in 1867 and in the
Second Reform Bill, the word "man" was employed and not the phrase "male
person." This meant that Brougham's proposed language faced a political test
in the decade following its enactment. An MP by the name of Denman asked
the following question when the Second Reform Act, which extended the
suffrage to a wider proportion of working-class men, was being debated:

> Mr. Denman said, he would beg to ask Mr. Chancellor of the Exche-
> quer, Whether, having regard to the Act 13 & 14 *Vict.*, c. 21, s.4, which
> enacts, "That in all Acts words importing the masculine gender shall
> be deemed and taken to include females," it is intended by the use of
> the word 'man' instead of the words 'male person' in Clause 3 of the
> Bill to amend the Representation of the People, to confer the suffrage
> on women qualified according to the requirements of that Clause?

The chancellor of the exchequer was clearly annoyed at having to answer this
query, and noted that the "learned Gentleman might have reserved for the
Committee on the Bill" his question when judges could be consulted. Also, if
he had studied it more closely, "he would have found it unnecessary to put his
Question." The chancellor of the exchequer then replied: "It is laid down in
the Act to which he refers that in all Acts the words importing the masculine

---

23. "An Act for Shortening the Language used in Acts of Parliament," [June 10, 1850], *The Statutes of
the United Kingdom of Great Britain and Ireland, 13 & 14 Victoria, 1850,* cap. 21, section 4 (London: His
Majesty's Statute and Law Printers, 1807–1869), 66–67. This law was passed as part of a number of
statutes reforming British law during 1851 and 1852.

gender shall be taken to include females unless the contrary is provided. But that is, I believe, provided in this instance." This ends the discussion of the relevance of Lord Brougham's bill to the Representation of the People Act, 1867.[24]

When 5,346 women attempted to register to vote following the passage of the 1867 act, their case was heard in the Court of Common Pleas to determine whether the word "man" in the act included women. The court decided that "man" did not include women, despite the legal reforms of 1851 and 1852, and Justice Byles undercut the common assumption that "man" was a generic term that included all humans. He stated: "No doubt, the word 'man,' in a scientific treatise on zoology or fossil organic remains, would include men, women, and children, as constituting the highest order of vertebrate animals. It is also used in an abstract and general sense in philosophical or religious disquisitions. But, in almost every other connection, the word 'man' is used in contradistinction to 'woman.' Certainly this restricted sense is its ordinary and popular sense."[25]

The importance of language, and of falsely inclusive language that can be interpreted to include or exclude women depending upon the persons interpreting it, and the occasion of the interpretation, is made explicitly clear in this case. Here lawyers argued for women's ability to register and vote if they did indeed constitute a part of "man" and met all of the other qualifications as set forth in the statute. The court had to reject the relevant statute through judgments about women's political capacities and past experiences. What seemed, then, like a simple issue of definition became embedded in the centuries-old pattern of failing to clarify when terms that represented all those who held a certain standing did, but more often did not, include women. Brougham had attempted to make it impossible for individuals to decide when the nouns they used to represent human beings would be inclusive or not. But political and judicial leaders were not willing to deal with the linguistic difficulties that

24. While Susan Kent discusses the act in *Sex and Suffrage,* she misidentifies it as Lord Romilly's bill and does not discuss its ramifications (187–88); *Hansard's Parliamentary Debates,* vol. 186 (March 18, 1867–May 3, 1867), 467–68. I have discussed *Chorlton v. Lings,* a women's suffrage case in the Court of Common Pleas, in "Women as Sextons and Electors," in *Women Writers and the Early Modern British Political Tradition,* 324–42, in which Brougham's statute was used unsuccessfully to justify a number of women voting in Manchester.

25. *Law Reports, Court of Common Pleas,* vol. 4 (November 9, 1868), 374–97. The court in debating the merits of the case went back to the various sixteenth- and seventeenth-century precedents for women's voting and office holding, and basically argued that recent usage was the key, and the Reform Act of 1832 was more significant than Lord Brougham's legislation, even though the latter followed it. In effect, the decision nullified Brougham's statute. It was common for courts to decide that women were included in inclusive language in criminal and taxation legislation, but absent in political statutes.

arose when they employed words that sometimes included women and sometimes did not. They retained the right to determine when words such as "person" and "man," or the masculine pronouns standing for them, would include one-half of the human race and when they would not.

Such realities have meant that even though there have been extraordinary changes in women's lives from the 1600s to the present, when we hear words such as "politician," "worker," "writer," "thinker," and so on, we are still apt to envision them as false universals which may include women but only stand for men. Altering economic and social realities will not ultimately bring an equal awareness of men and women's role in society so long as the words we use, and the images they evoke, mean something very different to the person saying or writing them, to the person reading them, and to the person envisioning the image that lies behind them.

Conclusion

This volume has attempted to explore the use of gendered, falsely universal terms in England from 1640 to 1832. It has also explored ways in which historians have taken these either to mean everyone when they meant only men, or to take terms such as "members" or "citizens" to mean only men when their authors and users intended them to include women. Whether failing to identify the gendered nature of language employed when speaking of the nation, or failing to understand terms, particularly in use in early modern guilds, which had modifiers (or analogs such as "freewoman" for "freeman") that clarified they did not refer only to men, historians continue to write in false universals about the history of England and Britain.

It is not clear why we fail to grasp when "all" is really all, and when we do so we do so more for class and race than gender. Women still seem more of a separate category to the historical narrative than is the case with the slow inclusion (and also continued exclusion) of other types of men. As the works analyzed in the last chapter on the Reform Bill of 1832 make clear, while African immigrants (whether from America or Africa) could be used as butts for jokes in the effort to keep working-class men from gaining the franchise, women were not even worthy of debate. Historical textbooks have integrated a range of materials in women's history over the last two decades, but that material has overwhelmingly dealt with domestic and sexual topics. When women are included in general histories in categories that would normally be filled by men, they are so included only when it is a movement or activity specifically identified as theirs, such as women's suffrage or occupations designated as theirs. What is almost always missing is an interactive analysis about major cultural, political, and social trends and how women influenced them and how they affected women's lives. Just as absent is any attempt to gender an analysis of men outside of supposed masculine characteristics such as sexual initiative or general aggression. While most anthropologists have long moved away from the "men in groups" type of analysis, historians who have just begun to study men as a gendered unit in the past look either to externals such as fashion or to the ways that masculinity affects their sense of war, the nation, or the self. Almost no one asks how their power position as a man affects their political participation and viewpoint, aside from economic standing and various ideological loyalties.

One of the reasons this is the case, I would contend, is that we have not integrated gender into a foundational category that continually affects our day-to-day decisions in a broad range of historical settings. We have not done so for a number of reasons, but one is the ubiquity of the false universal. We have no reason to pursue a gendered analysis of terms such as "citizen," "the English," "the nation," "artisan," "farmer," "all," and the like if we do not first ask just who we mean when we use these terms. If most general terms are spoken as if including women, but thought of as including only men, then we have no incentive to grapple with their gendered nature. And, just as scholars who study whiteness correctly note that white Americans and Europeans describe themselves without a color designation while terming others African-Americans, Latinos, or blacks, then in the same way those studying the past have had no reason to assess the gender of men because they have never identified them as males.

When such categorization exists, it does in those areas where masculinity is thought to be at play, not simply the fact of being a man. Maybe joining a sports team, or fighting in a war, can be seen as symbolizing one's sex if one is male, but voting, or holding office, or being in an occupation or profession, is not seen as being defined by the fact that one is male, nor is that fact considered an influence on one's day-to-day performance of those tasks.

For us as historians to write a fully gendered analysis of men as men and to study women in broad categories of national and global import, we need to move away from the ingrained view that sees men standing for the species and women standing for a specialized form of that species. Only through such a move can books, such as the two appearing on women's role in late eighteenth- and nineteenth-century British politics and the nature of political reform during a similar period be related to each other. While Gleadle's and Richardson's *Women in British Politics, 1760–1860,* and Evans's *Parliamentary Reform, c. 1770–1918,* cover overlapping issues and similar time periods, for example, they are written as if they were discussing totally different subjects.

The work on women gives slight attention to the nature of politics in general, or even to reform, while the work on reform speaks only about women when it deals with the topic of women's suffrage. This is the case even though political reform movements, whether or not they ultimately included women among the electors, had a major impact on England, and women lived in that society just as much as the men who were either included or excluded from the vote. Further, the ways that men defined their status as voters was consistently gendered in 1832, 1867, and beyond. Democratic arguments were encased in stereotypes against the effeminate upper classes who were monopolizing political access, even though they were weak and effeminate individuals. They were also geared against "petticoat politics," as a number of historians have pointed out. But too little scholarship has been devoted to why effeminacy (whatever that may be) has been equated with being female, beyond simply describing its use as an opprobrium. There is no similar stereotype as to the softness of professional men in comparison with common laborers that would disqualify them from political participation. Given the number of lawyers in representative bodies in North America and Western Europe, perhaps that is only to the good.

As historians become greater and greater specialists we may have difficulty in developing an analysis of the operations of gender in the past. Not simply are we divided geographically, chronologically, and topically, but we are also divided between those who primarily study the actions of the past and those who study the representation of those actions. One of the problems with such a division, which has mushroomed recently with the growth of cultural history, is that we best understand the workings of the false universal if we study its functioning in daily decisions by all of us in all aspects of our lives. I have problems with the phrase "cultural construction" because it makes it seem as if recognition of the meanings and significance of words is somehow distant from their everyday usage. But the false universal is a constant part of our word choice and continually affects our understanding of how we act and what we say. The constructed meanings of words are as much a part of our everyday thoughts and actions as the practical circumstances through which those thoughts and actions are carried out. To divide them is artificial and makes us miss how much we use words that theoretically could be generally inclusive, but in our particular usage means only a certain set of individuals.

Such realities exist as surely in early modern Britain as they do today, and they are brought to our attention only when explicit, public arguments are made concerning the place of women in falsely universal categories. In the decade following the *Athenian Mercury's* stating that women had to be clearly included in terms incorporating all humans, Mary Astell's *Serious Proposal to the Ladies* stressing the need for women's advanced education, and *An Essay in defence of the Female Sex,* which argued forcefully against men obscuring women's past, the following work altered its description on the title page to acknowledge such arguments. Originally published in 1678 as *The History of Man; or, The Wonders of Human Nature,* it was intended to present its subject through "many thousands of Examples" revealing "his Body, Senses, Passions, Affections," along with "his Quality, Vocation and Profession." The work was reissued in 1704 as "The Wonders of the Little World: Or, a General History of Man," and stipulates on the title page that it not merely discusses men but "both sexes" as well. While the works are close to identical (except for the latter being briefer), still the later printer felt some compunction to reference women specifically in this broad history of humanity.[1] Such compunction emerges only when the operations of the false universal are identified and become part of public discourse.

This book has intended, then, to provide some insight into how a gendered false universal influenced both actual decisions, and the way those decisions were framed by contemporaries and explained by later historians, and to argue that we need to analyze our word choice to make clear our meaning to ourselves, and as historians to our readers, and ultimately our students. When we say "people," but we really do not mean people, or we speak of "human" characteristics, but they are characteristics drawn only from one sex, or one

---

1. Nathaniel Manley, *The Wonders of the Little World; or, A General History of Man. In Six Books* (London: Printed for T. Basset, R. Cheswel, J. Wright, and T. Sawbridge, 1678); *The History of Man; or, The Wonders of Human nature; in relation to the virtues, vices and defects of both sexes* (London: Printed for R. Basset and W. Turner, 1704).

THE
WONDERS

OF THE

Little World :

Or, a General

HISTORY of MAN,

IN

Six BOOKS.

WHEREIN

By many thousands of **Examples** is shewed what MAN hath been

FROM THE

First Ages of the world to these Times.

In respect of his

Body, *Senses*, *Passions*, *Affections* : His *Virtues* and *Perfections*, his *Vices* and *Defects*, his *Quality*, *Vocation* and *Profession* ; and many other particulars not reducible to any of the former Heads.

Collected from the Writings of the most approved Historians , Philosophers, Physicians , Philologists and others.

By **Nath. Wanley**, M. A. and Vicar of *Trinity* Parish in the City of *Coventry*.

Quicquid agunt Homines Votum, Timor, Ira, Voluptas,
Gaudia, Discursus, nostri est farrago libelli. Juvenal. Satyr. 1.
Conamur tenues grandia. Hor. lib. 1. ode. 6.

LONDON,

Printed for **T.** *Basset*, at the *George* in *Fleet-street* : R. *Cheswel*, at the *Rose* and *Crown* in St. *Pauls* Church-yard : *J. Wright*, at the *Crown* on *Ludgate-hill*, And **T.** *Sawbridge*, at the three Flowers *de Luce* in *Little Britain.* 1678.

Figs. 7 a and b   "The Wonders of the Little World; or, A General History of Man" (1678); reissued as "The History of Man; or, The Wonders of Human Nature" (1704). Note the reference to "both Sexes" in the 1704 edition.

THE

History of Man;

OR, THE

WONDERS

OF

Humane NATURE,

IN

Relation to the Virtues, Vices
and Defects of both Sexes.

WITH

Examples Antient and Modern,
Alphabetically digested under their Proper
Heads. The whole Work being inter-
mixt with Variety of Useful and Diver-
tive Relations, never before Publish'd.

Ponitur Exemplum fugiendum sive Sequendum,
Cernitur hoc Oculis, Mente sed illud agit.

LONDON:
Printed for R. Basset, at the *Mitre* over-against *Chancery-
Lane End* in *Fleet-Street*; and *W. Turner*, at the
Angel at *Lincolns-Inn* Back-Gate, 1704.

Fig. 7b

race, or one class, or one nation; if we are to portray the past as honestly and as thoroughly as possible, then we need to think about how we are using falsely inclusive terms with the intent (either consciously or unconsciously) to obscure the existence of those persons excluded from our analysis and description of the past.

❖ *Bibliography* ❖

Primary Sources

Guildhall Manuscripts: 4656/7; 4657A/1 & 2; 4657A/4

An Account of the General Nursery or Colledge of Infants, set up by the Justices of the Peace for the County of Middlesex . . . London: Printed by R. Roberts, 1686.

Addison, Joseph. *Selections from the Writings of Joseph Addison.* Edited with introduction and notes by Barrett Wendell and Chester Noyes Greenough. Boston: Ginn & Co., 1905.

———. *Essays of Joseph Addison.* Chosen and edited with a preface and a few notes by Sir James George Frazer, vol. 2. London: Macmillan and Co., 1915.

An Address to the Females of Great Britain, 3d ed. London: J. G. and F. Rivington, Whittaker, Treacher and Co., and Roake and Varty, 1832.

The Adventurer. [1752].

Advice to a Son: Precepts of Lord Burghley, Sir Walter Raleigh, and Francis Osborne. Edited by Louis B. Wright. Ithaca, N.Y.: Cornell University Press for the Folger Shakespeare Library, 1962.

Ambrose, Isaac. *Redeeming the Time* . . . *A Sermon preached At Preston in Lancashire* . . . *at the Funeral of* . . . *the Lady Margaret Houghton.* London: Printed by T. C. for Nath. Webb and William Grantham, 1658.

Anglicus [pseud.]. *A Letter to the Right Hon. Lord John Russell* . . . *containing suggestions towards the improvement of the English Reform Bill.* London: Mills, Jowett and Mills, 1831.

Ascham, Anthony. *Of the Confusions and Revolutions of Governments.* . . . London: W. Wilson, 1649.

Ash, John. *Grammatical Institutes: Or, an Easy Introduction to Dr. Lowth's English Grammar, Designed for the Use of Schools,* 4th ed. London: Printed for E. and C. Dilly, 1762.

A Supplement to the Athenian Oracle, Being a Collection of the Remaining Questions and Answers in the Old "Athenian Mercuries . . ." To which is prefix'd the "History of the Athenian Society." London: Printed for Andrew Bell, 1710.

The . . . *Athenian Mercury Resolving the Most Nice and Curious Questions propos'd by the Ingenious of either Sex.* London: Printed by T. Darrock and sold by J. Morphew at most Booksellers Shops in Town and Country, 1710.

The Athenian News; or, Dunton's Oracle. London: Printed by T. Darrack, 1710.

B.,W. *Sacred To the Precious Memory of Mrs. Mary Boyleston, Daughter of Mr. Thomas Boyleston, of Fan-Church Street, London.* London: Printed for John Macock, 1657.

Ball, William. *The Power of Kings Discussed: or, An Examen of the Fundamental Constitution of the Free-borne People of England.* London, Printed for John Harris, 1649.

Baston, Edmund. *A Funeral Sermon on the Death of Mrs. Plaice, Late Wife of Mr. Joseph Plaice Merchant of Clapham.* London: Printed by Samuel Bridge, 1700.

Baxter, Richard *A Breviate of the Life of Margaret, The daughter of Francis Charlton* . . . *and wife of Richard Baxter* . . . *there is also published the character of her mother, truly described in her published funeral sermon, reprinted at her daughters request....* London: Printed for B. Simmons, 1681.

Bearcroft, Philip. *The Wise and Useful Institution of our Charity Schools: A Sermon Preached in the Parish-Church of Christ-Church, London; on Thursday April the 28th, 1748.* London: Printed by J. Oliver and sold by B. Dod, 1748.

[Bennett, John]. *Strictures on Female Education; Chiefly as it Relates to the Culture of the Heart, in Four Essays.* By a Clergyman of the Church of England. London: Printed for the Author, and sold by T. Cadell, J. J. G. and J. Robinsons, J. Murray and Dodfley, [1787?].

[Birkenhead, John]. *The Assembly-man, Written in the Year 1647.* London: Printed for Richard Marriot, 1662/3.

Bolton, Edmund. *The Cities great Concern,... whether Apprentiship Extinguisheth Gentry.* London: Printed by William Godbid, 1674.

Bramston, James. *The Man of Taste: Occasion'd by an Epistle of Mr. Pope's on that Subject.* London: Printed by J. Wright for L. Gilliver, 1733.

Brinsley, John. *A Looking Glasse for Good Women,... and Advice to such of that Sex ... led away to ... Separation.* London: Printed by John Field for Ralph Smith, 1645.

The Briton. [1762].

[Brown, David]. *The Naked Woman, Or a Rare Epistle sent to Mr. Peter Sterry Minister at Whitehall....* London: Printed for E. Blackmore, 1652.

Burton, J[ames]. *Lectures on Female Education and Manners,* 3d ed. Dublin: Printed for J. Milliken, 1794.

C., J. *A Handkercher for Parents' Wet Eyes.* [London]: Printed by E[liz] A[llde] for M. Sparkes, 1630.

Canne, John. *The Golden Rule, or, Justice Advanced. Wherein is shewed, that the Representative Kingdom, or Commons,... Have a Lawfull Power to ... Adjudge to Death the King....* London: Printed for Peter Coke, 1649.

Cartwright, H. [Mrs.]. *Letters on Female Education, Addressed to a Married Lady, By Mrs. Cartwright.* London: Printed for Edward and Charles Dilly, 1777.

Cavendish, William. *Ideology and Politics on the Eve of Restoration.* Edited by Thomas Slaughter. Philadelphia: The American Philosophical Society, 1984.

[Chamberlayne, Edward]. *An Academy or College: wherein Young Ladies ... may be ... instructed in the true Protestant Religion.* [London]: Printed by Tho. Newcomb, 1671.

The Charter of the Company of Clothworkers of London. London: Printed in 1648.

[Chesterfield, Philip D. S., Earl of]. *Lord Chesterfield's advice to his Son on Men and Manners:... To which are added, EXTRACTS from VARIOUS BOOKS, Recommended by Lord Chesterfield....* London: Printed for W. Richardson, 1788.

Cloathing for the Naked Woman, or the second part of the Dissembling Scot ... Being a Correction of Mr. David Brown.... London: Printed and sold by Giles Calvert, 1652.

Comenius. Edited, with an Introduction by John Sadler. London: The Macmillan Company, 1969.

Cook, John. *King Charls his Case or An Appeal to all rational men Concerning his Tryall at the High Court of Justice.* London: Printed by Peter Cole for Giles Calvert, 1649.

Cornwallis, Frederick. *A Sermon Preached in the Parish-Church of Christ-Church, London, April 29th, 1762: at the yearly meeting of the Children Educated in the Charity-schools [of] London and Westminster.* London: Printed by J. and W. Oliver, 1762.

The Country Journal or, the Craftsman. [1727].

Cuffe, Henry. *The Differences of the Ages of Mans Life.* Newly revised. London: Printed by T. H. and sold by Nathaniell Buster, 1640.

Defoe, Daniel. "An Academy for Women." *An Essay Upon Projects* (1697). Facsimile. Menston: Scholar Press, 1969.

—. *Conjugal Lewdness; or, Matrimonial Whoredom. A Treatise Concerning the Use and Abuse of the Marriage Bed* (1727). Facsimile. Gainesville, Fla.: Scolars' Facsimiles and Reprints, 1967.

—. *The Earlier Life and Chief Earlier Works of Daniel Defoe.* London: George Routledge & Sons, 1889.

—. *The Versatile Defoe: An Anthology of Uncollected Writings by Daniel Defoe.* Edited and introduced by Laura Ann Curtis. Totowa, N.J.: Rowman and Littlefield, 1979.

A Directory for the Female Sex: Being A Father's Advice to his Daughter. London: Printed by George Larkin, 1684.

Dufour, Phillipe Sylvestre. *Moral Instructions from a Father to his Son.* London: Printed for the author, and sold by W. Owen, 1760.

Dury, John. *Considerations Concerning the Present Engagement, whether it may be lawfully entered into....* London: Printed by John Clowes for Richard Wodnothe, 1649.

—. *The Reformed Librarie-Keeper with a Supplement to the Reformed School....* London: Printed by William Du-Gard, and sold by Rob. Littleberrie, 1650.

—. *The Reformed School.* London: Printed by R. D. for Richard Wodnothe, 1649.

—. *A Seasonable Discourse ... What the Grounds and Method of Our Reformation Ought to Be in Religion and Learning....* London: Printed for R. Wodnothe, 1649.

The dutifull Advice of a loving Sonne To his aged Father. London: Printed for Benjamin Fisher, 1632.

[Egerton], Sarah Fige (Fyge). *The Female Advocate: or, An Answer to a late Satyr against the Pride, Lust, and Inconstancy of Woman, written by a Lady in Vindication of her Sex.* London: Printed by H. C. for J. Taylor, 1687.

An Elizabethan Guild of the City of Exeter ... the Society of Merchant Adventurers. [Exeter, 1873].

The Englishman. [1779].

The Estate of the Poor in Sion College. London: Printed by George Dagget, 1688.

[Fielding, Sarah]. *The Governess; or, The Little Female Academy. Calculated for the Entertainment and Instruction of Young Ladies in their Education,* 4th ed, rev., and corr. London: Printed for A Millar, 1758.

A Friendly dialogue between two London-apprentices, the one a Whigg, and the other a Tory. London: Printed for Richard Janeway, 1681.

Gastrell, Francis. *The Religious Education of Poor Children, Recommended in a Sermon Preach'd in the Parish Church of St. Sepulchres, June 5, 1707 ... Promoting the Charity-Schools Late Erected in the Cities of London and Westminster.* London: Printed and sold by H. Hills, 1707.

The Gentleman's Magazine: and Historical Chronicle, By Sylvanus Urban, Gent. London: Printed by John Nichols for D. Henry and sold by E. Newberry, 1784.

Gould, Robert. *Love Given Over; or, A Satyr against the Pride, Lust, and Inconstancy, &c of Woman.* London: H. Hills, 1710 [a reprint of the 1682 edition].

[Great Britain. Army]. *An Agreement Prepared for the People of England, for a Secure and Present Peace....* London: Printed for John Partridge, R. Harford, G. Calvert, and G. Whittington, [1649].

[Great Britain. Sovereigns. Charles I]. *Orders and Directions, Together with a Commission for the better Administration of Justice ... the reliefe of the Poore, the well ordering and training up of youth in Trades....* London: Printed by Robert Parker and by the Assignes of John Bill, 1630.

[Halifax, Lord, George Savile]. *The Lady's New-years Gift: or, Advice to a Daughter.* London: Printed and sold by Randal Taylor, 1688.

Halkett, Anne. *Meditations Upon the Seven Gifts of the Holy Spirit, Mentioned in Isaiah XI. 2,3. As Also, Meditations upon Jabez his Request....* Edinburgh: printed by Mr. Andrew Sympson, and sold by him and Mr. Henry Knox, 1702.

Hansard's Parliamentary Debates: Forming a Continuation of The Parliamentary History of England, from the Earliest Period to the Year 1803, vol. 3. London: Printed by T. C. Hansard for Baldwin and Cradock et al., 1832.

Hobbes, Thomas. *Considerations upon the Reputation, Loyalty, Manners & Religion, of Thomas Hobbes of Malmesbury, Written by Himself, by way of Letter to a Learned Person.* London: Printed for William Crooke, 1680.

———. *De Cive*, the English Version. Edited by Howard Warrender. Oxford: Clarendon Press, 1983.

———. *Leviathan, Or the Matter, Forme and Power of a Commonwealth, Ecclesiastical and Civil.* Edited by Michael Oakshott. Oxford: Blackwell, 1947.

Hoole, Charles. *Childrens Talk, English and Latin.* London: Printed for the Company of Stationers, 1697.

Jackson, John. *The Blessedness of Communicating to Charity-Schools. A Sermon Preach'd at Dursely, in Glouchester-shire, Feb 19. 1710.* London: Printed for and sold by H. Hills, 1710.

[St. Jerome]. *Certaine Selected Epistles of S. Hierome as also the lives of Saint Paul The First Hermite ... Translated into English....* [Saint-Omer: Printed at the English College Press]. Permissu Superiorum, 1630.

Joceline, Elizabeth [Brooke]. *The Mothers Legacy, to her Unborne Child.* Oxford: Printed and sold by Jo.Wilmot, 1684.

Johnson, Elizabeth. "Preface to the Reader." [Elizabeth Singer Rowe]. *Poems on Several Occasions.* London: 1696.

The Ladies Diary; or, The Womens Almanack for the Year of Our Lord, ... Containing many Delightful and Entertaining Particulars for the Use and Diversion of the Fair Sex. London: Printed by J. Wilde, 1707 [1710, 1712].

The Ladies Library. 3 vols. London: Published by Mr. Steele, Printed for Jacob Tonson, 1714.

The Lawes Respecting Women, as They regard their Natural Rights, or their Connections and Conduction. 4 books. London: Printed for J. Johnson, 1777.

The Lawes Resolutions of Womens Rights: Or, The Lawes Provision for Woemen. London: Printed by the assignes of John More, 1632.

Leigh, Dorothy. *The Mother's Blessing, Being Several Godley Admonitions Given by a Mother unto her Children upon her Death-bed.* [London]: Printed by I. M. for I. Clarke, W. Thackery, and T. Passinger, 1685.

A Letter of Advice to the Petitioning Apprentices. London: Printed by N. Thompson, 1681.

The Levellers: A Dialogue between two young ladies ... proposing an Act for Enforcing Marriage. London: Printed and sold by J. How, 1703. Reprinted in vol. 5 of the 1765 edition of *The Harleian Miscellany.*

The Life and Age of Woman. Copyright secured. Printed at Barre, Mass., by A. Alden, n.d.

Lilburne, John. *The Freemans Freedome Vindicated.* [London]: June, 1646.

Locke, John. *Two Treatises of Government.* Edited with an Introduction and Notes by Peter Laslett. Cambridge: Cambridge University Press, 1988.

———. *Some Thoughts Concerning Education* (1705). *The Educational Writings of John Locke.* Introduction and Notes by James L. Axtell. Cambridge: Cambridge University Press, 1968.

London's Liberties; Or A Learned Argument of Law & Reason, upon Saturday, December 14, 1650. London: Printed by Ja. Cottrel for Gyles Calvert, 1651.

Maidwell, Lewis. *An Essay upon the Necessity and Excellency of Education, With an Account of Erecting the Royal Mathematical Schole.* London: Printed for S. B. and J. B. and sold by J. Nutt, 1705.

Makin, Bathsua. *An Essay to Revive the Antient Education of Gentlewomen, in Religion Manners, Art, and Tongues.* London: Printed by J. D., sold by Tho. Parkhurst, 1674.

Macaulay, Catharine. *Letters on Education: With Observations on Religious and Metaphysical Subjects.* Edited by Gina Luria. New York: Garland Publishing, 1974.

Man: A Paper For Enobling the SPECIES: Designed to be continued weekly. London: Printed by J. Haberkorn and sold by J. Robinson and A. Linde [1755].

Milton, John. *Of Education, To Master Samuel Hartlib.* [London]: Thomas Underhill, 1641.

————. *Milton on Education. The Tractate of Education.* Edited and with an Introduction and Notes by Oliver Morley Ainsworth. New Haven: Yale University Press; London: Oxford University Press, 1928.

The Monitor: or, British Freeholder. [London, 1755–56]

A Moral Essay Upon the Soul of Man. London: For A. F., 1648.

More, Hannah. *Strictures on the Modern System of Female Education, with a view of the Principles and Conduct prevalent among Women of Rank and Fortune.* [London], published in 1799.

More, Thomas. *St. Thomas More: Selected Letters.* Edited by Elizabeth Frances Rogers. New Haven, Conn.: Yale University Press, 1961.

Morgan, Octavius. *List of Members of the Clockmakers' Company: From the Period of their Incorporation in 1631 to the Year 1732.* Reprinted from the *Archaeological Journal,* vol. 40 (1883). Exeter: William Pollard, 1883.

[Neville, Henry]. *A Parliament of Ladies: With their Lawes Newly Enacted.* [London], Printed in 1647.

A New Marriage, Between Mr. King, and Mrs. Parliament. [London]: Printed in 1648.

The North Briton. [1762].

The Oath of every Free-man, of the Citty of London. [London]: Printed by William Jaggard, n.d.

The Old Maid, By Mary Singleton, Spinster. London: Printed for A. Millar and sold by S. Bladon, 1755–[1756].

"Chorlton v. Lings." *Law Reports, Court of Common Pleas.* Vol. 4 (November 9, 1868): 374–97.

The Ordinances of the clothworkers' company, together with ... fullers & Shearmen of the City of London. Transcribed from the Originals. . . . London: Privately printed, 1881.

[Parker, Henry]. *Observations upon some of his Majesties late Answers and Expresses* [1642].

Peters, Hugh. *A Dying Fathers Last Legacy to an Onely Child: or, Mr. Hugh Peter's Advice to his Daughter.* London, Printed for G. Calvert, 1660.

Prevost, John, M.A. *Instructions to a Nobleman's Daughter Concerning Religion. At first designed for One, now ... all of that Rank, ... and others of that Sex.* London: Printed by W. R. for D. Brown and L. Stokey, 1700.

Proposals for Raising a Colledge of Industry of all Useful Trades and Husbandry, with Profit for the Rich, a Plentiful Living for the Poor, and a Good Education for Youth. London: Printed and sold by T. Sowle, 1696.

"Prouse's Case," Croke, Car. 390. *English Reports,* vol. 79: 940.

Raleigh, Sir Walter. *Sir Walter Raleigh's Instructions to his Sonne: and to Posterity,* 4th ed. London: Printed for Benjamin Fisher, 1633.

Redivivus, Junius. *What the People ought to do, in Choosing their Representatives at the General Election, after the Passing of the Reform Bill,* A *Letter directed to the Electors of Great Britain.* London: Published by Effingham Wilson, 1832.

Register of Apprentices of the Worshipful company of Clockmakers of the City of London from its Incorporation in 1621 to its Tercentenary in 1931. Compiled from the Records of the Company by Charles Edward Atkins. [London]: Privately printed for the Company, [1931].

Report of the Proceedings of the Great Meeting of the Inhabitants of the Midland Districts, held at Birmingham, May 7, 1832. Birmingham: Printed by William Hodgetts, 1832.

Samuel Hartlib and the Advancement of Learning. Edited by Charles Webster. Cambridge: Cambridge University Press, 1970.

A Sermon Preacht Upon the Death of Mrs Anne Barnardiston, . . . at the Age of Seventeen. London: Printed by J. A. for Benjamin Alsop and John Dunton, 1682.

Shakespeare, William. *As You Like It.* Directed by John Hirsch and Edited by Elliott Hayes and Michael Schonberg. Toronto: CBC Enterprises, 1983.

———. *A New Variorum Edition of Shakespeare: As You Like It.* Edited by Richard Knowles, with a Survey of Criticism by Evelyn Joseph Mattern. [New York]: The Modern Language Association of America, 1977.

Stockden, John. *The seven women confessors . . . which lived . . . in Coven Garden* [sic]. London: Printed for John Smith, [1642].

Skelton, Anne. *Comforts Against the Fear of Death: Being some short meditations composed by that precious Gentlewoman, late of Norwich . . . A. Skelton.* London: Printed by J. M. for Nathaniel Brooks, 1649.

The Standard of Equality, in subsidiary Taxes and Payments, or a just and strong Preserver of Publick Liberty. London: Printed by D. H., 1647.

Stoughton, John. *Choice Sermons Preached Upon Selected Occasions. . . .* London: Printed by R. Hodgkinson for D. Frere, 1640.

Les Temps de la Vie. Catalogue for special exhibit, February–September 1995, Musée national des Arts et Tradition populaires, Paris.

To De Black Electors ob Emboro [1832].

The True-born English-woman. In a letter to the publick. . . . By a true-born English-man. [London]: Printed in 1703.

A Vindication of the Loyal London-Apprentices: against the false and scandalous aspersions of Richard Janeway. [London, 1681].

Wase, Christopher. *Considerations Concerning Free Schools as Settled in England.* Oxford: Printed at the Theater in Oxford, 1678.

Woodward, Hezekiah. *A Childes Patrimony Laid Out Upon the Good Culture of Tilling over His Whole Man.* London: J. Legatt, 1640.

Winstanley, Gerrard. *An Appeal to the House of Commons. . . . Whether the Common People Shall have the quiet enjoyment of the Commons and Waste Land. . . .* [London]: Printed in 1649.

———. *A Letter to the Lord Fairfax, and His Councell of War . . . That the Common People ought to dig, . . .* London: Printed for Giles Calvert, 1649.

———. *The Mysterie of God, Concerning the whole Creation, Mankinde. To be Made Known to every man and woman. . . .* [London]: Printed in 1648.

Wollstonecraft, Mary. *Thoughts on the Education of Daughters: A Mary Wollstonecraft Reader.* Edited by Barbara H. Solomon and Paula S. Berggren. New York: A Mentor Book, 1983.

Woman. Sketches of the History, Genius, Disposition, Accomplishments, . . . of the Faire Sex, By a Friend to the Sex. London: Printed for G. Kearleys, 1790.

Selected Secondary Sources

Acheson, Katherine O. *The Diary of Anne Clifford, 1616–1619.* New York: Garland Publishing, Inc., 1995.

Ariès, Phillipe. *Centuries of Childhood: A Social History of Family Life.* New York: Vintage Books, 1962.

Barker-Benfield, G. J. *The Culture of Sensibility: Sex and Society in Eighteenth-Century Britain.* Chicago: University of Chicago Press, 1992.

Beier, A. L. *Masterless Men: The Vagrancy Problem in England, 1560–1640.* London: Methuen, 1985.

Ben-Amos, Ilana Krausman. *Adolescence and Youth in Early Modern England*. New Haven: Yale University Press, 1994.

———. "Reciprocal Bonding: Parents and Their Offspring in Early Modern England." *Journal of Family History* 25, no. 3 (2000): 291–312.

———. "Women Apprentices in the Trade and Crafts of Early Modern Bristol." *Continuity and Change* 6, no. 2 (1991): 227–52.

The Birth of a Consumer Society. Edited by Neil McKendrick et al. Bloomington: Indiana University Press, 1982.

Brewer, John. *The Common People and Politics, 1750–1790*. Cambridge: Chadwyck-Healey, 1986.

———. *The Sinews of Power: War Money and the English State, 1688–1783*. New York: Alfred A. Knopf, 1988.

Brock, Michael. *The Great Reform Act*. London: Hutchinson & Co., 1973.

Burrow, J. A. *The Ages of Man: A Study in Medieval Writing and Thought*. Oxford: Clarendon Press, 1986.

Butler, J. R. M. *The Passing of the Great Reform Bill*. London: Frank Cass & Co., Ltd., 1964.

Butler, Judith, and Joan W. Scott. *Feminists Theorize the Political*. New York: Routledge, 1992.

Carlton, Charles. *Charles I: The Personal Monarch*. London: Routledge & Kegan Paul, 1983.

Carter, Philip. "Men about Town: Representations of Foppery and Masculinity, Early Eighteenth-Century Urban Society." In *Gender in Eighteenth-Century England: Roles, Representations and Responsibilities*, ed. Hannah Barker and Elaine Chalus, 31–57. London: Longman, 1997.

Clark, Anna. "Gender, Class and the Constitution: Franchise Reform in England, 1832–1928." *Re-reading the Constitution*, 239–53.

———. *The Struggle for the Breeches: Gender and the Making of the British Working Class*. Berkeley and Los Angeles: University of California Press, 1995.

Colley, Linda. *Britons: Forging the Nation, 1707–1837*. New Haven: Yale University Press, 1992.

Collinson, Patrick. *Godly People: Essays on English Protestantism and Puritanism*. London: Hambledon Press, 1983.

Colwill, Elizabeth. "Just Another *Citoyenne?* Marie Antoinette on Trial, 1790–1793." *History Workshop Journal* 28 (1989): 63–87.

Consumption and the World of Goods. Edited by John Brewer and Roy Porter. London: Routledge, 1993.

Crawford, Patricia. "The Challenges to Patriarchalism: How Did the Revolution Affect Women?" *Revolution and Restoration: England in the 1650s*, ed. John Morrill, 112–28. London: Collins & Brown, 1994.

———. "Charles Stuart: Man of Blood." *The Journal of British Studies* 16, no. 2 (1977): 41–61.

Cresswell, Beatrix F. *A Short History of the Worshipful Company of Weavers, Fullers and Shearmen of the City and County of Exeter*. Exeter: William Pollard & Co., 1930.

Deviant Bodies: Critical Perspectives on Difference in Science and Popular Culture, ed. Jennifer Terry and Jacqueline Urla. Bloomington: Indiana University Press, 1995.

Displacing Whiteness: Essays in Social and Cultural Criticism, ed. Ruth Frankenberg. Durham, N.C.: Duke University Press, 1997.

Di Stefano, Christine. *Configurations of Masculinity: A Feminist Perspective on Modern Political Theory*. Ithaca, N.Y.: Cornell University Press, 1991.

Dobson, William, and John Harland. *A History of Preston Guild; the Ordinances of various Guilds Merchant. The Charters to the borough, the incorporated companies*. Preston: W. and J. Dobson, [1862].

Education in Tudor and Stuart England, ed. David Cressy. New York: St. Martin's Press, 1976.

The Experience of Authority in Early Modern England, edited Paul Griffiths et al. New York: St. Martin's Press, 1996.

Elkington, George. *The Coopers: Company and Craft.* London: Sampson, Low, Marston & Co., [1932].

Epstein, James A. *Radical Expression: Political Language, Ritual, and Symbol in England, 1790–1850.* Oxford: Oxford University Press, 1994.

Evans, Eric J. *Parliamentary Reform, c. 1770–1918.* London: Longman, 2000.

"Fear, Myth, and Furore: Reappraising the Ranters." *Past & Present,* no. 140 (1993): 155–210.

Fletcher, Anthony. *Gender, Sex & Subordination in England 1500–1800.* New Haven: Yale University Press, 1995.

Folliot, Shelia. "A Queen's Garden of Power: Catherine de Medici and the Locus of Female Rule." *Reconsidering the Renaissance: Papers from the Twenty-first Annual Conference,* 245–56. Binghamton, N.Y.: Center for Medieval and Renaissance Studies, 1987.

Foreman, Amanda. "A Politician's Politician: Georgiana, duchess of Devonshire and the Whig Party." *Gender in Eighteenth-Century England,* 179–204.

Fruchtman, Jack. *The Apocalyptic Politics of Richard Price and Joseph Priestley: A Study in late Eighteenth Century English Republican Millennialism.* Philadelphia: American Philosophical Society, 1983.

Gardiner, Dorothy. *English Girlhood at School: A Study of Women's Education through Twelve Centuries.* Oxford: Oxford University Press, 1929

Gleissner, Richard A. "The Levellers and Natural Law: The Putney Debates of 1647." *Journal of British Studies* 20, no. 1 (1980): 74–89.

Grafton, Anthony, and Lisa Jardine. *From Humanism to the Humanities: Education and the Liberal Arts in Fifteenth- and Sixteenth-Century Europe.* Cambridge, Mass.: Harvard University Press, 1986.

Gregg, Pauline. *King Charles I.* London: J. M. Dent [1983].

Harris, Barbara. "Property, Power, and Personal Relations: Elite Mothers and Sons in Yorkist and Early Tudor England." *Signs: Journal of Women in Culture and Society* 15, no. 3 (1990): 606–32.

Harris, Tim. *London Crowds in the Reign of Charles II.* Cambridge: Cambridge University Press, 1987.

Hawkin, Richard Y. *A History of the Freemen of the City of York.* [York], 1955.

Hayes, T. Wilson. *Winstanley the Digger: A Literary Analysis of Radical Ideas in the English Revolution.* Cambridge, Mass.: Harvard University Press, 1979.

Hendrix, Scott. "Masculinity and Patriarchy in Reformation Germany." *Journal of the History of Ideas* 56, no. 2 (1995): 177–93.

Hill, Christopher. *The Intellectual Origins of the English Revolution.* Oxford: Clarendon Press, 1965; rev. ed., Oxford: Clarendon Press, 1997.

———. *The World Turned Upside Down: Radical Ideas during the English Revolution.* New York: Viking Press, 1972.

A History of the Worshipful Company of Coachmakers and coach harness-makers of London. Compiled by direction of the Lord Iliffe, Master. London: Printed for Private Circulation, 1937.

Hufton, Olwen. "Women in Revolution, 1789–96." *Past and Present* 53 (1971): 90–108.

Hughes, Ann. "Gender and Politics in Leveller Literature." *Political Culture and Cultural Politics in Early Modern England: Essays Presented to David Underdow,* ed. Susan D. Ammusen and Mark A. Kishlansky, 162–88. Manchester: Manchester University Press, 1995.

Hunt, Margaret. "Hawkers, Bawlers, and Mercuries: Women and the London Press in the Early Enlightenment." *Women & History* 9 (1984): 41–68.

Jones, M. G. *The Charity School Movement: A Study of Eighteenth-Century Puritanism in Action.* Cambridge: Cambridge University Press, 1938.

Kelso, Ruth. *Doctrine for the Lady of the Renaissance.* Urbana: University of Illinois Press, 1956.

Kelly, J. N. D. *Jerome: His Life, Writings, and Controversies.* London: Duckworth, 1975.

Kenyon, J. P. *Revolution Principles: The Politics of Party, 1689–1720.* Cambridge: Cambridge University Press, 1977.

Kent, Susan Kingsley. *Sex and Suffrage in Britain, 1860–1914.* Princeton: Princeton University Press, 1987.

Kramer, Stella. *The English Craft Gilds.* New York: Columbia University Press, 1927.

Kramnick, Issac. *Republicanism and Bourgeois Radicalism: Political Ideology in Late Eighteenth-Century England and America.* Ithaca, N.Y.: Cornell University Press, 1990.

Lake, Peter. *Anglicans and Puritans? Presbyterianism and English Conformist Thought from Whitgift to Hooker.* London: Unwin Hyman, 1988.

Lane, Joan. *Apprenticeship in England, 1600–1914.* Boulder, Colo.: Westview Press, 1996.

Laslett, Peter. *The World We Have Lost,* 2d ed. New York: Charles Scribner's Sons, 1965.

Lewis, Rein. *Gendering Orientalism: Race, Femininity, and Representation.* London: Routledge, 1996.

Lloyd, Genevieve. *The Man of Reason: "Male" and "Female" in Western Philosophy.* Minneapolis: University of Minnesota Press, 1984.

Lovejoy, Arthur O. *The Great Chain of Being: A Study of the History of an Idea.* Cambridge, Mass.: Harvard University Press, 1961.

Mack, Phyllis. *Visionary Women: Ecstatic Prophecy in Seventeenth-Century England.* Berkeley and Los Angeles: University of California Press, 1992.

The Making of Masculinities: The New Men's Studies. ed. Harry Brod. Boston: Allen & Unwin, 1987.

Mcentee, Ann Marie. "'The [Un]civill Sisterhood of Oranges and Lemons': Female Petitioners and Demonstrators, 1642–1653." In *Pamphlet Wars* ed. James Holstun, 92–111. London: Frank Cass, 1992.

McKendrick, Neil, John Brewer, and J. H. Plumb. *The Birth of a Consumer Society: The Commercialization of Eighteenth-century England.* London: Europa Publications, Ltd., 1982.

MacPherson, C. B. *The Political Theory of Possessive Individualism: Hobbes to Locke.* Oxford: Clarendon Press, 1962.

McRee, Benjamin R. "Bonds of Community: Religious Gilds and Urban Society in late Medieval England." Doctoral Dissertation, Indiana University, 1987.

Mendelson, Sara, and Patricia Crawford. *Women in Early Modern England, 1550–1720.* Oxford: Clarendon Press, 1998.

Ober, Josiah. *Mass and Elite in Democratic Athens: Rhetoric, Ideology, and the Power of the People.* Princeton: Princeton University Press, 1989.

———. *The Athenian Revolution: Essays on Ancient Democracy and Political Theory.* Princeton: Princeton University Press, 1996.

Offen, Karen. *European Feminisms, 1700–1950: A Political History.* Stanford: Stanford University Press, 2000.

Pateman, Carole. *The Sexual Contract.* Stanford: Stanford University Press, 1988.

Philips, J. A. *The Great Reform Bill in the Boroughs.* Oxford: Oxford University Press, 1992.

Plomer, Henry R. *A Dictionary of the Booksellers and Printers Who Were at Work in England, Scotland, and Ireland from 1641 to 1667.* London: Printed for the Bibliographical Society by Blades, East & Blades, 1907.

Plomer, H. R., et. al. *A Dictionary of the Printers and Booksellers who were at Work in England, Scotland, and Ireland from 1726–1775.* [Oxford]: For the Bibliographical Society, Oxford University Press, 1932 [1930].

Pocock, J. G. A. *The Ancient Constitution and the Feudal Law: A Reissue with a Retrospect.* Cambridge: Cambridge University Press, 1987.

———. *Virtue, Commerce, and History: Essays on Political Thought and History, Chiefly in the Eighteenth Century.* Cambridge: Cambridge University Press, 1985.

The Prerogative of Creating Peers. London: James Ridgway, 1832.

Race, Gender, and Rank: Early Modern Ideas of Humanity. Edited by Maryanne Cline Horowitz. Rochester: University of Rochester Press, 1992.

Rappaport, Steve. *Worlds within Worlds: Structures of Life in Sixteenth-Century London.* Cambridge: Cambridge University Press, 1989.

Rebellion, Popular Protest and the Social Order in Early Modern England. Edited by Paul Slack. Cambridge: Cambridge University Press, 1984.

Re-reading the Constitution: New Narratives in the Political History of England's Long Nineteenth Century. Edited by James Vernon. Cambridge: Cambridge University Press, 1996.

Ruether, Rosemary Radford. *Women and Redemption: A Theological History.* Minneapolis: Fortress Press, 1998.

Russell, Conrad. *The Causes of the English Civil War: The Ford Lectures Delivered in the University of Oxford 1987–1988.* Oxford: Clarendon Press, 1990.

Sapiro, Virginia. *A Vindication of Political Virtue: The Political Theory of Mary Wollstonecraft.* Chicago: University of Chicago Press, 1992.

Sanderson, John. *"But the people's creatures": The Philosophical Basis of the English Civil War.* Manchester: Manchester University Press, 1989.

Saxonhouse, Arlene. *Athenian Democracy: Modern Mythmakers and Ancient Theorists.* Notre Dame, Ind.: University of Notre Dame Press, 1996.

Schwoerer, Lois. "Women and the Glorious Revolution." *Albion* 18, no. 2 (1986): 195–218.

Scott, Joan W. *Only Paradoxes to Offer: French Feminists and the Rights of Man.* Cambridge, Mass.: Harvard University Press, 1996.

Seaver, Paul S. "Declining Status in an Aspiring Age: The Problem of the Gentle Apprentice in Seventeenth-Century London." In *Court, Country, and Culture: Essays on Early Modern British History in Honor of Perez Zagorin,* 129–48. Rochester: Rochester University Press, 1992.

———. *Wallington's World: A Puritan Artisan in Seventeenth-Century London.* Stanford: Stanford University Press, 1985.

The Seven Ages of Man. Edited by Robert R. Sears and S. Shirley Feldman. Los Altos, Calif.: 1964.

Smith, Hilda L. "Humanist Education and the Renaissance Concept of Woman." In *Women and Literature in Britain, 1500–1700,* ed. Helen Wilcox, 9–29. Cambridge: Cambridge University Press, 1996.

———. "A General War Amongst the Men [but] None amongst the Women: Political Differences between Margaret and William Cavendish." In *Politics and the Political Imagination in Later Stuart Britain,* ed. Howard Nenner, 143–60. Rochester: University of Rochester Press.

Smith, Toulmin, Esq. *Early English Gilds: From Original MSS. of the Fourteenth and Fifteenth Centuries.* With an Introduction and Glossary by Lucy Toulmin Smith. London: Early English Text Society, 1892.

Schochet, Gordon. *Patriarchialism in Political Thought: The Authoritarian Family and Political Speculation and Attitudes Especially in Seventeenth-Century England.* New York: Basic Books, 1975.

Some Account of the Worshipful Company of Clockmakers of the City of London. Compiled principally by Samuel Elliott Atkins and William Henry Overall. [London], Privately printed, 1881.

Sources of English Constitutional History: A Selection of Documents from A.D. 600 to the Present. Edited and Translated by Carl Stephenson and Frederick George Marcham. New York: Harper and Brothers, 1937.

Spence, Janet T., R. L. Helmreich, and J. Stapp. "Ratings of Self and Peers on Sex-Role Attributes and their Relation to Self-Esteem and Conceptions of Masculinity and Femininity." *Journal of Personality and Social Psychology* 32 [1975]: 29–39.

Stopes, C[harlotte]. C[armichael]. *British Freewomen: Their Historical Privilege,* 4th ed. London: S. Sonnenschein; New York: Scribner, 1909.

———. *The Sphere of "Man" in Relation to that of "Woman" in the Constitution.* London: T. Fisher Unwin, 1907.

Swanson, Heather. "The Illusion of Economic Structure: Craft Guilds in Late Medieval English Towns." *Past and Present* 121 (1988), 29–37.

Telling the Truth about History. Edited by Joyce Appleby, Lynn Hunt, and Margaret Jacob. New York: W. W. Norton, 1994.

Tensions of Empire: Colonial Cultures in a Bourgeois World. Edited by Frederick Cooper and Ann Laura Stoler. Berkeley and Los Angeles: University of California Press, 1997.

Thomas, P. W. *Sir John Berkenhead, 1617–1679: A Royalist Career in Politics and Polemics.* Oxford: Clarendon Press, 1969.

Trease, Geoffrey. *Portrait of a Cavalier: William Cavendish, First Duke of Newcastle* New York: Taplinger Publishing Company, 1979.

Turberville, Arthur Stanley. *A History of Welbeck Abbey and its Owners.* 2 vols. London: Faber and Faber, Ltd., 1938.

Underdown, David. *A Freeborn People.* New York: Oxford University Press, 1996.

Wahrman, Dror. *Imagining the Middle Class: The Political Representation of Class in Britain, c.1780–1840.* Cambridge: Cambridge University Press, 1995.

Ward, Joseph P. *Metropolitan Communities: Trade Guilds, Identity, and Change in Early Modern London.* Stanford: Stanford University Press, 1997.

Wedgwood, C. V. *A Coffin for King Charles: The Trial and Execution of Charles I.* New York: The Macmillan Co., 1964.

Weil, Rachel. *Political Passions: Gender, the Family, and Political Argument in England, 1680–1714.* Manchester: Manchester University Press, 1999.

Westlake, H. F. *The Parish Guilds of Medieval England.* London: Society for Promoting Christian Knowledge, 1919.

Wiesner, Merry. *Women and Gender in Early Modern Europe,* 2d ed. Cambridge: Cambridge University Press, 2000.

Willen, Diane. "Women in the Public Sphere in Early Modern England." *Sixteenth Century Journal* 19 (1988): 559–75.

Wilson, Kathleen. *The Sense of the People: Politics, Culture, and Imperialism in England, 1715–1785.* Cambridge: Cambridge University Press, 1995.

Wiseman, Susan. "'Adam, the Father of all Flesh': PornoPolitical Rhetoric and Political Theory in and After the English Civil War." *Pamphlet Wars,* 134–57.

Woman in Western Thought. Edited by Martha Lee Osborne. New York: Random House, 1979.

Women in British Politics, 1760–1860: The Power of the Petticoat. Edited by Kathryn Gleadle and Sarah Richardson. New York: St. Martin's Press, 2000.

Women Writers and the Early Modern British Political Tradition. Edited by Hilda L. Smith. Cambridge: Cambridge University Press, 1998.

Young, Iris. *Justice and the Politics of Difference.* Princeton: Princeton University Press, [1990].

Young, Robert F. *Comenius in England.* Oxford: Oxford University Press, 1932.

Young, Sidney. *The Annals of the Barber-Surgeons of London.* Two Volumes. London: Blades, East & Blades, 1890.

Index

Page numbers in italics indicate illustrations.

Tatler (Addison, Steele), 143
taxes, 91–92, 103–4, 105, 158, 186
terminology. *See* language
Thomas, P. W., 16 n. 17
Thomason, Elizabeth, 24
Thompson, Caessa (pseud.), 192, 194–97
Thoughts on the Education of Daughters (Wollstonecraft, 1983), 167
To De Black Electors ob Emboro (1832), 192, 194
Tompion, Thomas, 81
Tories
    competition for dominance, 174
    opposition to reform, 175–76, 184
    position on reforms, 188
    public resistance to, 181
Toulmin Smith, Joshua, 85
Tractate of Education (Milton, 1644), 33, 52, 52–55
training. *See* apprenticeships; education
Tristam Shandy, 83
True-born Englishman, The (Defoe), 145
True-born English-woman. In a letter to the publick by a true-born English-man (1703), 147

Unwin, George, 85

Veale, Elizabeth, 101, 102–3
Vernon, James, 177
Viet, Mariane, 97
Vives, Juan Luis, 68–69
voting rights. *See* franchise; suffrage

Wahrman, Dror, 176
Walker, Susan, 79
Wallington, Nehemiah, 74 n. 2
Wallington's World: A Puritan Artisan in Seventeenth-Century London (Seaver, 1985), 74 n. 2
Ward, Anne, 83
Ward, Caesar, 83
Ward, Joseph P., 74 n. 1
Ward, Paul, 98
Wase, Christopher, 32, 33
Washington Post, 36
"weaker sex," 19, 151–54
weavers, 75–80, 97–98
Webster, Anne, 82
Webster, George, 82
Wedgewood, C. V., 109

Westlake, H. F., 85
What People Ought to Do, in Choosing their Representatives at the General Election, after the Passing of the Reform Bill, 182–83, 184–85, 186–88
Whig Examiner (Addison), 143
Whigs
    Escott's view of, 189
    fear of reforms, 175
    ideology of, 145
    position on reforms, 188, 191
    tract writer's view of, 184–85
White, John, 81
whiteness as universal, 155–56
widows
    apprenticeships and, 45
    as contributors to guilds, 82
    as English citizens, 113
    as exceptions to exclusion of women, 96, 98
    guild membership for, 85
    as guild mistresses, 73, 76, 77, 80–81
    as publisher/booksellers, 82–84
Wildman, John, 103–4, 180
William, king of England, 146–47
William (late of Walker Minories), 79
Wilson, Hannah, 82
Wilson, James, 82
Wilson, Kathleen, 140–41
Winstanley, Gerrard, 119, 120–22, 186
Wisdom tradition, 25 n. 27
Wollstonecraft, Mary, 167, 173
women. *See also* exclusion of women; female maturation; gender issues; girls; mothers; political standing of women; stereotyping of women; suffrage; widows
    advice to children, 62
    apprenticeships for and to, 45–46
    in Christianity, 21–27, 65–67
    as consumers, 140–42
    definitional exclusion of, 2–6, 111, 116
    dependent status of, 120 n. 14, 122, 180
    discussions of training for, 40–41
    eighteenth century stereotype of, 143–45, 147, 166–67
    employment restrictions on, 96
    established roles of, 41
    as exceptions to the norm, 39–40
    funeral sermons for, 23–27, 67, 71 n. 50
    in Great Chain of Being, 17, 19